MW00578598

UNCOMFORTABLE

CONVERSATIONS

WITH A JEW

UNCOMFORTABLE

CONVERSATIONS

WITH A JEW

EMMANUEL ACHO

NEW YORK TIMES BESTSELLING AUTHOR OF
UNCOMFORTABLE CONVERSATIONS WITH A BLACK MAN

NOA TISHBY

NEW YORK TIMES BESTSELLING AUTHOR OF
ISRAEL: A SIMPLE GUIDE TO THE MOST MISUNDERSTOOD COUNTRY ON EARTH

SIMON ELEMENT
NEW YORK   LONDON   TORONTO   SYDNEY   NEW DELHI

**SIMON
ELEMENT**

An Imprint of Simon & Schuster, LLC
1230 Avenue of the Americas
New York, NY 10020

First Simon Element hardcover edition April 2024

SIMON ELEMENT is a trademark of Simon & Schuster, LLC

Simon & Schuster: Celebrating 100 Years of Publishing in 2024

For information about special discounts for bulk purchases,
please contact Simon & Schuster Special Sales at 1-866-506-1949
or business@simonandschuster.com.

The Simon & Schuster Speakers Bureau can bring authors
to your live event. For more information or to book an event,
contact the Simon & Schuster Speakers Bureau at 1-866-248-3049
or visit our website at www.simonspeakers.com.

Interior design by Davina Mock-Maniscalco

Manufactured in the United States of America

1 3 5 7 9 10 8 6 4 2

Library of Congress Cataloging-in-Publication Data has been applied for.

ISBN 978-1-6680-5785-8
ISBN 978-1-6680-5787-2 (ebook)

From Emmanuel:

To those hoping against all hope that our world will be healed.

From Noa:

To Ari

Contents

Preface

CHECK ON YOUR JEWISH FRIENDS

EMMANUEL: It was Friday, October 6th. I'd just finished up a late dinner with a friend, and by 11:30 p.m. I was ready to wind down and get some sleep before my usual 9:00 a.m. to 9:00 p.m. Saturday workday. As I got into bed, I opened Instagram and saw that Noa was on Instagram Live. The thing is, Noa doesn't go on IG Live. She just doesn't—and I don't know her to be wild, so 11:30 p.m. on a Friday was just kinda weird. I tuned in, if anything to make sure she knows she's actually on live and hasn't hit the button accidentally or some other scandalous business, and there she is, sitting at her desk. It's serious. It's tense. And she seems a little frantic.

NOA: At that point it was two and a half hours after thousands of Hamas terrorists had invaded Israel and were in the process of massacring what would end up being more than twelve hundred people—but we didn't know it at the time because things were still unfolding and we barely had any information. Anything we did hear—that they'd taken over entire towns, that they were slaughtering entire families and concertgoers—

seemed too extreme to be real. But I knew it *was* real, and I knew it was bad, and I knew it would be more significant and dangerous than one isolated event. It felt generational. And so, I was live on Instagram.

EMMANUEL: I could tell she was distraught, but I couldn't make out much from what she was talking about because I had no context. All I could wrap my head around was "Israel's been attacked"—but truth be told, I didn't really know what that meant because we've been here before; it's not like this is the first time we heard the words "Israel" and "terrorist violence" in the same sentence. And after about twenty minutes, close to midnight, I logged off.

NOA: I, on the other hand, did not. I stayed up and on Live all night, piecing together stories as they were coming in. These testimonies from the South of Israel were horrifying beyond imagination. They were the same stories I'd heard from my grandparents about what had happened to them in Europe, and it was now being done to Israelis in pastoral villages and at a music festival.

EMMANUEL: When I woke up the next morning, I saw that Noa had posted several times, each time wearing the same outfit—and Noa's not a same-outfit kinda lady.

NOA: The deadliest terrorist attack in decades had just broken out, and the last thing I cared about was changing my outfit. I just put on my Gaza Envelope Task Force T-shirt, which is part of the Jewish National Fund, a great old-school organization that, among other things, helps Israelis living in Gaza border towns. I didn't take that shirt off for, like, forty-eight hours.

EMMANUEL: She also kept posting from the same spot, which led me to believe she hadn't moved (or showered) in about twenty hours.

NOA: I hadn't.

EMMANUEL: I kept checking my phone at commercial breaks while I was hosting my Saturday college football show, and I'd see her posting, posting, posting about this tragedy that was unfolding in Israel. So, I texted her and said, "Hey, can we go on IG Live when I get off work? I want my followers to hear what's going on." It's worth mentioning at this point that Noa and I had been discussing writing a book together about antisemitism for about fifteen months prior to this. I had originally reached out to amplify her message of combatting anti-Jewish hate to an even larger, more diverse audience. And because Noa had literally written a book on the topic—Israel and how people perceive it—I wanted to expose as many people to that experience and that knowledge as I could.

NOA: And I, of course, said yes (on both counts). I was truly appreciative of such a powerful gesture.

EMMANUEL: Normally, I go straight home after work and decompress from the twelve hours of being on camera, but that night around 9:30 p.m., I set up my computer in my office and went live. I had so many questions for Noa, but my very first was simply, "Are you okay?"

NOA: I was very much *not* okay.

EMMANUEL: We spent about an hour talking through the events of the 7th, with Noa giving me all kinds of context—or at least everything she was able to know at that point. We knew that Hamas had started a war. We knew that hundreds of people had been slaughtered and/or kidnapped. We knew everything was in chaos . . . Then came my final question: *What can I do to help?* Which elicited the most raw and authentic answer:

Stop what you're doing and check on your Jewish friends.

A WORD FROM EMMANUEL

Wassup y'all, so here we are again, back for another Uncomfortable Conversation. I'll be honest with you; I had vowed to myself (and my literary agent) that I wouldn't write another book. After all, I am a TV host and sports analyst by occupation. But I once heard the saying, "Your career is what you're paid for, and your calling is what you're made for." I realized I had to answer that call once more.

My *Uncomfortable Conversations* books and YouTube videos were conceived from the desire to educate about another person's perspective. You all came into my figurative living room, took a seat, and we talked about what it was like to be a Black man in America. Well, I mostly did the talking but with an assist from questions I'd received from my online and real-life communities. It wasn't always easy, and some topics were definitely tougher than others, but we kept it honest and friendly and got through it together. This book is similar; only now I've invited a brilliant mind to join us. And rather than talking about racism and the misunderstandings of the Black struggle, we're going to talk about antisemitism and the misunderstandings of the Jewish struggle. Because just as Black people are not a monolith, neither are Jewish people. Your experience is your expertise, which is why we're going on this journey with my friend and expert Noa Tishby.

Above all, my objective for this process is to *understand*. I won't necessarily agree with everything that Noa has to say, and we may not come to a uniform point of view, but that's not the point. That's not how real conversation works anyway. I want to learn more, to see things differently, and I want the aperture of my mind to be opened to a new perspective. My hope for you is the same—you may not be aligned with everything in the pages that follow, but look for the personal connection and understanding. Noa is a deeply knowledgeable guide to the current landscape of the Jewish experience and antisemitism, plus she has a really good heart and a desire to see the best in the world—something I believe we have in common.

Did sitting down to write this book make us both uncomfortable at one moment or another?

Of course.

Did the post–October 7th world make me feel like I, a Black man, could be on the wrong side of history by helping a Jewish woman tell her story?

No doubt about it.

This collaboration will not be without backlash from my own community, who may just see this as me dancing for "the Man," and I'll be honest, that scares me. There is so much tension between the Black and Jewish communities right now, namely because each group and individual within it sees the Israel-Palestine struggle so differently. Honestly, some people probably even have an issue with the fact that I said Israel-Palestine and not Palestine-Israel—that's how high the tensions are. The Jewish community sees itself as the persecuted, while the Black community largely sees them as complicit in an oppressive system. And my discomfort comes from navigating the in-between because the truth lies somewhere in there.

That discomfort is woven into the fabric of this book, especially because my relationship with Noa was at stake. And because disagreement in this case wasn't just a matter of where to eat lunch—we were discussing very big, very complicated issues that have a very long history and, ultimately, life-and-death consequences at their core. But as I like to say, pressure bursts pipes, but it also makes diamonds. So as nerve-racking as it was asking Noa the tough questions and holding ourselves accountable for the truth, or making myself vulnerable by asking things I wouldn't have necessarily asked if I were sitting across the table from anyone else, I know that this is forging a path for new conversations. Healing conversations.

The world is in a far different place now than it was in 2022 when we were "simply" condemning the hateful statements that Kanye made about our Jewish brothers and sisters; this is now a community that is under heightened attack. Just as the Black community was under heightened attack when I wrote *Uncomfortable Conversations with a Black Man* in the wake of the murder of George Floyd. As it's been said: "Justice will not be served until those who are unaffected are as outraged as those who are."

One way to bring forth justice is through dialogue. Through respectful curiosity, asking, and listening. So, this book is also about modeling for people how to do something as simple as having a conversation in the first place. How to give someone else the space to speak plainly and communicate their own truth, while also examining your own—however inconvenient or even painful that might be. Because everything great, I believe, is birthed through discomfort.

I once had a friend ask me, "How come when we read the Bible, we always read it as being the oppressed and not the oppressor? Why do we always make ourselves Moses but never Pharaoh?" To which I replied: *Yo. That's crazy.* I've always thought of myself as Moses, begging the higher power to let my people go. I never once stopped to think that I could occasionally be Pharaoh. And that challenged me; it made me wonder, *In whose life am I the oppressor? And what if the line between oppressor and oppressed is not as clear as we thought it was?*

So, this time, instead of answering the questions, I'm asking them. I'm getting curious, getting vulnerable, and of course, getting uncomfortable. But before I could have any conversations with Noa or you, the reader, I had to look in the mirror. I had to remind myself—and you—that once again, *understanding*, not agreement, is the objective. Because if you can become aware of someone's experience, it allows you to be more compassionate. And if you can be more compassionate, it compels you to *do* something. To take action. To be an ally (something we'll be talking much more about later in this book). But most important, to see those in need of your support as deserving of it.

It's always bothered me how when someone is trying to elicit an emotional response, they'll say, "Imagine that person is your sister/brother/mother/father." I say that's part of the problem—this idea that we can't fully connect with someone else's experience until they're someone we know or are related to or look like we do. To me, understanding should come automatically because we are human beings. It should go unsaid that if tragedy befalls some of us, it befalls all of us. Because without that appreciation, the world suddenly becomes a very lonely and isolating, if not dangerous, place. Seeing all people as worthy of our compassion expands our capacity to create lasting change. And then suddenly the world is a much kinder, more tolerant, more beautiful place.

So, open up your mind, let's get educated, and, above all, let's get uncomfortable.

A WORD FROM NOA

A few things make me uncomfortable: Cilantro. Clothes with heavy prints. Hamas supporters on US college campuses. And needing to defend my right to be upset by one of the oldest forms of hate and discrimination that has caused the murder of millions of people: antisemitism, or "anti-Jewish racism." This age-old hate is clearly back (it actually never went away), and I'm uncomfortable with just how comfortable the polite, modern, and educated world has become with it.

Antisemitism is as old as Jews themselves (which is really old—we predate both Christians and Muslims by millennia), with the first written accounts of it dating back to Alexandria, Egypt, in the third century BCE. In 93 CE, the Jewish-Roman historian Josephus Flavius wrote his epic multivolume book *The Antiquities of the Jews* to fight Greco-Roman antisemitism. As in, people have been sounding the alarm about the danger of anti-Jewish oppression and racism for about two thousand years.

But things are different now, right? There are no more crusades or inquisitions or men in white robes and pointy hats freely roaming the streets and calling for the killing of Jews. There are no more country clubs publicly declaring "No Jews [or Blacks] Allowed." And the Nazi Party has long been defeated. Ruth Bader Ginsburg is an icon. Steven Spielberg is a three-time Oscar winner. Scarlett Johansson has been *Esquire*'s Sexiest Woman Alive—twice! People set their clocks to Jon

Stewart or Ben Shapiro. We've had a former president with a Jewish daughter and a vice president with a Jewish husband. It seems like the problem has been solved; Jews (at least in North America) are finally safe and accepted—case closed.

And yet, here we are, witnessing TikTok debates about whether Hitler and Osama bin Laden had some good points we should all appreciate.* Because just as the election of Barack Obama in no way means we're living in a post-racial society, the success of *Seinfeld* in no way indicates that we've overcome antisemitism. Quite the opposite.

The year 2021 saw the biggest spike in anti-Jewish rhetoric, violence, and vandalism in the United States since World War II. Verbal attacks by thought leaders, liberal politicians, pop stars, and athletes; physical attacks of visibly Jewish people; desecration of synagogues; neo-Nazi marches; and antisemitic programming spreading on college campuses. And on October 8th, twenty-four hours after the largest number of Jews were slaughtered in any single day since the Holocaust, hundreds of thousands of people around the world marched *in celebration* of that slaughter. And don't get me started on social media, where I'll sometimes post pictures of Shabbat candles and will almost always receive hundreds of messages wishing me, in one form or another, to "Die, you Zionist bitch." (Or "imperialist colonizer," depending on the mood of the day.) Hatred that used to be reserved for dark rooms or the dark web is now in your face on Instagram, Ivy League college campuses, and on the White House lawn on T-shirts

---

* In 2023, Osama bin Laden's "Letter to America"—originally published in 2002 to justify his targeting and killing of American civilians on September 11th—circulated on TikTok. It received more than fourteen million views and prompted dozens of viral videos featuring young Americans sympathizing with bin Laden.

that say "Camp Auschwitz" and "6MWE." As in, "six million wasn't enough," referring to the number of Jewish people murdered in the Holocaust.

Jews are just over 2 percent of the US population, but they are the target of *63 percent* of religion-based attacks. Antisemitism has reached epidemic levels. How can this be? Shouldn't our unprecedented level of interconnectivity thanks to social media ensure that this sort of behavior is a thing of the past? We've all seen this movie before, so why do we keep replaying it?

That's where Emmanuel and I come in—two friends, one Jewish, one not, unafraid to ask and answer the toughest, most uncomfortable-making questions about the Jewish experience with the hopes of increasing awareness and understanding of our religion, culture, history, and challenges.

The person asking all those uncomfortable questions is Emmanuel. If you've been part of the cultural conversation in the last three years, you know who he is. His Primetime Emmy Award–winning digital series *Uncomfortable Conversations with Emmanuel Acho* opened up dialogue in order to dismantle racism and other taboo topics and has reached over 11.9 million people per episode. And now, in response to the alarming rise in antisemitism, Emmanuel is at it again, this time with me, exploring this deeply burrowed, deeply pervasive, difficult-to-spot hate and tackling how not to repeat that persecution. In *Uncomfortable Conversations with a Black Man*, Emmanuel wrote: "We can all access the life-changing medicine that will cure the world's most ailing, long-lasting pandemic, but in order to access it, we're going to have to have some uncomfortable conversations." In other words—the way *out* is *through*. We are going in and going in hard, which just so happens to be my specialty.

The Jew answering these questions is me; lovely to meet you. My name is Noa Tishby, and I am probably one of the loudest voices in the world on all things Judaism, Israel, and anti-antisemitism. I was born and raised in Tel Aviv by a secular, liberal, and politically active family, and, like Emmanuel, I now live in Los Angeles. After being told at age twenty-one by a famous producer that "If you make wine, you live in France; if you make watches, you live in Switzerland; and if you are in show business, you need to live in Los Angeles," I moved here to act and produce. But after far too many well-intentioned people asked me things like, "If you're from Israel, where is your hijab?" And after drawing far too many maps of the region on napkins at dinner parties, I started to get a clearer idea of my real passion: advocacy for the Jewish people, the Jewish state, and the Middle East.

Eventually, I expanded the scope of my mission to include fighting antisemitism globally. In 2022, I was appointed Israel's first-ever Special Envoy for Combatting Antisemitism and the Delegitimization of Israel by Israel's then foreign minister, Yair Lapid. In that role, I was honored to work alongside legends in the field of fighting antisemitism such as American ambassador Deborah Lipstadt and the UK's Lord John Mann. I was eventually fired by Prime Minister Benjamin Netanyahu over my criticism of certain policies he was going to enact—which I was okay with, as it made no difference to my advocacy.

Through this work, my mission became clear: to be an unwavering voice for our people and against hate. I've been touring the world to do just that ever since, giving talks, meeting with communities, writing my bestselling book on the topic, *Israel*, and addressing the UN and Congress, twice each, about the unchecked torrent of antisemitism on social media and the connection between campus antisemitism and terrorism financing.[*]

That's my long-winded way of saying that I don't think there are two better people to have this conversation than Emmanuel and me. But I'd be remiss not to add that when Emmanuel and I first started talking about this project, I was just as concerned and anxious as I was excited. I mean, who would have thought that I, a non-historian, non-journalist secular girl who'd never been to synagogue until well into adulthood, would be telling the story of Judaism, the Jews, and antisemitism? How is that even possible?! *Israel* was one thing—it's the history of my homeland—but this was an entirely different beast with many different heads: religion, geography, history, and politics, spanning thousands of years all over the globe. In true Emmanuel form, he had the perfect thing to say: "God doesn't choose the prepared, he prepares the chosen." And if Emmanuel says so, who am I to say otherwise?

I am approaching this book with an extraordinary amount of humility and have made sure to consult the experts—rabbis, historians, my community. This book is not meant to be an exhaustive history of the Jews from Abraham to the present (i.e., I want you all to actually read and, yeah, enjoy it), and it is not meant to replace any other academic reading on this topic, but it is meant to reveal some uncomfortable truths about where we've been, where we are, and where we're going. It might even cover a few questions you've had but never dared to ask. I do not take this role lightly, but as my mantra goes: go deep or go home. So, let's get started and see what happens when a Black man and a Jewish woman sit down to chat.

---

[*] Yep, there is a connection; just watch my November 15, 2023, testimony on C-SPAN.

Part I

YOU
AND ME

1.

HOW THIS BOOK HAPPENED

NOA: I wish I had a better story of how Emmanuel and I met. I wish I could tell you that we ran into each other in some magical place. That the mysterious hand of God put us in the same room, on the same train, at the same demonstration for human rights. That we heard each other chant the same social justice slogan and our gazes caught each other's and here we are, writing this book together. But I can't. Because as so many other great stories begin, we met through our agents.

EMMANUEL: Hold on a second now, Noa. That's not exaaactly how it happened. Truth be told, I was on the hunt to find a partner for this passion project. I felt oppressed groups too often speak in silos. Black people fight for Black people, women fight for women, and Jewish people fight for Jewish people, but why don't we ever fight together? Imagine how powerful we would be if Black and Jewish people—two of the most historically oppressed groups—fought together. And like so many others in Hollywood, I do my best thinking while, you guessed it . . . getting a facial.

I walked into my appointment and said "Wassup" to my lovely esthetician, Ronit. But get this, before I could sit down, this sweet woman who was born in Israel says to me,

"I just saw your last Instagram post about antisemitism and I bought a book for you; it's in the mail. You are going to love it!" She goes on, "I forget the title, but it's written by an incredible woman."

I look at Ronit and say, "*Israel?*" She replies, "Huh?" I respond again, "*Israel.* Is the book called *Israel* by Noa Tishby?"

With a bewildered smile she says, "Yes! That's it."

I then told her I had just finished Instagram creeping on Noa, and I had planned to reach out to her shortly about co-writing a book . . . THEN . . . I called my agent, who called your agent and said . . .

NOA: "Read this," ordered my awesome (and yes, Jewish—we'll get to that eventually) agent, Jacob. "Read this now and talk to me after." I'd just signed with a new talent agency, and as my career took a turn toward activism, I'd asked my agent not to call me with anything that didn't have real meaning. I have been an actress and a producer most of my life, and this was the first time I had to tell anyone *not* to send me on any auditions or pass along any random projects. All I wanted to do was to be a powerful spokesperson for the Jewish people, against anti–semitism, and for social change. The cover of the book Jacob sent me piqued my interest: *Uncomfortable Conversations with a Black Man*. I read it in just a couple of days and was floored. The wisdom, the straight shooting, the no-punches-pulling honesty—I felt like I was finally seeing the matrix of how racism has been sewn into the fabric of our society while also getting to see life through the eyes of a Black man—and being genuinely entertained.

Within days, our agents set up a meeting. And on a warm LA night, Emmanuel and I met at Pace, the old-school Laurel Canyon restaurant.

I arrived with mixed feelings. A few months prior to our meeting, I had come to that same restaurant with my sister, Mira. We sat outside at a two-top right on the canyon, along the street. A white car was standing at the light, honking aggressively. The driver was trying to push his way through traffic, disturbing everyone eating outside with his outbursts.

"He must be Jewish," a voice behind me said.

Mira and I froze. I turned my head to the table. A couple was sitting there, and since I hoped I might have misheard or maybe misunderstood, I asked the man politely, "Excuse me, sir, what was that?"

"He must be a Jew," the man repeated bluntly. "You know, the Jews, they think they own everything."

I took a deep breath and turned to face him, making sure he could see the Star of David necklaces I proudly wear around my neck. "Do you understand that what you said is hurtful, hateful, and is, in fact, antisemitic?"

The woman the guy was with went pale. "Nahhhh," he said, "I am not antisemitic! I have a ton of Jewish friends!"

EMMANUEL: Sigh.

NOA: I went home and did what every human of my generation would do—I posted a bunch of stories on Instagram and basked in the glory of love and care pouring out at me from friends and followers. And that was pretty much it . . . until the dinner with Emmanuel.

There I was at the same restaurant, but this time, instead of sitting next to an antisemite, I was sitting with a champion for the truth and a genuinely nice guy. Draped in a Jim Morrison vibe, feeling like the Jewish Daisy Jones, I found myself asking, once again, "Excuse me, sir, what was that?" Emmanuel had just asked me to be his partner on his next journey—to write his next book together. I could barely process the proposal before I said, "I do." I mean, yes. I said yes.

And so, it began. From that first conversation, we didn't hold back. Emmanuel asked me whatever was on his mind.

EMMANUEL: You're right, I did. I needed to ask you questions about being Jewish the same way white people asked me questions about being Black. (Or at least how I wished white people would ask me questions about being Black.) Is being Jewish a race or an ethnicity? Why do some Jewish people wear the caps on their head? Why are there so many Jewish people in Hollywood? If your agent is Jewish, and my agent is Jewish, is it unfair to say that Jewish people control the entertainment industry? When's the next Shabbat dinner? And also, after the events of October 7th, what in the world is going on in Israel?

NOA: The chapters that follow are the result of those conversations. It's a no-judgment space to answer the questions you've thought about but might have been too nervous to ask. It's a real space for me to give uncensored answers. Because I don't believe in "safe spaces"; I believe in *real* spaces. In other words—bring it on.

EMMANUEL: Well, in that case, here's my first question: Why was it so important for you to have the book be called *Uncomfortable Conversations with a* Jew? Because if I'm being honest, it made *me* uncomfortable at first. When I started speaking on race, I made a conscious decision to say, "Black people," not

"Blacks." Asian people, not Asians. Jewish people, not Jews. It just sounds offensive. So why "Jew"?

NOA: Exactly because of your reaction. That word, *Jew*, has been used as a slur for thousands of years but not because there's anything inherently wrong with being a Jew. The problem is with the meaning that people have assigned to it, the dehumanization and humiliation associated with it. So, I am now reclaiming this word and owning it proudly. I'm a Jew, and I love it.

There is a term in the Jewish tradition called *bashert*, which usually refers to a romantic soulmate. The actual word translates to "destiny," "meant-to-be," "inevitable," or "preordained." The fact that Emmanuel asked me to write this book with him at the same place I was subjected to antisemitic harassment was, indeed, *bashert*. But more than that, it felt like a lifeline. About fifteen months after our first meeting was October 7th, when the world began roiling with more antisemitism than Jewish people have seen since the Holocaust. As a community, we have had to put our mourning, grief, and anxiety on pause in order to hold the front lines of combatting anti-Jewish hate. So, you can imagine how I felt when Emmanuel said simply:

EMMANUEL: Relief is on the way.

2.

THE NAME GAME
Who (or What) on Earth *Is* a Jew?

EMMANUEL: I believe we need to start from the absolute beginning. Some people might not understand what being a Jewish person means, and specifically, who is a Jewish person?

NOA: I think that's a great place to start—if anything because it just so happens that most people in the world have never met a Jew by *any* definition of the word, seeing as we're just under 0.2 percent of the population and are most densely clustered in North America and Israel. It's also true that the less people know Jews, the more antisemitic they are.

This topic also gets right to the heart of the argument of how Judaism is different from Christianity and Islam because it's not just a religion, it's an *ethno-religion*. Meaning being Jewish is not solely about being observant or practicing daily rituals. It's about a shared story and history, a shared culture, and a shared ancestral homeland—in Hebrew, it's an *Am* and *Uma*, a peoplehood and a nation. And yeah, a religion, too. But to me, it's mostly a peoplehood.

EMMANUEL: I have been led to believe that a Jewish person is either:

A. Someone of the Jewish faith, or
B. Someone of the Jewish heritage and/or culture.

From my knowledge, which I know is limited, you can be Jewish by religion, or you can be Jewish by birth, right?

NOA: Yes and yes! So, the simple answer is that a Jewish person is someone who was born to a Jewish mother (or father, for some branches of Judaism), or who has converted to Judaism. From there we have a lot more to unpack because actually *being* Jewish is not a one-size-fits-all experience. There is no one way to qualify as a Jew. We come in all flavors of denominations (or levels of observance—and sometimes none at all) and ethnicities. In fact, Jews have been debating (one of our favorite pastimes) over the issue of what it means to be a Jew for thousands of years.

Another interesting thing to understand about Judaism before we start is that it's not a missionary religion. Unlike other Abrahamic traditions such as Christianity and Islam, we're not out there trying to convert people. Traditionally, Judaism makes it really hard to join on purpose because, well, being a Jew isn't a walk in the park. It includes rules and restrictions, not to mention membership to a group with a long history of ongoing oppression. So, we don't want to just build numbers; we want people who understand what it means to commit to this crew. Plus, we don't believe that people have to be Jewish in order to have a connection to God or have a sense of purpose in the world. If people are out there building a just society and want to be partners in that work? Fantastic—no need to be a Jew, too.

EMMANUEL: Okay, this is all fascinating—complex, but fascinating. Break this down for me.

How Do You Jew?

NOA: It *is* fascinating *and* complex. Judaism is a religion, a culture, and an ethnicity; it's a belief system, a tradition, and a bloodline. In one way or another, it can be all those things. Every Jew Jews differently.

My dad was a full-on atheist, and he was just as Jewish as the most observant Jew you can find. One is equally Jewish whether they are a devout practitioner of the faith or if they're a part-timer for the High Holidays. It's also safe to say that the Jewish community as a whole is a mishmash. We represent almost every color and ethnicity. With all due respect to the unofficial representatives of American Jewry, Barbara Streisand and Adam Sandler, the international Jewish community is *way* more diverse.

EMMANUEL: See, this is confusing for me. Because as a Christian—I'm actually the son of a pastor—I grew up going to three church services every Sunday, and not like three different church services, the same church service three times. Sunday morning at 7:50 a.m., 9:50 a.m., and 12 p.m. I was there in the second row, hoping communion would be taken so I could sip on the grape juice. I don't know why, but that church communion grape juice tastes extra good . . . maybe it's anointed. But back to the point—when someone says they are a Christian, it implies that they adhere to a specific set of beliefs. So, when you say that you can be an atheist but also be Jewish, that makes no sense to me. Wouldn't that mean you are not any religion, let alone Jewish?

NOA: You'd think, right?! And sure, there are most likely some spiritual advisors out there cringing as I say this, but believing in God is not a requirement when it comes to being Jewish. Because Judaism is about more than just our belief system. It is something we can be born into; it can be something that connects us to a geographical place; and it can include rituals that aren't necessarily associated with God. But before we get too far into the weeds, let's start with the actual religious elements of Judaism, because that's the part most people think of when they think of, well, a religion. And as the oldest surviving monotheistic religion in the world, whether you're Orthodox or only in it for the bagels, you gotta respect that.

Never Losing My Religion, Just Adjusting It Over Time

NOA: The Jewish religion dates back to the 2000s BCE, when a visionary guy named Abraham jump-started the monotheistic revolution. Believing there was one God (and later, that we are all created in God's image) was a disruptive concept, since polytheism was the trend, and everyone from the Egyptians to the Sumerians to the Greeks were on that bandwagon. As we now know, this new and exciting idea of monotheism would go on to become the foundation not only of Judaism but also of Christianity and Islam. But at the time, that new construct was a game changer.

How it went down, according to the Bible, is that God ordered Abraham to go forth, get circumcised, and lead a people. This became known as his covenant, or agreement, with God, who promised him the land of Canaan for his descendants in exchange for following His word. And Canaan, a historical geographical term for a piece of the eastern Mediterranean region of West Asia, now includes, you guessed it, most of modern-day Israel.

About four thousand years ago, when Abe and his newly minted band of Jews were building their homeland, it was a sovereign Jewish state, referred to in the Old Testament as Israel, in the Bible as the United Monarchy, and in the Quran as, well, Israel.* It was this covenant between Abraham and God that eventually, hundreds of years later, culminated in the handing down of the Torah, or the first five books of the Old Testament that included the Ten Commandments and the written Jewish laws. This is when God revealed himself to Moses at Mount Sinai and made a covenant with the people of Israel then and there.

EMMANUEL: You know what's crazy is that as a Christian, this topic has always raised unanswered questions for me since the very first day I came to faith. I won't say that it has made me uncomfortable, necessarily, but I've definitely felt . . . some type of way. Because the Bible, which I believe in firmly, always talks about the Jews being God's Chosen people or getting priority with God (Matt. 15:24, Rom. 1:16). Based upon what I believe and the text, it's as though God had a sort of soft spot for the Jews . . . I'm just not exactly sure what that means in totality or practicality. But the Bible is pretty clear about the favor that Jews have with God.

---

* This can also be corroborated with carbon-dated archaeological findings, such as remains and artifacts in Jerusalem associated with the First Temple, also known as the Temple of Solomon, which was built by King David's son Solomon between 957 and 959 BCE. These include a 2,700-year-old seal (called a *bulla*) with a name written on it in Hebrew, "Natan-Melech, Eved Ha'Melech," a doozy of a moniker that appears in the Second Book of Kings.

NOA: It is a mind-blowing concept, to be "chosen"; I'll give you that. But it's important to point out—because this idea of somehow being better than anyone else has been used against us—that we don't see it as being superior to anyone. If anything, this "chosenness" is understood and experienced as humility, an aspiration to do better, and/or an eternal sense of guilt—not a self-satisfied favorite-child complex. And the fact that anyone can technically choose to become Jewish speaks to the fact that this chosenness is just as much about human choice as divine choice. It's not some mystical genetic elitism (we'll get to that later) but a way of life that was codified thousands of years ago.

What is also amazing to me is that you don't even have to believe in the biblical stories to understand that so much of this history did, in fact, happen. Even if you think this is the stuff of myth or fairy tales—and remember, I did not grow up sitting in synagogue on Saturday mornings—we can stick to the facts: We know, objectively, historically, and scientifically, that Israel, the birthplace of Judaism, existed somewhere between 1200 and 1400 BCE. We know that Judaism gave us this radical idea of a relationship between one person and one God. We know that there are hundreds of rules and regulations that have been passed down for millennia. Together they tell this foundational story (and we love us some good stories) about how Abraham considered his relationship with God to be a covenant, or oath-bound relationship, not just with himself, but with his children and their children's children, too. So literally that covenant was made with *me*—and my children. And if you identify as a Jew, regardless of your current religious status, that covenant was made with you, too.

So, What Is Judaism?

NOA: In order to condense thousands of years of religious texts into a bite-sized snooze-proof snack, I asked Rabbi Jeremy Borovitz whether we could summarize what people spend entire lifetimes studying into the basic pillars of Judaism. His response? "No. Impossible."

But then he walked it back: "Or at least impossible to identify the tenets that everyone can agree on." Because, as you'll see in just a moment, there is nothing more Jewish than dissent and disagreement—the unofficial Jewish superpower. But for now, for the sake of us understanding what it is exactly that we Jews all have in common, Rabbi Borovitz explained that, to his mind, the main pillar of Judaism is a connection to the two covenants that are specific to the Jewish people. These are:

1. *The covenant you enter simply by being a descendant of Abraham and his wife Sarah.* (Aka our *genealogical* connection to Judaism versus one just in practice.) Which, for the record, is why my dad, the atheist, was very much a Jew.

2. *The covenant of Sinai.* This is often symbolized through the Torah, or the actual laws and religious practices of Judaism. And actually, we Jews have not one but *two* Torah traditions. The first is the written Torah, also called the Hebrew Bible, which was, again, as the story goes, handed down to Moses by God on Mount Sinai. And then there's the oral Torah, codified as the Talmud, which includes a whole other

set of statutes and interpretations (and thousands of years of heated debates about them) that were put forth by rabbis over time.

So, as far as an agreed-upon definition of what it means to practice Judaism, that's about as concrete as it gets. However, Rabbi Borovitz adds this: "To see the pillars of Judaism, consider the words of Shimon the Righteous from Pirkei Avot 1:2 in the Talmud:

"The world stands upon three things: the Torah, work, and charity."
לע הרותה לעו הדובעה לעו תולימג םידסח

Some modern scholars interpret this to mean that Judaism is, in a nutshell: study, practicing that study in real life, and being good to others.*

EMMANUEL: My life is based upon the same instructions; they are just presented in a different way. In church, I was always taught that the two most important things I can do are:

1. Love God with all my heart, mind, and soul.
2. Love my neighbor as I love myself.

As you were talking, I realized that Jews live by the same

---

*A famous story from the Talmud has it that a non-Jew who wanted to convert to Judaism came to the sage Hillel the Elder (an early Talmudic sage and all-around Jewish baller) and asked to be taught the entire Torah while he stood on one foot. The wise man replied, "That which is hateful to you, do not to your fellow. That is the whole Torah; the rest is interpretation."

principles that Jesus told his disciples are the greatest commandments to follow (Matt. 22:37–39).

Ya know, Noa, maybe we actually have more in common than we thought.

NOA: Of course we do. Similar to what you've just described, I like to say that being Jewish is very much about your actions in the here and now, both personally in your life and collectively as a people. Being Jewish is not theoretical.

On every level, Judaism prompts you to be present in your actions every second of the day. It would not be wholly inaccurate to say that Judaism, in its most observant form, is essentially an obsessive-compulsive version of an awareness and gratitude practice. From the moment you wake up to the moment you go to bed, there's a prayer and ritual for that. The day you're born, the day you get married, and the day you die—there's a practice for that. What foods you eat and in which order, how exactly to consummate your relationship, even pooping (and giving gratitude for it!)—Judaism has a say in that, too.

Because the more present you are—with yourself, with your spouse, with your family, with your community—the more connected you become to who you are. And the more you understand yourself, the more you understand the world and God (whatever that happens to look like for you). As a secular Jew, even I can appreciate how amazing it is that we have thousands of years of wisdom and stories and traditions that connect us with ourselves and a higher power and that give us a deeper meaning to life. They also connect us with one another, which we know is one of the most powerful sources of health and happiness for humans.

There is a lot to Judaism that makes it special and unique, and it's all worth knowing in the name of demystification and understanding. But I've narrowed it down to a few of my favorite things:

- **It's a decentralized religion.** Meaning you don't really need a single designated place, such as a synagogue, to practice it. Our temples had a nasty habit of being destroyed, and Jews tended to be kicked out of most places they lived. So, Judaism went through a sort of rebrand that made the *community* the center of the sacred, as well as the individual—meaning (most of) our rituals could travel with us and be just as sanctified.

- **It emphasizes community.** One only has to join a Jewish family for Shabbat or a Passover Seder to understand the value of togetherness in Judaism. The idea of our connection to one another originates in the Torah, and some of our holiest prayers, such as the mourner's prayer we say after someone dies, require that ten people, or a minyan, be present; nine other people who can say "Amen; I see you in your pain; I see you in your grief."

  Basically, the idea behind these rituals is that life, healing, and growth do not happen in a vacuum. They happen in a community—Judaism is the greatest team sport there is. (Not unlike Little League—we all get to play and everybody gets a trophy.) And that kind of solidarity, that idea that none of us can go through life alone, is probably what has sustained us collectively as a people.

- **It celebrates nature**. Jews were some of the original nature-loving woo-woo spiritualists. Our scripture is full of stories devoted simply to noticing the beauty of the mountains and the trees and seeing nature as a reflection of God's greatness in the world. Our holidays are synced to nature—such as Sukkot (a seven-day celebration where we build outdoor huts to remember how Jews lived after escaping slavery in Egypt) or Tu Bishvat (a literal celebration, like an actual birthday, of trees) and other customs like Tashlich on Rosh Hashanah, the Jewish New Year, where we toss bread crumbs into a moving body of water to symbolize throwing away the crap from the year before and letting go of the things that no longer serve us. Also, we're moon people. Our calendar is guided by the lunar cycle, with each new moon marking a new beginning. We see every new lunar cycle as an opportunity to heal the wounds from the previous month and to create something new and beautiful in the coming month. Rabbi Sharon Brous puts it this way: "As a people, we've come to understand that hope and light wax and wane, and that often in the moments that appear to be the darkest and most bleak, we are actually standing at the cusp of something completely new." How beautiful is that?

- **It evolves as we do**. Even though every branch or denomination of Judaism is different, what they all have in common is change. Some believe in small changes over time while others believe in debating until we all agree on *some* change, and some advocate for lots of change all the time. What we get as a result is a religion that is pretty much always evolving in some way, or what my activist-writer friend Gidi Grinstein refers to as "flexigidity." Meaning Judaism is rigid in some ways and flexible in others, which is yet another superpower and a source of Judaism's long-lasting resiliency. That's also what allows it to be inclusive and progressive. For example, a hundred years ago, girls wouldn't have been educated or even bat mitzvahed—a Jewish rite of passage when you turn twelve or thirteen—but now, of course, they are. And women certainly would not have been rabbis but are now leading congregations around the world.

- **It's a big tent.** As in, no matter who you're married to, how often (or not often at all) you go to synagogue, or which Jewish laws you observe, there's still a place for you under the big Jewish tent. That's mainly because Judaism has over time evolved to include four main branches with varying levels of observance and adherence to the Halacha (pronounced ha-la-CHA; really let that back-of-the-throat *cchhh* sound rip), or Jewish law. As the circumstances of our Jewish forebears changed (i.e., depending on which countries they'd gotten kicked out of and where they needed to make another go of it), the Jewish religion underwent divisions and reforms to help keep it alive. These main branches are:

  - **Reform Judaism:** One of the first offshoots of the OG Halachic Jewish practice, it started to pop up in Germany in the beginning of the nineteenth century with the original goal of helping Jews assimilate by making Judaism more "modern" and less of the complicated socio-religious-ethnic group it had historically been. (See also: assimilated whiteness, which is a topic for another chapter.) In terms of acceptance, these folks are the chillest with the idea that you might consider yourself Jewish even if your connection is through your father or if your conversion was less than traditional. Secular Jews who practice nothing at all might most easily vibe with these folks.

- **Orthodox Judaism:** In response to Reform Judaism softening their relationship with rabbinic law, Orthodox Judaism doubled down on it. They are the belief purists who maintain that the Torah was written by God. They are firm on abiding by age-old traditions and religious laws. In the Orthodox world, you're a Jew if your mother is Jewish. Period. Your dad could be the Jewiest Jew straight out of *Fiddler on the Roof*, but his faith alone couldn't secure your Member of the Tribe (MOT) membership if your mother isn't Jewish.

- **Modern Orthodox Judaism:** This also sprouted up in response to Reform Judaism as a way to blend orthodox traditions with more modern, secular sensibilities. There's more adherence to Halacha as well as still engaging with society at large, like wearing modern clothing, getting university degrees, and holding modern-day professions.

- **Conservative Judaism:** Aka the ongoing marital mediation between Modern Orthodoxy and Reform. Conservative Judaism has nothing to do with conservative politics; conservative Jews can be right-leaning Republicans or left-leaning Democrats. They find value in the traditional Halachic laws but actively debate how to properly merge the old world with the new. Called "continuing revelation," it means that a law committee of Conservative rabbis and scholars, called the Committee on Jewish Laws and Standards, has the right to decide modern-day law and practice.*

THE FOUR PILLARS OF JUDAISM

NOA: One of my favorite ways to think of Judaism comes from my aforementioned friend, Gidi Grinstein. He says that Judaism can be viewed through four pillars: religion, peoplehood, *tikkun olam*, and nationhood. Religion and faith are personal and are observed differently by different individuals. Peoplehood can be described as shared stories: legacy, history, family, and educational traditions, which link many generations. *Tikkun olam* is the Jewish mandate to make the world a better place, literally to "mend it." And nationhood is the modern manifestation of a basic human need: a connection to a land and the need for self-determination and self-governance. Not every Jew practices or identifies with all four pillars, but I think they are a great prism to use when thinking about one's Jewishness.

---

* A great example is when, in 1950, the Committee on Jewish Laws and Standards realized that not driving to synagogue on Shabbat was an issue because of the realities of suburban life. They handed down a new legal decision, or *teshuvah*, and now Conservative Jews can drive to synagogue on Shabbat. (Which then led to many Conservative Jews just driving everywhere in addition to synagogue on Shabbat, because you might as well.)

When you look at Judaism through the lens of these pillars, it's easier to see how Jews can each relate to their Judaism in different ways. It's the same genesis story and history, and yet we don't all share the same relationship with our faith and/or Jewish identity and practices.

EMMANUEL: I'll be honest . . . you just said a whole lot—

NOA: Oh, you mean condensing an *entire* religion's worth of teachings into a single chapter?

EMMANUEL: Exactly. But how does this relate to you personally? Which Judaism sleeping bag do you fall into beneath this proverbial "big tent" of Judaism?

NOA: I usually find myself snuggled into a more secular sleeping bag, but that's not to say that religious and spiritual elements of Judaism don't play a role in my life. A big way they do is through the culture those things have shaped over time, like the other three pillars Gidi described: peoplehood, *tikkun olam*, and nationhood. Take this story, for example:

When I was in my early twenties, I traveled to Australia for the first time and went to Melbourne to visit my friend Lauren's family. They weren't particularly religious—at least as far as I could tell, considering they didn't keep kosher or wear head coverings—but we still sat down to Shabbat dinner the first Friday night I was there. What shook me was that, as a person living a very secular life and who grew up in a very secular family, it all felt super *familiar*. Lauren's father, whose family was Australian many generations over, could just as easily have been my dad or an uncle. Her mom, also Australian, could have been from central casting for "Jewish mother." Not in an over-the-top "Eat! Eat! You're skin and bones!" kind of way, but again, in that seen-it-before, felt-it-before, familiar kind of way. It was hard to explain to myself even back then, but I just knew that I *knew* these people. That they were *my* people. I was halfway around the world and yet it felt like home.

It occurred to me then that there was a through line between Jewish families around the world, this je ne sais quoi that we all share and can immediately recognize. Not necessarily in the shape of the same exact traditions but a similar vibe. Similar attitudes. That's where the culture of Judaism comes in.

3.

THE CULTURE CLUB

NOA: Here's something you'll hear a lot from secular Jews around the world: "I am not *Jewish*-Jewish, I am *culturally* Jewish." Come again? How is it possible to have a religious identity without actually practicing the religion? How can you be Jewish while not believing in God or stepping foot inside a synagogue? The answer is: It's in the culture. Or, alternatively—as is the case with most things Jewish-adjacent—it's complicated.

EMMANUEL: That word *culture* you just mentioned means everything. Growing up in a Nigerian household and attending a primarily white high school, yet also belonging to a church in the inner city of Dallas, Texas, I constantly heard the insulting remark, "Acho is Black, but he's not really *Black*-Black." Or "You're an Oreo—Black on the outside and white on the inside." They were trippin', and what they meant was that I was not culturally Black, even though my skin color was Black—as though that somehow made me less Black.

Now as an adult, I understand that not fitting into the stereotypical norms doesn't make one any less Black or change their ability to identify as Black. And I can educate people that there is not one way to be Black. Honestly, there isn't one way to be just about anything.

NOA: Exactly—so for us, there is an undeniable, not specifically religious thread that passes through the entire Jewish community, all around the world from the US to the UK, Turkey to Thailand. When you meet a Jew, you tend to *know* that you've met a Jew (and not just a New Yorker with an affinity for therapy, everything bagels, and NPR—although that's all very Jewy). No matter where you're from, or the color of your skin, that thread connects you to the same tribe and nation.

The reason Judaism has as much culture as it has rich religious tradition is because of the ever-evolving nature of its laws. The culture exists *because* the religion exists. Take lighting Shabbat candles, the practice that many Jews partake in on Friday nights to mark the beginning of Shabbat, or the sabbath. This tradition evolved from the Torah, where we were told to not work on Saturday, followed immediately by: and don't even *think* about starting a fire! Probably because back then, starting a fire was legit work. So, the tradition developed such that you light symbolic beautiful candles *before* Shabbat starts. Most Jews probably aren't aware of where this progression of tradition came from, but for many Jews, candles + challah (traditional, and tasty, braided bread) = insta-Shabbat. What started out as a religious observance is now a cultural practice that Jews around the world share and that I love.

EMMANUEL: As someone on the outside, this is all so fascinating. What are some other hallmarks of the Jewish culture?

NOA: While I usually try to avoid generalizations about Jews, a sense of humor and a deep desire to feed people are indeed hallmarks of being culturally Jewish. In fact, I can't tell you the level of anxiety I get when somebody tells me they're hungry.

EMMANUEL: I've witnessed this personally.

NOA: In addition to a compulsive need to feed you, there's also:

- **Storytelling**: Remember how I told you that we Jews love a good story? It's actually at the core of the Jewish tradition. Because we were always getting uprooted and exiled and couldn't rely on our synagogues to stay intact, *we've* had to keep the traditions of our people alive. Which means that we're not only in charge of telling those stories but we're also *commanded* to share them so that our children and their children can learn them, understand their place in the world, and see how they connect to a much larger Jewish narrative. These stories teach us how we overcame persecutions and thrived as a nation, in addition to lessons that we can still apply to our lives today.

  This storytelling happens at every Jewish holiday— we recount something that happened to the Jewish people way back in the day, and so the holidays become rituals for remembering. As the comedian Alan King joked, most Jewish holidays go something like this: "They tried to kill us, we won, let's eat." And each holiday tells a different story: Passover (aka the matzoh holiday) recounts the exodus from slavery in Egypt to freedom and self-determination. Hanukah, the December holiday celebrated with menorahs, dreidels, and latkes (competing with, and losing to, Christmas), celebrates the Jewish revolt against the ancient Greeks, the consequent recovery of Jerusalem, and the reclamation of the Second Temple.

Heavy track record aside, there is something pretty magical about that repetition, knowing Jews have been doing the very same thing for thousands of years. I mean, we *still* don't eat leavened bread on Passover because of Pharaoh.

- **Questioning (and arguing with)** *everything*: One of the first friends I made after moving to the United States was a guy from Australia. (I have a soft spot for Aussies; what can I say?) From time to time, he would tell me stories from when he went to Catholic school, where it's safe to say he didn't have the best time. One day he told me that when the kids in his class learned about the Immaculate Conception, he challenged his teacher about it, trying to figure out what it all meant. After all, to an eight-year-old kid who knows enough about how babies are made to not exactly take this story at face value, it merited at least a follow-up.

"What did the teacher say?" I asked him.

"Nothing," he replied. "He spanked me with a ruler for asking a question."

I was blown away.

Now, he went to school in the '90s and I'm pretty sure, or at least hope, that they don't use a ruler down under for anything other than drawing a straight line anymore, but at the time, I was shocked. I, on the other hand, was taught that everything needs to be questioned in order to be better understood, even stories from the Bible. I was taught to *always* ask questions, *always* doubt, and—if there's another point of view to be had—*always* argue. As I grew up, I learned that the entire Jewish culture is built on these qualities and that they go back to the foundation of our religion.

Take Abraham, for example. After making his covenant with God, God informs him that he and his wife Sarah are about to have a son. As the story goes, Abraham was ninety-nine years old at the time, and the mom-to-be a fresh eighty-nine. Instead of blindly believing this all-knowing wisdom, Abraham essentially responds with, "Excuse me, what's that now?"

When something doesn't seem right, we've been instructed to question it, argue over it, and debate it until truth prevails. In a way, it's about never being content with the status quo (or just never being content). It's like the joke about the waiter in a Jewish deli: when he approaches a table of old ladies, he asks, "Is *anything* all right?" Which is funny to the Jewish community because the answer is almost always: "Meh. We can do better."

- **Education**: The directive to read and write is woven into Judaism. It goes all the way back to the Talmud saying to educate one's children. But also, it was sort of a necessity. The moment our second temple was destroyed by the Romans in 70 BCE, we realized that if Jews were going to keep passing on those crucial Jewish stories and rituals, then they were going to have to learn how to read and write. It was a pretty radical idea, too, because at that time in the ancient world, mostly religious leaders, the monarchy, and the wealthy were allowed to be literate. Now Jewish parents were commanded to educate their children—well, let's be honest, *male* children—and they'd send their sons from as young as four to primary school or synagogue. (One of the first if not *the* first instance of compulsory education!) The teachers would smear honey over each letter on their little tablets so that the children could lick it off, forming a sweet association with the written word, and it's been love (with a hint of obsession) ever since.

- **Valuing the Here and Now**: Jews believe that after they die, their spirit once again becomes one with God. But you find very few mentions of the afterlife in the Hebrew Bible, and that's because, according to Rabbi Jonathan Sacks, one of the most prominent spiritual leaders in the world, "Judaism is an extraordinarily this-worldly, this-life-focused religion." That's part of what made it different from other ancient religions, which were hyper-focused on the afterlife (just look at all those pyramids decked out with pets and snacks for the next otherworldly chapter). Judaism doesn't deny that something pretty rad is coming after we die, but it teaches instead that, to quote Rabbi Sacks again, "If we are to come close to God, if we are to really grow as human beings, if we are to make a difference to the world, then let's do it here. Here and now, not in some other world, in some other life."

NOA: Now, some Jewish people might hear all this and say, "But you can't inherit culture!" or "Judaism will never survive if we don't maintain the religion!" But I think celebrating our unique culture is important. For starters, it's essential for understanding what we Jews value. It also illustrates how beautifully per-vasive Judaism is in a Jew's life, even if some, like me, hardly ever go to temple or were raised by a father who didn't believe in God.

Whether we recognize it or not, Judaism has seeped into almost every nook and cranny of our lives because of these traits, values, and behaviors. We have this lovely universal shared identity *because* we're Jewish—and that's not something to take for granted if we want Judaism to have a future.

Our tiny population (which, remember, is less than 0.2 percent of the world's total) relies on *us* to keep the flame of our peoplehood glowing through tradition, whatever that might look like for each of us. All to say, this is my little noodge (one of my favorite Yiddish words) for Jews to reflect on what it means to them to be Jewish, especially as we are now so clearly seeing how crucial it is for us to hold our heads a little higher and shine a little brighter. Together.

4.

THE JEWISH . . . RACE?

EMMANUEL: Let me ask you this: Is it accurate to refer to Jewish people as a race, meaning is somebody Jewish in the same way that somebody would be Black or white?

NOA: Actually, one of the biggest misconceptions about Jewish people is that we are a race—in fact, it's what got us into a sticky situation with a guy named Adolf Hitler. So, I can cut to the chase on that one: the answer is a definitive No. To understand *why* is to first acknowledge that, as you know, we use race to group people by shared physical traits and behaviors. And it's often a loaded notion, giving us a way to compare these groups against one another in a society-wide power ranking.

So, the key reason why it's important to establish that there is no such thing as a Jewish race is because the idea that it *is* a race has been foundational to antisemitism for decades. You only have to look at the most famous political group to lump people from around the world together and call them a race: the Nazis. As the Aryan-supremacist Nazi Party so . . . *help-*

fully demonstrated, people can be labeled, marginalized, and slaughtered based purely on this mythical construct.* Those who saw—and still do see—Judaism as a race are suggesting that there is something inherently biologically distinct about Jews that can't simply be washed away.

We share a lineage, but not a biological identity. If I were to introduce you to an Ethiopian Jew, an Asian Jew, and a Russian Jew—looking at them, you would see no similarities. But they are all still 100 percent Jewish. Kinda like how people descended from the passengers of the *Mayflower* are not of a specific Mayflower race.

EMMANUEL: So, what you're saying is while all Black people share their Blackness and all white people share their whiteness, all Jewish people don't have one uniform thing that makes every single one of them genetically the same.

NOA: Precisely. Many Jews have a lot in common with one another—a love of arguing, mixed feelings about pork and shellfish, a passion for laughing and learning, and membership in a tribe that we can all trace back to Abraham and Sarah. But while there are many things we share, a single genetic code is not one of them.

It is important to add the disclaimer, though (because, remember, Nazis), that while there is some shared ancestry

---

* The Nazis lusted after a "pure" Aryan race, which had a surprisingly murky definition but was essentially synonymous with non-Jewish, non-Black, and non-Roma (formerly known as Gypsy). Therefore, the inferior Jewish "race" was deemed one of the primary Master Race polluters and needed to be cleansed.

among a percentage of Jews, it's a footnote* in the grand genetic scheme of things and far from proof of a distinct Jewish race. A more appropriate and nuanced concept for understanding how all Jews are related is that of an *ethno*-religion, which is a vast group of people who do happen to share a distinctive culture, ancestry, belief system, and/or language.

So, no matter how many Jewish Jeans, Genes, or Eugenes you meet, the existence of a singular Jewish *gene* is more folklore than fact. And trying to collapse all of our differences in our expansive, intersectional peoplehood and shove them into a box is not only problematic but also flat-out wrong.

EMMANUEL: Okay, so I hear all that . . . but you know what, I'm just gonna go ahead and ask it: Are Jewish people white?

---

* There have been several studies pointing to a shared genetic ancestry for Jews that can be traced back to the Middle East. And this also shows up in a predisposition for certain types of genetic diseases that disproportionately affect Jews. But, as most scholars of race would explain, race is a social, not biological, construct.

5.

SOOO, ARE JEWS WHITE?

EMMANUEL: When I think about race in America, I think about two simple terms: Black and white. It's crazy; we've simplified so many colors and cultures and groups of people in America into just those two primary groups: white people and people of color. A lot of identity gets lost in that. Every week at 12:30 p.m., Monday through Friday, I have a production meeting at the Fox Studio Lot with the talent and producers of my daily sports show, *Speak*. It's about twelve people in total. I sit in this meeting with my three cohosts, all of whom are Black American—the American piece being an important distinction. One of my cohosts, LeSean, who goes by "Shady," makes it a point whenever discussing Black athletes to specify whether they are Black or Black American. Because Shady is acknowledging a more accurate racial identity by saying Black American athletes, as opposed to Black athletes who could be from the Caribbean, Africa, or Europe.

So, for Shady, there is a pride he takes in differentiating his specific race (Black American) from the larger race of Black people. That's part of what makes race so interesting to me, the idea that while it brings a micro group together, it ultimately separates the macro group of all of humanity. Which is why I think forcing all races to fall under the header of "Black" or "white" does a major disservice to mankind.

But if race, particularly in the Western world, is largely Black and white, then where do Jewish people fit in?

NOA: If they are of European descent, which is the majority of Jews in America, then they do tend to look white. But many Jews in the world, and certainly the majority of Jews in Israel, do not resemble a white person.

EMMANUEL: Then for the purposes of this conversation, between two people who are currently in America, is it fair to say that Jewish people *are* white? And, as a result, have access to the privilege that comes with it? Because I feel like this is part of the disconnect. In America, my Jewish brothers and sisters have the privilege of being perceived as white. Historically, they have not been discriminated against in America based upon the color of their skin; they did not have to suffer Jim Crow laws, or public abuse without justice at the hands of the police. So, when Jewish people in America say that they are not white, it sounds to me like they're trying to have it both ways. They get the benefits of being members of the oppressive class while also claiming minority membership. So, all that said—how would you answer my original question? Are Jews white?

NOA: You might not like this response, or you might say I'm trying to have it both ways, but my answer is yes and not at all. Because to some people, we are not white enough. And to others, we are too white.

The yes part is that Jewish people, especially the ones of Eastern European descent, are indeed white-*passing*. But there is a difference between being white-passing and WASP-y (White Anglo-Saxon Protestant) white. Because after decades of being kept out of the white racial majority here in North America, Eastern European Jews were only allowed to integrate into white society in the last two generations—assuming they'd done their best to assimilate, or blend in with the way they dressed, spoke, and lived. It was kinda like "don't ask, don't tell" for Jews.

So, it's alarming for us, after so many years of persecutions and inequity, to find out that we are too white to be seen as an imperiled minority because, from an outsider's perspective, we've benefited from white privilege and run Wall Street and Hollywood. And you can imagine how infuriating it is that the majority of the American population insists we're fully white, even as we're told by white nationalists that we're not.

EMMANUEL: I hear that, and I don't disagree. But I still wrestle with the fact that a Black person has to worry about inherent disrespect and daily danger by law enforcement, and you don't—and I think that's a point of great tension.

NOA: One hundred percent. Even though I don't look totally white and always get asked "Where are you from?" (as in, you don't look American or European), I don't have to worry about being shot if I run a stop sign, whereas you do.

But here is the thing, Emmanuel. Not only were Jews shunned and murdered for two millennia, white-passing or not, but Jews are also not *all* white. So now we have the Jewish experience being painted with a waaay too large paintbrush. Assumptions about our collective experience are being drawn from the portion of us who happen to have the lightest skin and benefit from it, which diminishes the experience of non-white Jews. Ask any of my Moroccan, Iranian, or even Israeli Jewish friends (including myself), and they resent the idea of Jewish whiteness to the core. My friend Shanni Suissa, a proud Moroccan Jew, said it best: "I'm white? I have one eyebrow— screw you, I'm not white!" As in, no one is mistaking her for a blue-eyed, blond-haired *Mayflower* descendant. Also, Drake is a Jew. So, there's that.

Ultimately, my answer to "Are Jews white?" remains "Yes and no." And as we know by now, the only way out is through, so let's grab you a snack, prepare to open your mind, and jump in.

EMMANUEL: Happen to have any more of those peaches you gave me the first time I came over to your house?

NOA: I'm all out, babe, but I've got the entire nut and dried fruit aisle of Trader Joe's in my pantry, so we're covered.

6.

YOU'RE NOT WHITE ENOUGH

NOA: The story of how Jews, originally a small band of desert folk from ancient Israel, ended up as white Americans is, like most Jewish sagas, filled with subjugation and violence. Because Jews wouldn't have made it all the way to America if it weren't for a centuries-long cycle of war, enslavement, massacre, and exile.

From the minute things got heated in Judea (now modern-day Israel), which started all the way back in 586 BCE, when the Babylonians helped themselves to everything there, the Jews started to leave for greener pastures. Some stayed, but many scattered—a period in our history called "the exile." And for the next two thousand or so years, they wandered: they crossed into Africa, made their way to Europe and Asia, and settled in places like India, Yemen, Ethiopia, Morocco, Spain, Germany, Poland, and Russia.

Because Jews were so spread out during this time after being exiled from Israel, they ended up separating into four main ethnic communities, also known as the Jewish Diaspora: There were the *Ashkenazi Jews* of Central and Eastern European descent,

Sephardic Jews from Spain (who mostly resettled in other parts of Europe, the Middle East, and North Africa after getting kicked out of Spain), *Mizrahi Jews* from North Africa and the Middle East (think Egypt, Morocco, Libya, Yemen, Iran, and Iraq), and *Beta Israel Jews* from Ethiopia. Honorable mention also goes to the Cochin Jews of India, the Kaifeng Jews of China, among many others. All Jews, all with a covenant with Abraham, all with ancestral ties to Judea, but if you put them next to one another, they look about as alike as you and me, Emmanuel.

To fully grasp how any of them ended up as "white," you have to look at when they arrived in the United States and the plans white Protestants had for them.

The Immigrants Are Coming!

NOA: During the first couple decades of the twentieth century, America was the place to be for immigrants from all over the world. At this point, about *two million* Eastern European Jews had shown up at Lady Liberty's doorstep. They came to escape the political volatility in Eastern Europe, the rampant violence against Jews in the Russian Empire, the rise of fascism, and everyone accusing them of attempting world domination. And all these new weird-acting, weird-sounding foreigners were starting to make white Protestants nervous.

Part of that was because these newcomers were driving up the competition for low-skill jobs and accepting lower wages. But also, America, a country made up of immigrants, has a history of hating on immigrants.

Despite the fact that this was the Progressive Era, or a time of prosperity and progress for the United States, the thinking of the day was that immigrants were holding the country back from achieving its true potential. In many Anglo-Saxon Americans' minds, these poor, huddled masses were nothing more than criminals and charity abusers. And "scholars" of the time put forth that people of certain ethnicities—namely Jews, Asians, and Africans—were genetically inferior and therefore particularly detrimental to this blossoming tween of a global power.*

Also, the Jews were walking into a post–Civil War societal construct that was literally Black and white, and so someone had to decide: Which one were they?

If You Teach a Man to (Gefilte) Fish: Learning to Be White

EMMANUEL: Well, that would have been pretty easy to decide based on skin color, no? I get that these immigrants weren't like Hallmark-style white people, but wouldn't their whiteness still have been relatively clear?

NOA: You would think. But in the late nineteenth century, widely accepted ethnological literature considered Jews to be

---

* Charles Davenport, a Harvard-educated zoologist, was a major contributor to the widely influential study of eugenics, or the idea that you could "breed out" undesirable traits from a population. In 1910, he established the Eugenics Record Office at Cold Spring Harbor Laboratory in New York, where he was keen to demonstrate how immigrants would only pollute the Anglo-Saxon bloodline, saying, "I believe in such a selection of immigrants as shall not tend to adulterate our national germ plasm with socially unfit traits" and warning that "those who could pass as White would pollute the White gene pool." As a reminder, this was 1900s America, not 1930s Germany. Although, Hitler and the Nazis eventually took this theory and "research" to the bank.

"Black," or at the very least *swarthy*. Also, during that time, British researcher and "pigmentation authority" John Beddoe crafted an "index of nigrescence," essentially ranking the population of Great Britain from most white to least. Jews scored a full 100 percent "nigrescence" on his scale. And racist anthropology throughout the nineteenth and twentieth centuries asserted that Jews had Black skin, Black blood, and Black origins.

However, by the time this big wave of Jews got to the United States in the first couple of decades of the 1900s, it was conceded that they were not fully Black—but they also weren't considered fully white either. They were Black-adjacent or maybe white-*ish*. Like the Italians or Irish immigrants—white-looking enough, but totally off-brand. As a result, they were subjected to legal and de facto barriers. Think prohibited access to living in certain neighborhoods, quotas at colleges and universities, bans on applying for certain jobs, barred entry from stores, restaurants, and social clubs, stereotypes in the media—all the classics.*

EMMANUEL: Got it. So, they're aesthetically white, but they're not fully accepted into white society at this point.

NOA: Somewhat accepted, but with a grudge. They had essentially become the white Protestants' makeover project. The white Protestants thought immigrants were strange and disagreeable—and they treated them as though they were

---

* Henry Ford even got into the action, promoting antisemitic propaganda and conspiracies that the Jewish cabal wouldn't stop until it took over the world. He eventually apologized (because he was being sued for libel), but he'd already made quite an impression. In 1931, when Adolf Hitler was asked by a reporter why he had a portrait of Ford over his desk, he said, "I regard Henry Ford as my inspiration."

strange and disagreeable—but they also decided that they'd be a lot more comfortable if there were *fewer* strange and disagreeable people. And they did that through pressure to be just like them—to assimilate.

But even though Jews were seemingly in the clear in terms of practicing their Judaism without being, well, killed for it, that didn't undo generations of trauma and a deep belief that suggested it's safer to blend in and not rock the boat if they wanted to see their grandbabies born. And when the Nazis started rolling through Europe in the 1930s, the writing on the wall became clear in a very Eddie Izzard fashion: cake or death. (Or, in this case, assimilate in America or bust.) So, fitting in was a matter of survival, and the only option on the menu was "white."

EMMANUEL: I totally understand everything you're saying; it's just hard to hear. If Black people had the luxury of becoming "white" to avoid the existential threat of being targeted for the color of their skin, I'm sure that option would've been taken as well. I guess I'm just frustrated, that's all. It's like being a kid and your class having to go back inside from recess, but another teacher's class getting to stay outside for longer. You're going to resent them for that, even though it's not their fault that their teacher was more lenient.

NOA: I hear you. This is for sure a privilege that white-passing Jews have. Yes, many Jews can and do claim whiteness in order to protect themselves from overt racism. Undeniably, there is a construct of white privilege in this country. And yes, we have to accept as fact that white folks have built many, many systems that have exclusively benefited them over the years. We must recognize that we are white enough not to be second-guessed at hospitals or to not get pulled over and brutalized for no reason. Because of the privilege of not having that as our experience, we have a responsibility to be aware and to right the wrongs of systemic racism.

At the same time, assimilation has not and will not keep us safe from hate. I'm going to put a pin in how that shows up currently because I want to take a minute to go back to 1950, to those Jews who had just gotten set up as white in America. They'd barely finished mourning the deaths of their entire extended families in the Holocaust when Jews became the focus of Senator Joseph McCarthy's witch hunt for Communist influence—and potential espionage—in American institutions. Progressive Jews across the country came under suspicion, and it didn't help their PR campaign that Ethel and Julius Rosenberg were charged and executed as spies.

Granted, Joseph McCarthy was one part anti-Communist crusader and one part antisemite. (Apparently his favorite party trick was pulling out his copy of Hitler's *Mein Kampf*, calling it "inspirational," and saying "That's the way to do it.") But any American citizen suspected of being sympathetic to the Soviet Union, where many Jews had recently emigrated from— or who were thought to have subversive political views in general—were investigated, arrested, imprisoned, fined, fired, blacklisted, and otherwise humiliated.*

---

* Ninety percent of teachers blacklisted from working in public schools were Jewish, as well as the majority of actors, directors, and screenwriters blacklisted from Hollywood or pressured to "name names" in front of investigative panels. Even prominent Jewish organizations such as the Anti-Defamation League (ADL), the American Jewish Committee (AJC), and the American Jewish Congress (AJC) felt like they had to take a visible stand against Communism and declare their American patriotism in order to avoid public opinion conflating Jews with Communism.

My point is that while our whiteness did allow us some protection in the past eighty years, it has not been the silver bullet against persecution. In fact, it often has come back around to hurt us.

7.

YOU'RE TOO WHITE

EMMANUEL: Okay, you've lost me—how in the world has being white hurt Jews in America?

NOA: Believe me, I know how it sounds. But to understand the double standards we experience as Jews, including our relatively newly assigned whiteness, is to understand antisemitism.

Let's begin with this: to be a white-passing Jew in America can best be described by this quote from Eric Goldstein, an associate professor of history at Emory University:

> Jewish identity in America is inherently paradoxical and contradictory…What you have is a group that was historically considered, and considered itself, an outsider group, a persecuted minority. In the space of two generations, they've become one of the most successful, integrated groups in American society—by many accounts, part of the establishment. And there's a lot of dissonance between those two positions.

EMMANUEL: This reminds me of the plight of being a light-skinned Black person in America. Historically, there was the "one-drop" rule, which was used to oppress anybody with even one drop of Blackness in them. Therefore, even light-skinned Black people were treated like the rest of the marginalized Black community. Now, many of those light-skinned people can be white-passing, which affords them more privileges than darker-skinned Black people. Just think about the Black actresses in Hollywood even today. How many of them are darker skinned? Viola Davis, Gabrielle Union . . . that list is short. But there is a much more extensive list of those whose skin tone resembles that of Halle Berry. However, it's not like lighter-skinned Black people belong to the white community—because they're not white, they're Black, especially if they have two Black parents. And they still most likely experience prejudice.

NOA: In many ways it does feel similar. Jews have been told for decades by outside groups who they should be in order to fit in, and then are either shunned for not being enough of that thing (too ethnic! too poor!) or blamed for being too much of that thing (too white! too successful!). People really know how to make us Jews feel special, I'll tell you that.

On one end of the spectrum, you have what is beautifully summed up by an experience the comedian Alex Edelman describes in his one-man show *Just for Us*. For reasons I won't share because I don't want to spoil anything, and you should go see this masterpiece for yourself, Alex attends a meeting of white nationalists in Queens, New York. Alex Edelman is Jewish, and these folks espouse white supremacist ideologies, meaning they consider nonwhite people to be inferior. Jews happen to be very high on that list. The meeting transpires, Alex's hilarious narration unfolds, and then—the group sniffs him out as a Jew. Instead of embracing this equally melanin-challenged man as one of their own, they jeer him. "You're not white, you're *Jewish*."

Those of us who came from Europe didn't step off the boats onto American shores and immediately collect our white permits. That was highly conditional. When the white Christian majority decided we were finally worthy of being accepted, we consciously assimilated. We changed our names, our language, our clothing, and our culture. Eventually, we made some money, straightened our hair, did our noses, and sometimes even splashed our names across a museum or university. We gave back to charity, joined social justice movements, and raised our kids with good Jewish values. We figured if we just played by the rules, everybody would love us. NOPE!

EMMANUEL: But I feel like there wasn't a white permit to "accept," it was simply given to you because of the color of your skin?

NOA: Outwardly maybe. But it was never to be forgotten that we are not *really* accepted, not like everyone else. And then, all of a sudden, we were *too* white for their liking. Too successful. Too threatening. Particularly for the far right.

And on the far left, the rules of the game have also been changing. The criteria for whiteness has shifted to not only being about melanin but also about dividing the world into the oppressor and the oppressed. And the resulting conclusion of "Black and Brown = oppressed" and "white = oppressor"—which is historically true when speaking about the white Christian majority—created a context in which white-passing Jews don't fit.

This all boils down to one uncomfortable-making truth:

Jews are both not white enough and also way too white. We are seen as an "other" by some and as abetting an oppressive system by others. It's a "both/and" situation.

EMMANUEL: "Both/and"?

NOA: Meaning more than one thing can be true at one time.

Many Jews are both white-passing *and* our experience can only fully be understood through the prism of ongoing persecution, expulsion, and execution; plus, the collective trauma of what's been done—*plus*, the never-disappearing anxiety of what could come next.

We have benefited from that perceived whiteness *and* we continue to be the subject of some of the most vicious violence and hate.

And here I might piss off some people, but I'm not here to be polite; I'm here to be honest: Being a white-passing Jew in America is not a ticket out of the cycle of danger. As I said earlier, a majority of religiously targeted hate-crime offenses are committed against Jews, which has been the case every year since the FBI started reporting hate-crime statistics in 1995. After the Hamas attack of Israelis on October 7th, 2023, antisemitic events increased by *388* percent. In October 2023, FBI director Christopher Wray testified to a Senate panel that antisemitism terror threats were reaching "historic levels." Communities were advised against keeping up their mezuzahs (small cases containing traditional prayer scrolls) on their doorways during Halloween; the Israeli government issued an international travel advisory suggesting that Jewish travelers avoid displaying any sign of their Jewish or Israeli identity for their own safety; synagogues and religious schools have had to hire extra security to guard the entrances and students have been advised not to play outside; Jews everywhere have been making sure their passports are up to date; and I've been asked by far too many friends: "Where will we go if we have to leave again?"

Getting the Full Picture

EMMANUEL: I guess I understand it like this: Being a white-passing Jew in America is not a ticket out of the cycle of oppression, but it is a ticket out of the cycle of skin color–based oppression. It's not to say that white-passing Jews are not discriminated against, but that discrimination, in America, is not based upon their skin color.

NOA: Beautifully said—just a couple asterisks I'd add:

> **Our whiteness is conditional.** As in, some groups do not consider us white in the first place, which is why when we are "obviously" or visibly Jewish—such as attending synagogue, dropping our kids off at religious school, or working at Jewish organizations (not to mention wearing a yarmulke, or head covering, or other Jewish garb)—we rely on two sets of locked doors and an armed security guard to keep us safe. Also, as you'll see when we discuss antisemitism and Jewish hate in greater depth, we have been allowed white membership *so long as it serves the white Christian majority*. But when it is inconvenient—when we're a little *too* threatening to their agenda, a little *too* powerful for their comfort—it has a tendency of being snatched away. In both instances I just described, we are no longer white, we are only Jewish.

Not all Jews are white. When you use that giant paint-brush to designate all of us Jews as white, you are also marginalizing a huge group of us that does not get the attention it deserves. Remember when I told you that there were four predominant branches of Jews—the diaspora? Many of them are non-European; they're Asian, African, Latin American—a variety of Black and Brown Jews.

When you assume that all Jews are white and/or privileged, you erase an entire people's history. It also makes it a lot easier to assume the worst about Jews.

8.

THE MYTHICAL ME
Where Truth Ends and Stereotypes Begin

EMMANUEL: You mentioned that extra-wide paintbrush and how using it to paint the experience of all Jews has negative effects. Well, as you know, that same paintbrush has been used for Jewish stereotypes, too. Whether we like to admit it or not, there are a lot of stereotypes or generalizations about Jewish people, like the stingy Jew, the wealthy Jew, or the powerful Jew. But in my mind, there are reasons stereotypes exist. People don't just create them out of nowhere, so I think sometimes there's a little bit of truth to it. And sometimes a lot of bit of truth. Some stereotypes are more offensive than others. But some stereotypes seem to reinforce not-so-bad things, like "Nigerians always become doctors, lawyers, and engineers." My parents are doctors, and there are nine academic degrees between me and my three siblings, so that's not entirely off-base.

NOA: First, that's amazing. Second, interesting—so you would put forth that, say, Jews being wealthy or Jews having positions of power would be beneficial stereotypes?

EMMANUEL: Wouldn't they?

NOA: Not necessarily. In fact, the main reason why I wanted to go deeper into Jewish myths and stereotypes is because of how historically damaging they've been and continue to be—even when they seem "positive."

Everyone's a Little Antisemitic Sometimes

NOA: I love that you brought up stereotypes. I also love that you asked me flat out, despite how uncomfortable it must have been, "But since Jews are so rich, how can they *not* be cheap?" But what I love the most is that we have the kind of relationship where we can have these conversations—because I know that you have nothing but love in your heart.

So yeah, this is a prime example of how even the best-intentioned people still grapple with these mythologies. There have been generalizations, stories, and stereotypes attributed to the Jews for literally thousands of years. Of course they've made their way into the collective consciousness. And of course they're damaging, if not for any other reason than the fact that they're generalizations. They allow people to see us as being all the same. *If one Jew does X, then all Jews must agree.* They also form the basis for dehumanizing and vilifying Jews.

I can 100 percent speak from experience—after all, I've been called a Shylock, a hurtful, gross reference to a Shakespearean character defined by his greed and love of money, and it was a punch in the gut. I'm also well aware of the stereotypes of Jewish women and how, consciously or unconsciously, people might be seeing me through that lens—as just another loud, dominating, discontent, high-maintenance, manipulative Jewish woman running her mouth and taking up too much space. But hey, to quote a very funny song from the Broadway musical *Avenue Q*: "Everyone's a little bit racist [or antisemitic] sometimes!"

All to say, we can't move beyond our unconscious biases if we don't recognize them. (And yes, I am pretty intense. But FYI, I can be ready to leave the house in about five minutes. So there; not so high maintenance after all.)

Understanding how these tropes came to exist is one thing—and I'm going to give you the fascinating history- and globe-spanning lowdown on all of them—but noticing how they've followed us and morphed over the centuries is another. You'll start to see how they're still actively feeding the way people, and maybe even you, think and feel about the Jews, even though, to you, some of these claims might sound ridiculous. Because some stereotypes—like what you're suggesting—have been wrapped around kernels of truth, which makes the other, more unbelievable ideas seem more believable.

That's when seemingly harmless "facts" like "Jews control the banks," "Jews control Hollywood," or "Jews are wealthy" become like gateway Jew hate. They're *partially* based in truths, which leaves a sliver of your mind open to related *un*truths. And that's when you start to hear that tiny voice in the back of your mind say, *Maybe the Jews are to blame for X or Y after all.*

You Don't Look Like a Jew

NOA: Let's play a game: If I tell you that someone is "Jewy looking," would the first thing that comes to mind be someone with an appealing appearance?

I'll spare you the awkward silence; the answer is Nope! I get the classic backhanded compliment all the time—"You don't look Jewish!" When I first moved to America and people would tell me that, I straight-up took that as a compliment. I would actually say *thank you*! But eventually I realized that I had internalized that Jews are ugly and therefore *not* looking like a Jew was a good thing. I don't even know how I would react if someone said that to me today . . . maybe I would ask them if they mean not looking like Gal Gadot, Natalie Portman, or Scarlett Johansson was a compliment?

The reality is, over the generations, Jewish people—especially Eastern European Jews—have been characterized as having distinct and unflattering physical attributes—none of them applicable to every single one of us, and all of them used to spread antisemitic ideas. It's a lot easier to dehumanize and marginalize a group of people when they're seen as monstrous, ugly, and revolting. In fact, if you reinforce this thinking enough, it seems not only acceptable to persecute or completely wipe out those individuals but potentially even *necessary* to protect yourself from their negative influence.

Among the first of these myths was that Jews had devil-like horns, which we can credit to Saint Jerome, priest, theologian, translator, and, yes, saint. Around 400 CE, when translating the Hebrew Bible into Latin, he kicked off the rumor of the ages:

There is a line in Exodus 34:29 that tells us that after Moses received the two stone tablets on which the Ten Commandments were engraved and came down the mountain to the Hebrews, Moses didn't realize that ‏וְרַק רוֹע וִינְפּ‎. I am writing this in Hebrew because this line can be misinterpreted if you don't speak the language. How it is officially translated is that after chatting with God, Moses didn't realize that the skin of his face "qāran," or glowed/was radiant/emitted light. Qāran comes from the word qeren, which means "ray of light." However, qeren can also mean "horn." So, Saint Jerome took the liberty of translating this statement as "Moses grew horns"—an error that someone with even a basic understanding of Hebrew would have avoided, but the hornish description stuck. From that point forward, early influencers such as Michelangelo depicted Jewish people with these demonic appendages.

Was it ridiculous to assert that Jews, as human beings, had horns? Yes. Did that stop people from associating Jews with the Devil? No. Have I had a number of friends tell me that their roommate/band campmate/random acquaintance has asked to see their horns? You bet. It's the perfect example of how gateway Jewish hate or suspicion opens the door for bigger, more outlandish ideas.

So, by the Early Middle Ages, no one was shocked when Church leaders distorted Old Testament verses to teach their disciples that Jews were direct descendants of the mega horn-bearer himself, Satan.* They'd often be depicted with tails and hooves, conspiring with the Devil, and as torturing Jesus. And occasionally in these images, the Devil was surrounded by a Jew crew.

That Jewish horn myth also paved the way for what is one of the most popular and dehumanizing tropes we've seen: the hooked Jewish nose.

---

* This eventually influenced Martin Luther, the father of Lutheranism, to publish an only *subtly* antisemitic work called *On the Jews and Their Lies*.

This hurtful caricature of Jews is believed to have taken off in 1233 CE with a sketch depicting a horned, beak-nosed demon tapping the freakishly long noses of individuals understood to be Jews—as if to say "twinsies!" It is considered to be graphic evidence that "race"-based antisemitism was starting to become a thing as early as the thirteenth century. But it wasn't just a petty aesthetic insult somewhat rooted in truth—because, yes, for some Jews, the schnoz is a thing. What it created was the idea that one only had to look for the nose to "spot the Jew," and, like the horns, it created an unflattering visual that made all Jews seem evil, calculating, and untrustworthy.

Governments eventually realized they could use that as propaganda. When the Soviet Communists wanted to call out Jews as capitalist infiltrators, spies, and saboteurs; and when the Nazis wanted Germans to see how repulsive Jews really were, they didn't have to look any further than that sinister hooked nose to immediately connect malignant qualities to Jews.

And it all had the desired effect: when you consistently demonize the Jews, when you lump them all together as being the same, and then you make a lampoon out of their humanity, you *diminish* it.*

---

* You can still see echoes of these stereotypes today in popular culture. Take Watto from *Star Wars*. Described as a junk dealer, Watto is a blue-skinned creature with a large, hooked nose and a prominent belly. The director George Lucas and his film company Lucasfilm Ltd. have denied any malicious intent behind Watto's design, but his line "Mind tricks don't work on me, only money," spoken in a deeply accented English, didn't help alleviate any of these concerns. There's also the goblins from Harry Potter, seemingly designed in the image of Nazi propaganda with their short stature, hooked noses, large, hairy ears, close-set beady eyes, and male-pattern baldness. And they are—what's that now?—the *bankers* at Gringotts Wizarding Bank. So. Freakin'. Original.

My Accountant Is Jewish

EMMANUEL: Let me personalize things a little bit. In my experience and my circles, Jews do tend to be lawyers and accountants and powerful talent agents. Jews tend to be wealthy. I grew up in Dallas, adjacent to a suburb called Highland Park, which is where a lot of Jewish people live. A good number of those kids went to my private school, and whether it was the Cohens or Rifkins or all the Steins or Michael what's-his-name—

NOA: Probably something Jewish—

EMMANUEL: They were all fairly wealthy. Also, the hand of the wealthiest man I've ever shaken was a Jewish man—Jeffrey Lurie, the owner of the Philadelphia Eagles. So, I never had reason to think Jews weren't, like, Crazy Rich Jews. I just never asked anyone about it until now.

NOA: Why not? Did you have a sense you shouldn't touch that?

EMMANUEL: I think part of it was that when I was growing up, it just seemed like everyone around me was rich. That's the culture I was immersed in. And to be honest, we were well-off, too—not the richest; I mean, I knew kids who had bowling alleys in their houses—but my parents are doctors. So, I didn't really make the connection between Jews and wealth until I got older and went *Huh*. Because, like I said, some stereotypes have kernels of truth—there must be something that got the ball rolling on the "Jews have money"/"Jews are stingy" myths.

NOA: Of course they have a basis; they have a basis of *antisemitism*. I hate to break it to you, but just like not *all* Nigerian immigrants have multiple advanced degrees, not all Jews are rich. And the fact that some are well-to-do is also a new chapter for us. It's not like the Jewish people came to America from Europe, or wherever else, swimming in cash. They were mostly dirt-poor refugees escaping generations of persecution.

What they *did* have, though, was thousands of years of culture, tradition, and dedication—not to money, not to global domination, but to the sacredness of education and family values and community. And while it's true that Jewish people do earn more income relative to people of other religions and ethnic groups, it doesn't stack up to some glaring disparity—Jews do not control huge amounts of global wealth. A private global wealth firm has estimated the figure at about 1.1 percent. According to that same firm, the wealthiest people on this planet by religion are overwhelmingly Christian, controlling about 55 percent of worldwide wealth.

Here comes the *but*.

But when you think of Jews (especially Jewish men), you think of money, success, and power. As in, we have all of it and/or want all of it—and not in a sexy way; in a greedy, nefarious me-me-me way. You think of "the chosen people," but not in a positive way; in a literal "holier than thou" way. Because these Jewish stereotypes have existed for thousands of years and have become deeply embedded in our collective unconscious. They *seem* totally real. And it's a very complicated chicken-soup-or-the-egg conundrum that is begging to be untangled.

9.

THE MATH AIN'T MATHING

Jews, Money, and Power

NOA: Jews and money are like the really antisemitic version of peas and carrots. It's an association that seems totally natural but has its roots in the Middle Ages. Before we can really get into it, though, you'll need a brief history of banking.

EMMANUEL: I'm still here with all my snacks.

NOA: Back in the twelfth and thirteenth centuries, the Church interpreted the Bible as saying that one should not charge interest on money loaned. The Talmud, however, allowed it so long as the money was lent from Jews to non-Jews.* Especially

---

* Though, Jew-to-Jew lending with interest was forbidden. In fact, the Talmud interpreted this so strictly that even saying an extra hello to or doing something extra nice for someone from whom you'd borrowed was verboten.

when it was absolutely necessary for making ends meet, the Talmudic Sages cosigned.

From here, there are a couple versions of what happened next. The first scenario is that the Christians created a work-around by forcing Jews to become the bankers, or "money-lenders," which had a less honorable connotation. This made a convenient "middleman" out of the Jews, and because Jews often had restrictions around the types of jobs they could hold and were often not allowed to own land, it was pretty much an offer they couldn't refuse.

The system looked something like this: The town no-bleman would lend money to the Jew without interest, and then the Jew would lend that money to the non-Jewish peas-ants with nobility-dictated interest rates as high as 30 or 40 percent. Sometimes the money was paid back and conve-niently placed back into the nobleman's pocket with ample profit and zero sacrilege. But if the Jew couldn't collect, the nobleman killed him.

It was a major win for those in power—they profited at the peasants' expense while the Jews took the blame. Meanwhile, the peasants rarely blamed those in power for being taken ad-vantage of; their frustration and anger was most often directed at the moneylender—and pretty much all the Jews.

The second scenario of how this all went down is that some Jews decided *themselves* that it was necessary to start lending so that they could afford to pay increasing taxes. It made sense as a professional route because they already lived in more urban centers (because in many cases, they couldn't own land), and they were literate. Either way, Jews got blamed for political and economic turmoil and gained a reputation as predatory, usuri-ous lenders. Awesome.

Now, not all moneylenders were Jewish; in fact, most

weren't. That's just another stereotype, because while Jews were not the backbone of the credit industry or the motor of European capitalism, their involvement in these practices led to the rampant spreading of stereotypes about Jews being thrifty, cheap, or money hoarders—that we simply *loooove* our money. Shylock—that awful Shakespearean character I mentioned a little while ago was a straight-up Jewish moneylender and the central villain of *The Merchant of Venice*. Shylock lends money to the protagonist Antonio on the condition that he gets to cut off a pound of Antonio's flesh if he defaults on the loan. Whether Shakespeare actually meant for this depiction to be antisemitic is up for debate, but suffice it to say that *The Merchant of Venice* was one of the most popular productions in Nazi Germany, with more than fifty runs there between 1933 and 1939.

And *allll* of that followed the Jews to America.

When Jews started becoming more prominent as bankers and lawyers—jobs that were uniquely available to them as an antisemitic side effect that we'll get into in a minute—the imagery of Shylock and the money-loving Jew was already firmly implanted in the collective consciousness, informing people's opinions about Jews, whether they knew it or not. For example, it birthed the term "to Jew down," meaning to haggle or bargain for a lower price, which you still hear today.*

And then there's one of my favorite/not favorite stereotypes around Jews and money: the JAP, or Jewish American Princess. This not-so-cute nickname took off in the mid-1950s

---

* In March 2023, Florida Republican county commissioner Sam Parker was recorded telling a store owner he would have to "Jew him down." I hope he paid triple.

and was a dig at upwardly mobile Jewish women. It sounded a little bit like this: "Those bratty, entitled JAPs are spoiled rotten with Daddy's money until they marry rich." It was a stark reminder that the white majority *still* didn't consider us as fully part of their group and that Jews were either not enough (poor, dirty) or too much (Jappy, nouveau riche). And not only that, but one could also hear the subtext loud and clear: "Those grasping Jews."

Jewish women eventually co-opted the term for themselves in the '80s and '90s—proudly calling *themselves* JAPs—but I, for one, still can't go along with it. Because even though it feels like this idea is now ours to own, and it's not exactly a danger-ous *feeling*, snuggled down deep inside of it is a damaging antisemitic (not to mention sexist) insinuation: it's all about money for the Jews.

So yeah, things get pretty murky when it starts to look like these tropes are, to most eyes, accurate. Or when a kernel of truth is coated in antisemitic myth. That's when you end up with this all-too-familiar scenario:

Jews feeling attacked, and the (sometimes) unwitting commentator feeling gaslit or manipulated into doubting something they believe is true.

It's a dynamic that's never been more apparent than when it comes to Jews and success and Jews and power.

I Say Tomato, You Say Jews Have Too Much Power

EMMANUEL: If I'm being honest, I wrestle with this notion that Jews don't have a lot of power, especially in Hollywood.

NOA: Tell me why, and then I'll give you my side of the story.

EMMANUEL: Well, first of all, when I say that I do believe Jewish people have the most power in Hollywood, it's an observation, not an indictment. In my entire adult working life, everyone who has been in control of my life has been Jewish. I was drafted into the NFL in 2012 by the Cleveland Browns, and their owner was a Jewish man, Randy Lerner. I spent the majority of my career (from 2013 to 2015) with the Philadelphia Eagles. As I mentioned earlier, the Eagles' owner is a Jewish man, and the Eagles' general manager, Howie Roseman, responsible for hiring and firing every player in the building, was also a Jewish man. In 2016, I stepped away from the NFL and pursued television and my television agent was a Jewish woman. I left that talent agency and moved to another talent agency, and the head of my current talent agency is Jewish; the head of my speaking agency is Jewish; my agent is Jewish; and four out of the six people on my team—who are extremely influential with regards to my career and its success—are Jewish. Basically, from the moment I graduated college until now, Jewish people—particularly Jewish men—have had some level of authority and power over my life and employment. This isn't my opinion or some inflammatory speech, this is just fact. And when I was weighing whether or not to sit down with a Palestinian and do that interview—

NOA: Which we'll get into more later.

EMMANUEL: Yes, we will. For now I'll just say that when I called my Jewish talent agent to ask him about it, he told me I shouldn't do it. When I told my Jewish speaking agent about it, she said people had gotten dropped for less. When I called one of the most powerful Black people in the world about it, they warned cryptically but sagely, "If you have this conversation, you won't be able to get into places where you used to go." Here I was, wanting to simply have a conversation in a fair and measured way on my own platform, and I felt like my hands were tied.

I recognize that part of their motivation was protection of my career. I can give them credit for that. But that wasn't all there was to it. It is not a secret that these individuals are Jewish, nor is it a mystery what their own interests were in this situation. So, it made me feel scared, there was an implied threat of career danger. These people, people in power, could impact my income; they could impact my *life*.

NOA: Granted, this was right after one of the rawest moments in Jewish history since the Holocaust, so you can understand why the issue was touchy.

EMMANUEL: Yes, I can see that. Though, it was never coming from a malicious place, and I had no political agenda; I just wanted to have a conversation with someone who represented another involved party in the situation. But aside from all that, nobody knew what I was about to say! To me, as somebody who is not Jewish, having a group of Jewish people preemptively shutting that down or inciting fear of what the Jewish community could do to my career, and by extension, my life, seemed righteously unfair, but more importantly, exposed me in that moment to the true power Jewish people do have, at least in my life.

NOA: Let me tell you a joke: It's 1932 and there are two elder Jews in Germany reading the morning paper. One was reading the Jewish newspaper, and the other the German newspaper. "Why are you reading the German paper?" asked the Jew reading the Jewish newspaper. "Well," the other man replied, "in the Jewish newspaper, we are being persecuted and hated. In the German one, we control the banks, the media, and the entire world. It makes me feel so much better."

The thing is, when people intimate—or say outright—that Jews run anything, it snaps us back to those antisemitic dog whistles (or megaphones) accusing us of having too much power, too much control—and it's making things bad for everyone else and therefore needs to be taken away. So, we freak the hell out because that kind of talk is what has typically preceded some pretty gruesome disasters, such as one hundred thousand Jews being slaughtered in Russian and Ukrainian pogroms and millions in Germany during the Holocaust. Plus, it's not accurate to say that we have power. It's more accurate to say that we hold *positions* of power—which is a far cry from this cabal you are describing.

EMMANUEL: This feels like semantics. I feel like you're almost gaslighting me—if you hold a position of power, then you have power. If you hold a position as owner or CEO, then you can hire and fire as you please. To me, they are practically synonymous. It's my lived experience, my truth. And the reason why these people in my life are as influential as they are is because they're in power.

It's fascinating to me that Jewish people don't want to claim the power that they have. I'm more than happy, as a Black man, to say, "I am wealthy." I have worked tirelessly to get where I am in life. But it's like y'all are Superman but want to act like Clark Kent. But I can see that "S" on your chest underneath the suit! I see the cape! I'm not saying that y'all run the world, but at least acknowledge that you're Superman.

NOA: I hear you! And, in fact, feel the same as you—I also think the Jewish community should be thrilled that we are now free to hold any jobs we want and be proud to be influential. But there is a difference between saying "there is more Jewish representation in X industry than the relative population" and "the Jews *control* X or Y." There's nothing antisemitic about being factual, and of course there are a lot of Jews working in Hollywood. But the jump from representation to control is where you start to dabble in stereotypes and dangerous mythology. And when you look at those facts without seeing or understanding the entire picture, without knowing the historical context for *why* these truths seem to exist, then these statements develop negative, antisemitic undertones—or are outright antisemitic. Because, as it turns out, our involvement in industries like Hollywood, law, and finance has its roots in systematic discrimination. So, in a way, it feels like we're being blamed for holding these positions and succeeding in them, when we didn't have a lot of choice about which jobs we could hold in the first place.

EMMANUEL: Tell me more about the antisemitic roots of these professions. I'll admit, I had heard that Jews were forced into Hollywood, but I never looked into why there are so many Jewish people in those industries other than interest, geography, or maybe nepotism.

NOA: Again, why I'm so glad that we're doing this. First of all, the Jews weren't forced *into* Hollywood so much as they were forced *out* of many other industries. We've already been over how banking and finance-related professions were often dumped onto Jews, or how they were the only viable economic opportunities because Jews weren't allowed to own land or work in factories. Well, because many Jews couldn't own land, they moved to cities where they could continue practicing moneylending and trade, in addition to emerging professions like law. Similarly, many Jews got into theater to make a living, since it was considered "unsuitable" for white Christians.

Then, when Jews started coming to the States in the late 1800s/early 1900s, they had a little more freedom to run with these trades. Sure, they were banned from the elite "white-shoe" law firms, but they could start their own (usually after enlisting a non-Jewish partner to lend their more *palatable* name to the door). And the big hospitals refused to hire Jewish doctors, but that didn't stop Jews from starting their own (it's called Mount Sinai for a reason!). It was the same story for theaters. The best ones in town wouldn't employ the Jews, so the Jews turned to vaudeville, or stage productions with specialty acts like slapstick comedy, puppets, and trained animals—too low-rent for good Protestants to get mixed up with.

When more Jews started heading west to California in the first couple decades of the 1900s because there was a booming Jewish community there and booming antisemitism on the East Coast, they brought this enterprising spirit with them. Since diversity hires weren't a thing at the few non-Jewish movie studios such as Disney, they slowly but surely built their own—Metro-Goldwyn-Mayer, Warner Brothers, Paramount, Loew's, and Universal.

And in the most ironic twist of all, these European Jews who had just fled persecution only to arrive, broke and rejected, in a new country created the iconic imagery of the dazzling American Dream. They weren't telling Jewish stories or featuring Jewish movie stars—except for a handful of undercover Jews such as Betty Joan Perske (Lauren Bacall), Issur Danielovitch (Kirk Douglas), and Nathan Birnbaum (George Burns). No, they continued to leave their own heritage and history out of the conversation, put their heads down, and make as little noise as Jews as possible.

And that *still* didn't keep the white majority from coming for them. Hollywood was one of the first places the US government terrorized with its Communist witch hunts. It's also still one of the first places people point to when they start grumbling about the Jews having all the power. To which I have two things to say:

1. We have it because we built it! Because we had no other choice! Fair and square. And 2. Overrepresentation is *not* control. In any industry. Jews holding prominent positions is not this white-knuckled grip on all the power. Nor is it a plot to replace the influence of the entire white majority (aka the neo-fascist "Great Replacement Theory").

But I would also argue that it's not that we're taking over, it's that we're—duh duh duh—over-*contributing.* Meaning relative to our tiny population, we've, yes, made huge contributions. Jews are just shy of 0.2 percent of the world's population and yet they are the recipients of *22 percent* of Nobel Prizes, plus we have left our mark in finance, law, medicine, media, literature, music, and the arts. I mean, when *Oppenheimer* (a Jew) and *Barbie* (invented by a Jew) swept the box offices in 2023, all I could think was *Talk about the gamut of Jewish contributions to our country!* But not as part of a worldwide Jewish agenda or at the expense or exclusion of anyone else. That's something we Jews should be very proud of—but again, we try to hide it because the idea of Jews having too much control has been a very, very convenient reason to kill us.

---

* Thank you, Eric Weinstein, for introducing me to this idea.

The Octopus

EMMANUEL: I don't really think there's such a thing as overrepresentation, unless that community is working to keep other groups out, which I don't believe the Jewish community is doing. So, I would agree with you there. I can also understand the reason for trying to hide it, or what comes off as denying it. This is all really fascinating, honestly. It's as if we see the same thing differently, and that's okay.

NOA: But here's the thing—we're not usually given the benefit of the doubt. Instead, it's *assumed* that these things are true—and that they're all part of our attempt to take over the world. The best example of Jews being accused of having too much power is the trope of the Jew-as-octopus. It's a common image in antisemitic cartoons, where Jews, and Israel, are depicted as an octopod, tentacles wrapped around the globe (or the White House, as you'll see floating around the internet these days). It's used as a symbol of our desire to control global politics, the world economy, and the media. I'd say it's funny that they chose such an un-kosher animal, but there is nothing laughable about this indestructible cockroach of a myth. It is still reached for today, usually by referring to Jews as innocent-sounding "globalists." To use this term when referring to a Jewish person also suggests that Jews hold a higher allegiance to a global conspiracy than to their country of origin. Or, as is in fashion now, to *Israel* over their country of origin—which, according to a 2023 survey by the Anti-Defamation League (ADL), four in ten Americans believe in some part to be true.

This all contributes to that just barely perceptible whiff around Jews as untrustworthy, conspiring traitors with an alternative agenda. That same ADL survey found that one in five people believe Jews have too much power in the United States and are more willing than other Americans to use "shady practices to get what they want." So yeah, when Dave Chappelle goes on *Saturday Night Live* and makes a joke about Jews running Hollywood, it strikes a nerve.

But if you scan the Fortune 500—as in, the people who run the biggest industries in the world—it reads more like an Easter dinner RSVP list than a Passover Seder invite. I can almost hear people waving this away saying, "Yeah, but Michael Bloomberg; yeah, but Mark Zuckerberg." Are 0.2 percent of the world's people and their 1.1 percent of the money and power going to be able to stop a white majority—and anyone else who wants to join them—if they decided to take everything away like the Germans did in the 1930s? I'd hope so, but I'm not totally optimistic. So for now, let's agree that the Jewish bank president isn't the captain of a cabal and is just a president of a bank.

———

I want to go back to the Jewish people on your team. What that sounded like, to me, is that those Jews in positions of power were finally using their gatekeeping abilities to make an important judgment call against something that could be damaging and hurtful to Jewish people—and potentially to your career. People who make their living by being in the spotlight, whether celebrities, athletes, politicians, or business leaders, say and do antisemitic things *all the time*, and they are very rarely blackballed or canceled—especially in sports and entertainment, two industries where there are many Jews in positions of power. Kyrie is back to playing basketball, Adidas is back to selling Yeezys, and Prince Harry is on Netflix.

This experience of Jewish people putting their foot down is new because up until now they've been staying out of the fray. Or being Clark Kent. Because that's essentially our survival instinct. Despite the fact that we've made some incredible achievements that seem unlikely from a small group of people who, until the past seventy-five years, have not had the consistent freedom to own a home, live where they want, hold any job they want, have equal citizenship, get elected to office, or live day to day without the fear of being murdered. We are still plagued by the biologically ingrained fear of being rounded up for that success. Because every single Jewish person is a descendant of someone who was sitting in a kitchen somewhere in the world, looked around at the family, and said, "We have to get the f**k out of here; sh*t's about to hit the fan." We carry that with us, and as a result, we've internalized this knowledge that if we sit quietly, not drawing too much attention, not ruffling any feathers, and not upsetting anybody, maybe we'll be left alone.

10.

WHO GETS TO LAUGH AT US?

EMMANUEL: Okay, let me ask you this: When someone inadvertently says something antisemitic publicly, or it's intended as a joke and everyone who hears it knows it's just a joke—at what point are other people no longer responsible for that trauma response you described earlier? The biologically ingrained fear? I'm not Hitler; I have no plan to annihilate Jews, so when I say Jewish people have power, it stops there for me.

Ya know what, let me put it another way: The other day, when I was at your house, your son came in and you said, "Come here, you little monkey," and it reminded me of the time I was at a cookout in Austin a few years ago with about ten of my closest friends, some Black, some white. My Black friend's youngest daughter, Kaidence, comes over and starts climbing on the table, to which my white friend says, "Aww, she's such a little monkey."

Silence. Nobody says anything. The Black people were all just texting one another saying, "Who the hell gonna check her?" "E, you say something." "I'm not gonna say something; it'll be awkward!"

So later on, I called my friend and said, "Hey, you can't call Black people monkeys. You gotta understand the context of 'porch monkey' and how that term was used to describe Black people as lazy and unintelligent. As well as the fact that white people would say that our lips looked like monkeys'. So, when you called this beautiful Black girl a monkey, we all had a trauma response to that. And I'm telling you this because if you were to say that in a less safe environment, hands would be laid on you, and not for praying."

In theory, I made this person responsible for our trauma response. They weren't being racist; they were just saying monkeys are cute and like to climb, and so did this little girl. I couldn't really blame her for saying that.

NOA: First, thank you for sharing that with me. Second, to your question of who is responsible for a trauma response—that's impossible to determine because who is to say where the line is for something to feel hurtful or dangerous to someone? I defer to that person or that group to know when language can be problematic for them—even if the person using that language didn't mean anything by it or was "just trying to be funny." For me, that goes *double* when non-Jewish people use anti-Jewish tropes as the basis for humor, because repeating these stereotypes only drives them deeper into people's minds. And for some reason, it's gotten really easy to make fun of the Jews with few to no repercussions.

Amy Schumer did a fantastic sketch about the high tolerance for comments made at the Jews' expense on her show *Inside Amy Schumer*. Amy plays an unwitting participant in a DEI-training session. The moderator, played by the hilarious Chris Parnell, has roped her into demonstrating workplace no-nos. The other participants needle her with antisemitic taunts ranging from saying her handwriting is so bad it looks like Hebrew to flat out saying, "Hey, Fiddler on the Roof, can't you make it stop raining, ya old Jewbag? The Rothschilds control the weather."* With each increasingly absurd epithet, Parnell waves them off as admissible because they're not violating HR policy—they're just simply "not nice." Meanwhile, Amy's asking, "Why is everyone fine with making fun of Jews?!" It's not until a Black woman in the room calls out this behavior as completely unacceptable that things take a turn, but at that point, instead of Amy saying, "Yeah, you're right, it *is* antisemitic," she *apologizes*. She apologizes to the Black woman for what she's had to endure, apologizes for Israel—"I've never even been there, but I know I'm supposed to be sorry about it, and I'm sorry that there are terrorist attacks there and nobody wants to talk about them"—and apologizes for Bernie Madoff (and Bernie Sanders—all the Bernies), Harvey Weinstein, and Jeffrey Epstein. Finally, she apologizes for being Jewish and explodes into a puff of Stars of David.

First of all, thank you, Amy, for so beautifully illustrating how Jews tend to disappear from the Diversity, Equity, and Inclusion conversation because, through that lens, we're not really considered a minority group. Second of all, it's a great example of how humor and the ability to laugh at ourselves and our experiences are critical to the Jewish identity. The Sages of the Talmud had some pretty solid bits, and nothing says traumaprocessing quite like a good belly laugh. Humor has been one way for us to try to make sense of the incomprehensible and reclaim our persecution. Mel Brooks made fun of everything

---

* A reference to a wealthy Jewish family in Europe that rose to prominence in the banking world and was, of course, suspected of trying to take over the world.

from the Inquisition to the Holocaust; Sarah Silverman has us in tears (in a good way) about self-loathing Jews and how *Mein Kampf*—or "My Struggle"—is actually the Jewiest-sounding book there is; and even I couldn't have a conversation about antisemitism without throwing in a few jokes. But that does not mean that it is open mic night for everyone else.

EMMANUEL: I do feel like the hardest concept for people to grasp is why one group can do something that another group cannot. It's like everybody wants to be included in everything. Sorry, but everybody is not invited to every party; that's just not how it works. I learned that lesson the hard way when I was fourteen and wasn't invited to the Winter Formal, the middle school dance—but this isn't about my unhealed childhood trauma.

The most frustrating conversations I've had revolve around usage of the N-word—why Black communities can use it, based on a cultural and historical connectivity, along with a repossessing and redefining of the word, while white communities can't use it based on the historical context of how they used the word as a demeaning weapon. In the same way that you might call your significant other "Shnookums" (eww, I really hope you don't), but a stranger who doesn't share that intimate relationship with them wouldn't dare. There are certain jokes, words, phrases, et cetera, that communities and people who share a relationship can use with one another that outsiders can't and shouldn't.

NOA: Exactly! And yes, it's true that there may be grains of truth in some Jewish stereotypes—especially the less-damning ones. Like the overbearing mother, which has more to do with gender-role stereotyping than anything else. The neurotic Jew—

they've been trying to kill us for thousands of years; what do you expect?! The fact that we talk with our hands, which is most likely an outgrowth of gestures used in Jewish prayer. The nice Jewish boy, the result of Jews getting boxed out of physical labor and therefore putting more emphasis on academia than physical strength, plus, back in the shtetl days, the smartest student got the girl, not the mensch-y quarterback.

But that doesn't diminish that these generalizations—like all the stereotypes we talked about above—cut a little close to the bone when held in non-Jewish hands, just like the monkey incident. And that's because Jews carry with them the keen awareness that beneath these sentiments lies a deep vein of anti-Jewish hate, and one that never lies dormant for long.

Part II

US AND THEM

11.

DID THE JEWS KILL JESUS?

EMMANUEL: You know, we've talked a lot about race, but let's turn up the heat a little bit and shift back to religion. One of the most fascinating areas of tension in society, as it pertains to how the world relates to Jewish people . . . or at least how my world—being a Christian—relates to Jewish people, is the question surrounding who killed Jesus.

NOA: Ahh. We're going hard-core, aren't we? I love it. Growing up in Israel, I actually had little to no exposure to Jesus. Which is sad, considering he was a local. When I moved to the US, though, I realized that, to some extent, Jesus's life and death were historically the source of a good amount of antisemitism—and this was a shock to me. I'd always thought of Jesus as this cool OG Jew, yet here were a bunch of people who, throughout history, were using the death of that Jew as a reason to kill us. And even now, almost two thousand years later, it still forms a lot of the basis of antisemitic sentiments. This makes no sense to me.

EMMANUEL: Growing up in Bible Belt Dallas, Texas, I can tell you that every sermon ever preached ultimately culminates with the story of the death, burial, and resurrection of Jesus.

We always celebrate the resurrection aspect of Jesus's life because our faith is dependent upon it—it goes back to the book of Isaiah in the Old Testament. The prophecy was that a Man would come and live a perfect life and die for the salvation of the world. But we don't talk too much about the death aspect, in part because it's gruesome and not something we celebrate. But I would also say it's because it typically leads to an argument. An argument that is, of course, centered around the question of who killed Jesus. I have gotten into hyper-tense debates with my Christian friends, my Jewish friends, and even my nonspiritual friends about this topic.

NOA: Yeah, I mean that question has historically been the basis for some premium Grade A antisemitism. That combination of Jews being classified as "God killers" coupled with scapegoating Jews for something (anything) that a society dislikes is Jew Hate 101. That thinking, in some form or another, has been used to persecute, discriminate against, and ultimately murder millions of Jews over the course of history. And that suspicion of Jews, that seeing Jews as traitors, that hatred toward Jews has continued to linger. So, how did people get this idea in the first place?

EMMANUEL: Let me clarify—many argue that the Jews didn't *literally* kill Jesus, but that they *contributed* to his killing. Jesus had been traveling around town performing miracles, turning water into wine, walking on water, healing the sick, among other things. He and his disciples were proclaiming that He was the Messiah, and Jesus's teachings and proclamations were rubbing some of the Jewish scribes and leaders the wrong way. So, they had Jesus arrested and He was put on trial and set to face the death penalty. Pontius Pilate, the Roman governor of Judea, had authority to make the final decision—hence why the Jews did not literally kill Jesus (as in, nail him to the cross); they were not in military control, the Romans were.

At first, Pilate attempted to wash his hands of the decision, saying, "I find no fault in this man" (Luke 23:14). But many people hold the Jews of that time responsible because after Pilate said he found no fault with Jesus, the Jews cried out for Pilate to release a man named Barabbas, who had been imprisoned for murder, and to crucify Jesus instead. "But they were urgent, demanding with loud cries that he should be crucified. And their voices prevailed. So, Pilate decided that their demand should be granted. He released the man who had been thrown into prison for insurrection and murder, for whom they asked, but he delivered Jesus over to their will" (Luke 23:23–25).

NOA: Let me ask you this: Even if Jesus had literally been physically killed by a Jew—which we all, including a Pope,* agree he wasn't—why would another Jewish person who lived thousands of years later be blamed for that? That still doesn't excuse blaming an entire people for what, say, fifty Jews might have done two thousand years ago.

EMMANUEL: Not to mention, as a Christian, Jesus had to die. The purpose of Jesus being born was to die and become the ul-

---

* Pope Benedict XVI and the Catholic Church have said that there's no basis in Scripture to honestly believe that the Jews were responsible for JC's death.

timate sacrifice for all of our sins, so that everyone could have the opportunity for right-standing with God. So, who killed Jesus is a worthless argument to begin with. And correct, saying the Jews did kill Jesus still shouldn't excuse hatred toward millions of people until the end of time. The fact that a death, which had to happen, has been utilized to murder people for thousands of years is the dumbest thing in the world.

NOA: And also, probably, Jesus wouldn't like that.

EMMANUEL: Exactly.

12.

THE ANTISEMITISM LAYER CAKE

EMMANUEL: You mentioned "Jew Hate 101." If you were teaching that course, I'd take it—as in I'd like to learn more about what "antisemitism" actually means and what it looks like in the real world. Because even though it feels pretty straightforward—hating Jews for being Jews—it also seems like there's something else at play that I can't quite put my finger on. It's almost like antisemitism is either the belief that Jewish people have excess power and influence, or it's the marginalization and persecution of Jews.

NOA: You are 100 percent spot on. Antisemitism, or Jew hatred, is not a straightforward brand of hate. Antisemitism is both looking *down* at a Jew as inferior (Hi, Nazis!) but also kinda looking *up* at them, mostly with fear or resentment, and attributing to them a larger-than-life power and control (Heya, Marjorie Taylor Greene and your Jewish cabal space lasers!).

That can't-quite-place-it feeling you get about antisemitism is because it is, in essence, a shape-shifting conspiracy theory. And it is the cumulative effect of thousands of years of rumormongering and myth inventing in the name of being able to blame the Jews for just about anything.

But before we can get into how any of that shows up today, we need to start with the foundational basics: antisemitism's unique definition and qualities. Namely so you can see how the same exact tropes that have been used against Jews for millennia *still* show up now. Because antisemitism most certainly did not fade away with the Nazis and you'd be surprised to see where it's lurking again these days. Believe me, people thinking that Jews killed Jesus—which they very much still do!—is the least of our worries.

EMMANUEL: Tell me more.

Jew Hate 101

NOA: Ever since Abraham and God had their bromance, Jews have been the odd guys out. It wasn't easy being the first to do the one-people, one-God monotheism thing; and it's definitely not easy being different, especially because the world tended to hyper-fixate on those differences—primarily *not* being Christian or Muslim—instead of celebrating what we had in common. And not surprisingly, when people or things don't fit into the shapes they're "supposed" to, it's all too common for people to:

1. Make assumptions (or just make things up), or
2. Lay blame (aka scapegoat), generally pegging any passing tragedy and hardship on the Jews.

That special flavor of Jewish hate has its own special name: antisemitism. And it often ends in the call for the spilling of

Jewish blood to make things better. It's a cycle that has been ongoing for thousands of years, spreading around the world, and always following the same pattern.

IT'S IMPOSSIBLE TO BE ANTI-SEMITIC

NOA: Quick semantics tangent: Ironically, after Hitler's ideas about a superior Aryan race dissolved after World War II, European society replaced the idea of a "Jewish race" with the even more inaccurate "Semitic race," an idea that sprouted up in antisemitic circles back in 1879. But referring to people as "Semites" or "Semitic" is actually totally wrong if used to describe any group of *people*, including any ethnic, cultural, or racial group associated with the Middle East. That goes for both Arabs and Jews. The word *Semitic* was first used in the late 1700s to describe all the languages of the Middle East and Africa that have linguistic similarities, such as Arabic, Hebrew, Aramaic (historically spoken in Lebanon, Syria, Israel, Iraq, and Iran), and Amharic (spoken in Ethiopia). But the speakers of those languages didn't otherwise have any shared heritage or history, and you could speak a Semitic language and be an antisemite (and I'm not just talking about internalized antisemitism). Just like rugs can be oriental but people can't, languages can be Semitic but people can't. Which is why we express anti-Jewish oppression and discrimination as "antisemitism" and not "anti-Semitism" and why antisemitism doesn't automatically apply to hating on all people from the Middle East. Antisemitism is a club you don't wanna be a member of, and it's for Jews only. Ya with me?

A Slippery Little Sucker

NOA: The thing to understand about antisemitism is that it evolves and changes with the times. It is sometimes hard to spot or hidden from view, but it always leads to the same conclusion: Jews are to blame for society's problems.

I like to cite author and journalist Yossi Klein Halevi, who says that Jews are always used to describe whatever it is that is the worst, most loathsome in society at any given moment. Under Christianity, they were the Christ killers. Under the Nazis, they were the race polluters and economy-crippling money hoarders. Under the Soviets, they were either the conspiring Communists or the capitalist pigs, depending on who you're asking. As for the shape it's shifted to today, well, we're getting to that.

So, the spread of antisemitism hasn't happened overnight. On the contrary, it has been the culmination of centuries of whisper campaigns, propaganda crusades, and government-led movements—all of which injected antisemitic ideas directly into the veins of mainstream society.

You can think of antisemitism like a layer cake—which is maybe why so many people want a piece of it or have accidentally helped themselves to some. The layers have been added over time through history, and each layer has a different flavor of discrimination. There are religious, ethnic, racial, cultural, and political layers. Some of it is individually based (driven by stereotyping and mythology) and some of it systemic (policies, practices, and procedures that make it "official" in a society). But it all makes up one cohesive, multilayered slice with one cohesive message:

The Jews are different, and therefore bad/not to be trusted, and therefore to blame for [pick an unfortunate event], and therefore we'd be doing everyone a favor by getting rid of them.

Understanding what some of these layers have been is what will ultimately help you understand what antisemitism looks and sounds like now. What you'll notice is that there are common themes—or tropes—that loop back again and again, reinforcing new stereotypes while keeping the old myths alive. You might even find that you actually hold one of these invented layers of hate as self-evident truth.

We're going to run through them now, but keep in mind that this is, shockingly, not an exhaustive list. Please enjoy a delicious serving of antisemitism's finest:

- *There are too many Jews and they're making me nervous!* One of the earliest known forms of what was then called "Judeophobia" dates back to the Egyptian pharaoh Amenhotep III or Ramses II, depending on which historian you ask. Either way, this particular Egyptian didn't like the look of the Israelites' thriving numbers so he enslaved them and had the male babies thrown into the Nile. Done and done.

- *Jews are godless and bloodthirsty!* In 30 BCE, after the Romans took over Egypt, the Greek immigrants living there were cranky that they were now considered second-class citizens like the Jews who had stuck around. So, they started a smear campaign to make the Jews look even less desirable or deserving of certain freedoms. They accused the Jews of being God-hating, lawless cannibals who ate humans in secret rituals. Then they riled up the native Egyptians to hate the Jews, too, and even goaded certain Roman senators by saying they had given favor to the Jews because they themselves were Jewish. (They were not.) Appalled by the idea that they could have anything in common with those filthy Jews, let alone *be* Jewish, the Romans threw their lot in with the Greeks, and went on to join forces to murder tens of thousands of Jews.

In fact, the Greek-Roman tag team can be credited with kicking off antisemitic propaganda in the West. The Greeks and Romans spread suspicion about how Jews negatively affected everything from politics to the economy to religion to the culture at large, and word traveled throughout the Roman Empire. By the time the first (unsuccessful) Great Jewish Revolt broke out in 66 CE in Judea—when the Jews put their foot down about unfair taxation and Roman rulers draining resources from their temple—there was a surge in antisemitism. That evolved into Jews living under oppressive Roman Empire policies that limited things like land and property ownership, as well as many Jews getting kicked out of Judea (pre-Israel), a practice that we would go on to experience ad nauseam from then on.

- *Jews killed Christ!* Now we're caught up to where we started out with this conversation, the allegation that the Jews killed Jesus, and the resulting centuries of bad PR about killing God's son.

  These issues only got worse about three hundred years after His death when the Roman emperor Constantine formally joined the Christians and made Christianity the official religion of the Roman Empire. Because, as we know by now, if there's one thing the Romans really didn't have time for, it was the Jews.

- *Jews are dirty interlopers!* Now we're at about 300 CE. Over the next three hundred years in Europe, Jews were institutionally discriminated against: they were not allowed to marry Christians in some instances (300 CE), could not hold positions in government (439 CE), and could not testify against Christians in court (531 CE). Then, doubling down on their narrative that Jews were interlopers—and foreshadowing modern American politics—Christian nobility curried favor with their constituents by restricting economic opportunities for Jews.

- *Jews are the Devil!* In the Middle Ages, the Jewish community was regularly linked to devilry and black magic— mainly because of Saint Jerome and his viral "Jews have horns" theory, plus there were still hard feelings about that whole God-killing miscommunication. And with the First Crusade ramping up in 1096 CE, nothing was more important around Europe than Jesus. The idea that Jews were the Devil or Devil worshippers resulted in vehement antisemitism, which led to organized violent assaults on Jewish communities—after all, why not rid the country of the evil Jews? Called the Rhineland Massacres, mobs of French and German Christians pillaged Jewish homes for valuables to "fund the Crusades," and mass murdered the Jews on their way out. In fact, you can trace a straight line from this moment in antisemitic European history all the way through to the Holocaust.

- *Jews are bloodthirsty murderers . . . again!* In 1144 CE, the body of a twelve-year-old boy was found in a forest outside Norwich, England. Nobody thought much of it until a few years later when a local monk, Thomas of Monmouth, wrote his version of how things went down. According to him, it was the Jews who had kidnapped the boy and brutally tortured him in celebration of Passover. (Note: this is not how we celebrate Passover.) Nobody knows if this was Tommy's simple misunderstanding of Jewishness, or if he was simply trying to establish the boy as a patron saint for the city. Regardless, "blood libel" was born, the accusation that Jews murder Christian children to use their blood for various types of rituals, specifically making the Passover cracker called matzoh. (Also note: humans are *so* not kosher.)

This horrific lie created a difficult-to-resist conspiracy for anyone who had a bone to pick with the Jews. And it led to open season on Jewish communities all over Europe, with outbursts of drive-by (horse-by?) Jewish slaughter, rape, and vandalism, also known as pogroms. Ever since Thomas of Monmouth first planted the blood libel seed, Jews have consistently been rounded up and executed when children have died or gone missing—or have just been blamed for every passing tragic event.* And in the wake of the October 7th attack, all these classic, age-old blood libels exploded back into society and social media, but we'll come back to that antisemitic Mad Libs a bit later.

---

* In 2014, in an interview with a Lebanese television channel, a Hamas spokesman said: "We all remember how the Jews used to slaughter Christians in order to mix their blood in their holy matzohs. This is not a figment of imagination or something taken from a film. It is a fact, acknowledged by their own books and by historical evidence."

- *Jews are untrustworthy, disease-spreading demons!* The year 1228 CE is when we see the introduction of another familiar term: "the Wandering Jew." Coined by Christian leaders in Europe, it was a reference to Jews being doomed to forever wander as punishment for rejecting and killing Christ, and being both dirty and untrustworthy as a result. It was a brilliant self-fulfilling prophecy—the Christian leaders could make an example of the Jews' misery, while perpetuating the rampant antisemitism that actually caused the Jews to have to leave everywhere they lived in the first place! I imagine it sounded a little like this: "Look at those dirty, untrustworthy, God-killing Wandering Jews—they should really hit the road."

  Then, in the 1300s, when the bubonic plague was bulldozing its way across Europe and killing as much as 60 percent of its population, Europeans needed a fall guy. Medical explanations were coming up short, so religious ones would have to do. And the most popular diagnosis was this: the Devil had recruited the Jews to destroy Christianity. Even though the Jews were also dying from the plague—although at lower rates because Jewish law mandates frequent handwashing—that didn't stop Europeans from accusing the Jews of poisoning the wells, and Christian governments from ordering the massacre of their Jewish communities and that thousands of Jews be burned alive.*

---

* After thousands of years of Jews being brutally murdered for being God killers, only in *1965* did the Catholic Church get around to making an official declaration (*Nostra Aetate*, Latin for "In Our Time") denouncing antisemitism and formally rejecting the charge of Jewish culpability for Jesus's death.

- *Jews are not Christian!* The Spanish Inquisition, which started in 1478 CE, was particularly brutal for the Jews. The Church, which had big plans for an all-Catholic dominion, called for the forced conversion, torture (burning at the stake was a favorite), and expulsion of Jews.* For centuries after the Inquisition, the Church loved letting people know that the Jews had rejected Jesus, killed the son of God, and were agents of the Devil.

- *Jews are money hoarders!* Sound familiar?! Now we're up to when Jews were forced into banking roles. Episode recap: Jews were in a "middleman" position between the peasantry and their rulers, who would levy large, often unpayable taxes on their constituents. The peasants hated the Jews because they were the ones collecting those taxes, and the rulers hated the Jews because they were Jews. But they also loved how convenient it was to place blame on the Jews for any economic hardships. This moment in history is pretty much ground zero for every antisemitic association between Jews and the Benjamins (I'm not *not* looking at you, Ilhan Omar[†]).

---

* This birthed a movement of "Crypto-Jews," or Jews who converted to Catholicism but secretly practiced their Jewish traditions such as keeping kosher and lighting candles on Shabbat. Fascinatingly, I know Catholic people who never knew why their families observed certain Jewish practices—it's because they were once Jews!

[†] In 2019, in response to a tweet about then House GOP leader Kevin McCarthy calling her out for being critical of Israel, Omar responded: "It's all about the Benjamins, baby." This reference to a line about $100 bills from a Puff Daddy song was an antisemitic double-whammy: the suggestion that Jews are buying political support, and that when it comes to the Jews, it's all about the money. Some Jews gave her the benefit of the doubt about her intentions, but others—like me—remembered that in 2012 she had tweeted that "Israel has hypnotized the world," and have

- *Jews are too powerful!* The late-nineteenth-century politician and mayor of Vienna Karl Lueger was one of the first modern leaders to use antisemitism as a political tool. He perpetuated the idea of blood libel against the Jews and blamed them for disproportionate influence in academia and the press. (I'd ask you if *that* sounds familiar, but I won't insult your intelligence.) He was pretty much exploiting existing antisemitism to rile up his nationalist base and unite them in the shared hatred of Jews taking up too much space. Lueger eventually gets his flowers as one of the main inspirations for one Adolf Hitler.

- *Jews are disloyal!* By the late nineteenth century in France, we have the Dreyfus Affair. Captain Alfred Dreyfus, a high-ranking Jewish military officer, was falsely accused and convicted of treason. He was eventually exonerated, but the nationalistic French ran with the idea that Jews were more likely to be loyal to foreign interests than to their own. It was the most famous example of the "dual loyalty," "fifth column," or "globalist" tropes—the suspicion that Jews will never truly be loyal citizens and that they're most likely working for the enemy. Once Israel entered the scene in 1948, this idea evolved into the accusation that Jews were only truly loyal to Israel, and therefore should not be trusted.

- *Jews are evil rogues and cheats!* Antisemitism has *long* had a place in the Russian Empire, an underrated hub

---

been feeling less benefit and more doubt when it comes to her ability to objectively legislate.

of Jew hate. Whether it was simply because Jews were not Christian or because as Peter the Great, who ruled from 1682 to 1725, declared, "[The Jews] are rogues and cheats; it is my endeavor to eradicate evil, not multiply it," the Jews had a particularly rough go of it in this part of the world. In fact, until the Russian Empire began to expand in 1774 and gobbled up places where Jews just happened to be, Jews hadn't been allowed to live there because they had been expelled under the Order of Expulsion.

So, in 1791, no one batted an eye when Catherine the Great decreed the Pale of Settlement, forcing all the Jews in the Russian Empire to live in segregated areas along the empire's border (where they could be a replaceable buffer in the event of attacks by outsiders). She also removed their citizenship, enforced double taxation to keep them financially oppressed, and spread the propaganda that they were the ultimate evil, just to make it all stick. Also surprising no one was when her grandson Nicholas I drafted Jewish kids as young as twelve into the military, or when organized pogroms kicked up around 1821. Oh, and when Nikko's son Tsar Alexander II was assassinated in 1881, who took the blame? Why, them Jews, of course.[*]

---

[*] Alex had been using his time in power to make small but much appreciated improvements to Jewish life in Russia, such as allowing some of them to live outside the Pale of Settlement. So, his murder was an anti-Jew two-for-one: His notoriously antisemitic son Alexander III blamed his father's death on the Jews and then repressed the Jews even more under the May Laws. When a counselor to the newly appointed tsar was asked, "What will become of the Jews?" he said: "One third will be killed; one third will immigrate; one third will assimilate." And it

- *Jews are conniving conspirators for world domination!* But the Russians' biggest, most enduring contribution to the antisemitism saga was the publication of *The Protocols of the Elders of Zion* in 1903. It was a collection of documents (allegedly but almost certainly) forged by tsarist secret police in Russia, and was the original Jewish fake news. These writings told of a cloak-and-dagger plot by rabbis to take over the world as an all-controlling global cabal. This narrative came in handy for the Russian tsars and ruling class, who could deflect growing unrest among their constituents during the Russian Revolution and blame the Jews instead.

  To really twist the knife—and allow the peasants to let off a little steam—tsarist police largely looked the other way as mobs raped, murdered, and looted their way through Jewish villages. The Russian Orthodox Church, bless their hearts, often fueled these endeavors through anti-Jewish sermons. Between 1917 and 1921, after the October Revolution, more than five hundred Jewish communities in Ukraine were wiped out and more than one hundred thousand Jewish men, women, and children were murdered.

- *Jews are race polluters!* With secularism spreading through Europe in the nineteenth and twentieth centuries, antisemitism changed from hate for the Jewish *religion* to hate for the Jewish *people*—literally, their filthy Jewish blood. Whereas before, one solution to cleansing one's

---

was so. Coincidentally, this—coupled with the pogroms of 1881, is what piqued Russian Jews' interest in Zionism.

society of Jews was through conversion to Christianity, now there was no escaping your Jewishness because you couldn't convert from your bloodline. Jews were perceived as a distinct, inferior racial group that threatened the purity of, say, the Aryan race.

- *Jews are conniving conspirators for world domination . . . again!* As Europeans set out across the globe in the name of *actual* world domination, they brought all their antisemitic ideas with them. And around 1900, all the newer, more modern iterations of Jew hate got to take their very first trip back to the Middle East. Although, the Europeans shouldn't get all the credit for antisemitism in the Middle East and North Africa. Jews had consistently been forced to convert, exiled, beheaded, assassinated, murdered en masse, pillaged, and otherwise persecuted in this part of the world since they had been taken as slaves to Babylon in 586 BCE.

So, when Islamic regimes started feeling put out by the West, the Jews and their "ritual murders" took the blame. Blood libel had officially become the universal language of Jew hate. Then, in 1908, when the "Young Turks" took over the Ottoman Empire and started spreading their liberal ideas of religious freedom,* Muslim conservatives found a convenient scapegoat in that old European saw: a secret Jewish plot to take over.

---

* "Young Turks" was a nickname the Europeans gave this diverse group of Jews, Arabs, Albanians, Greeks, and Armenians—though mostly young Turkish men—who wanted to prioritize scientific advancement and modernization.

- *Jews are too powerful . . . again!* After World War I ended in 1918, Germany was in the gutter. Its economy had bottomed out after the war, and the reparations they had to pay France and England made matters worse. Then came the onset of the Great Depression in 1929. Unemployment surged, and the Germans felt that their new postwar democratic government (aka the Weimar Republic) had failed them. And guess who was responsible for all that? Say it with me now: the Jews. Economic and financial ruin + perceived racial inferiority + hundreds of years of dehumanizing and demonizing the evil Jew across Europe = recipe for disaster for the Jews. The Nazis took over, enacted restrictive laws that stripped Jews of all but a handful of civil rights, then carried out the most horrific systematic slaughter of a people. It was an event so unprecedented and unheard of that a word had to be invented to describe it: *genocide*. (For an extended version of this not-so-tiny footnote in our history, see chapter 14.)

Where does that leave us now? Well, we all know how much America likes to "borrow" culture, and antisemitism is no exception. By the time Jews started arriving in large numbers at Ellis Island in the early 1900s, thousands of years of tropes showed up with them: that Jews are conspiring to take over the world. That they are dirty and disease-spreading. That they are clannish, disloyal, and can't be trusted. That they are money-hungry and greedy. Which explains why, as we fast-forward to the present, the entire buffet is still being served.

It's Coming from Inside the House: Internalized Antisemitism

EMMANUEL: Answer this for me: Can Jewish people be anti-semitic? Kyrie Irving, a Black NBA superstar said in 2022, "I cannot be antisemitic if I know where I come from." He got suspended by the NBA for posting a link on his social media (broadcast to roughly five million people) to the 2018 film *Hebrews to Negroes: Wake Up Black America*. The movie contains countless antisemitic tropes, among other incredibly offensive things, about the Jewish community. But Kyrie insinuated that regardless of his post, he cannot be antisemitic because he, as a Black man, is the original Jew. Thus, as a Jew, he cannot be antisemitic. There is a lot to unpack there, but I'm curious—can Jewish people be antisemitic?

NOA: Well, what Kyrie is saying is a *whole* other issue—so let's come back to that. But as far as Jews being antisemitic? Yes. *Internalized* antisemitism is just as insidious as the other forms we've discussed so far, and it's another undeniable factor in how antisemitism looks and sounds today. This is the part where I might piss off a few Jews—and people are welcome to disagree with me; as I said before, disagreeing is in our culture. So here it is: Jews can most definitely be antisemitic, both toward themselves and to other Jews. As with other oppressed groups, after generations of being a target of hate and being told that there is something fundamentally wrong with us, some of that rhetoric has seeped into our self-identity and affects how we see ourselves and stand up (or don't) for ourselves.

A great example of how this happens in another community is Hannah Gadsby's stand-up comedy performance called

Nanette. And by stand-up comedy, I mean the set they do that starts with your usual jokes then takes a gut-wrenching turn to authentically sharing about self-loathing in the LGBTQ community. Hannah grew up in middle-of-nowhere Tasmania, where Hannah felt they had to hide who they were until they were an *adult*, all the while marinating in the homophobic rhetoric they were surrounded by. After a couple decades of that, there's little wonder why they're dealing with self-hate. They internalized society telling them that there was something wrong with them. Here's how they put it:

"Seventy percent of the people who raised me, who loved me, who I trusted, believed that homosexuality was a sin, that homosexuals were heinous, subhuman pedophiles. Seventy percent! And by the time I identified as being gay, it was too late—I was already homophobic. And you do not get to just flip a switch on that."

When I heard Hannah say that, I thought, *OMG. That sounds exactly like the Jewish experience in the diaspora.* For thousands of years, Jews have been told that there's something wrong with us. No matter where we went, those anti-Jewish myths and smears followed closely behind: *Jews are greedy, Jews are dirty, Jews are evil, Jews are not to be trusted.* As Jewish men were excluded from farm and factory labor and forced into nonphysical professions, they were labeled weak. As those same men were made to look on as their families and communities were destroyed in pogroms, they were labeled as impotent. Our faces and bodies were literally used as examples for what was ugly and disgusting.

In addition, for thousands of years we learned that in order to survive, we basically had to change everything about ourselves. To suppress what made us so easy to hate. To change our names. To not be *us*. And that internalization doesn't just go away; it turns the self against itself. It creates the self-loathing Jew.

EMMANUEL: This conversation reminds me of something, too. Every summer my family and I, along with forty American doctors and nurses, travel from Atlanta to Lagos, Nigeria, as part of a medical mission with our nonprofit Living Hope Ministries. We stay at the compound that my dad built in 1995, then we travel to rural villages so the doctors can perform medical procedures and administer medications. The fourteen-hour days are grueling—honestly, more intense than my NFL summer workouts used to be. Every day we're up at 6:00 a.m., load up on scrambled eggs with fried plantain (my favorite Nigerian breakfast delicacy), then take buses out to the mission field. The medical professionals are from all over the country—some from Texas, some from Florida. And some are Black, some are white. But whenever we deboard the buses, the primary thing we hear from the crowds of three thousand–plus local Nigerian villagers is the plea to be seen by the "white American doctors." Every year, the same thing happens. And I am dejected by the fact that these Nigerians have been convinced by society that the Black American doctors are not as qualified or capable as the white doctors. Even they, from across the Atlantic, have been conditioned to believe the lie that the white man is more educated or qualified than the Black man.

NOA: I got the chills hearing that. That's such a powerful example of how insidious internalized racism can be. There is, shockingly, not a ton of research that has been done about internalized antisemitism or racism, but there *has* been a lot of attention paid to internalized misogyny. This is when women, who have been drenched in society's prejudice against women their entire lives, go on to minimize the value of women, mistrust women, and show gender bias in favor of men. Because when a group is ingrained with the stereotypes perpetuated by the dominant society about that group, it leads to feelings of self-doubt, disgust, and disrespect for one's group and/or oneself. And who does that end up serving? The very people who are the source of those ideas and that agenda.

Systems of power use that self-hatred as a tool to continue to reinforce a group's suppression. As Sander Gilman demonstrated in his 1986 study of Jewish "self-hatred," the power majority can continue to subdue a group by dangling in front of them the idea that "if you're more like us (and less like *you*), you can join us." But it's a trap. A double bind. Because when a group takes them up on that offer, assimilates, and embraces the rules of the majority, they're also cosigning on a system that's not designed to share any power with them. And never will be.

At its best, internalized antisemitism looks like Jews being *way* too quiet about our needs. It's putting our heads down and trying to not rock the boat while we tend to everyone else with the self-deprecating hypervigilance of a dutiful eldest child. But at its worst, it's actually agreeing with the people who have the nastiest things to think or say about us. It's not questioning what is right because someone else is telling us it's wrong. And as you'll see in just a moment, this brand of internalized antisemitism may just be what sinks the ship during this next big wave.

Why Are We Still Talking About Antisemitism?

NOA: Yes, both as in why I'm still talking about it right at this moment when I know you're ready for a stretch break, and also why in the big-picture sense it's necessary to keep having this conversation. Because the thing is, after World War II, with a brief detour through the McCarthyist '50s, it *did* start to feel like antisemitism was largely a thing of the past in America. Many of us were lulled into believing that we lived in a post-antisemitic world.

Maybe your family moved to a house in the suburbs, where people didn't care so much about your religion as where you went to college or where you worked or what your golf handicap was. Maybe your bat mitzvah was the social calendar highlight of your seventh-grade class. Maybe you and your family were simply left alone to live in peace. Whatever it looked like for you—or around you, whether or not you are Jewish—chances are that for some stretch of time, most people thought antisemitism was a thing but not like a *thing* thing. Unless you were *really* paying attention—more on that shortly.

In reality, antisemitism never went away. Irish writer and politician Conor Cruise O'Brien once said, "There are always people around in whom anti-semitism is a light sleeper." And that's the thing about antisemitism—it's always there, below the surface and at the ready, but it's not always at a full roar. This gives the illusion that antisemitism has ended (hooray!), so it's even more difficult to sound the alarm bells when old Jew-hating patterns start to creep in again (ugh). Consider that just before two of the most heinous instances of Jewish expulsion and mass murder (the Spanish Inquisition and the Holocaust), Jews were considered to be one of society's most successful, well-integrated minorities. No one would have guessed that the slowly rising antisemitic temperature would actually amount to anything too terrible because of how good the Jews had it, but alas, we've been sorely proven wrong.

In today's world, it's safer than it's ever been to be Jewish, and yet, it still can be unsafe to be visibly Jewish in major cities like New York, where Hasidic Jews are physically attacked in broad daylight. Jewish cemeteries have been the target of vandalism, such as in Philadelphia and St. Louis, where headstones were marred or toppled. The Pittsburgh Tree of Life synagogue shooting in 2018 left eleven Jewish worshippers dead, the deadliest attack on Jews in American history. Anti-Jewish slogans and swastikas are plastered across Jewish places of worship, homes, and schools. A recent survey found that a quarter of American hiring managers and recruiters wanted fewer Jewish people in their industry and/or are less likely to advance Jewish applicants. Among the top reasons given: perceptions that Jewish people have too much power and wealth already and don't need their job. And then there's the wilderness of social media: 84 percent of Jewish hate–related messaging is not taken down from Facebook, Twitter, TikTok, Instagram, and YouTube, where it spreads like wildfire.

Which leads me to the point of *all* of this: the modern face of antisemitism.

Clowns to the Left of Me, Jokers to the Right

NOA: Up until now, modern antisemitism has pretty much looked similar to the extreme right-wing rhetoric most of us have heard, seen, and called out—cult-favorite chart toppers like there's too many of us, we're gross, we're God killers, and so on. And for the last seventy years or so, it's been at about the same radio frequency, often in a fringe-y, conspiracy theory sort of way. People have blamed the Jews and their cabal for everything from mass shootings to 9/11 to the financial crisis of 2008 to the "false flag" insurrection on January 6th. The "disease-spreading Jew" trope also had another moment in the sun in 2020, when American white supremacists claimed the Jews created COVID-19 to increase their control and profit financially (which many social media users ate up). Some conspiracy theorists conjectured that the virus was manufactured by the US and Israel to target political rivals such as China and Iran.

Granted, all these accusations—as absurd as they are—are damaging. They continue to reinforce people's conspiratorial notions about the Jews, as well as throw little treats to that lightly sleeping beast. But all of this suddenly feels a little passé, a little old-fashioned. I mean when I think of the "Unite the Right" crew marching through Charlottesville in 2017, chanting "Jews will not replace us"—don't get me wrong, I cringe; I have seen its danger—but something else, something with the potential to ignite an entirely new crisis for the Jews has been quietly brewing on college campuses and in liberal-leaning communities throughout the country for the past thirty years. And I've been warning people about it in interviews, on social media, on television, and in front of Congress. That's because "classic" anti-Jew rhetoric from the far right is somewhat of a familiar boogeyman by now—something most reasonable people can recognize and rightfully shoo away. But the shape antisemitism has been morphing into makes it much more difficult to detect and easier to spread. It's being seen as acceptable, if not *cool*, and as a result it has the capacity to be far more destructive and far more dangerous. And the world finally got to see it for itself on October 8th.

13.

OCTOBER 8TH

EMMANUEL: October 8th? Don't you mean October 7th?

NOA: I mean October 8th. I mean the day *after* 3,000 Hamas terrorists invaded Israel and butchered 1,200 people—the largest number of Jews in one day since the Holocaust—and took more than 240 hostages, including babies and the elderly. I know you would love for me to pause here and unpack this— why it happened, what exactly happened, how I feel about it all—and we will. For now, though, we're not talking about what happened on the 7th.

And that's because in order to clearly see what thousands of years of cumulative antisemitism currently looks like, you only have to look at what happened on October 8th. It's because no matter what you think about the politics and policies of Israel, what happened on the 7th was an act of pure barbarism and should have been condemned as such by the entire civilized world.

Instead, on October 8th, before Israel had taken a single action against Hamas, drowning out any condolence, support, and outrage Jews received from some allies were *cheers*. People rallied and chanted in the name of "Palestinian liberation," in the name of "freedom fighting," and in the name of the dissolution of Israel. At any cost. The Chicago chapter of Black Lives Matter, the political antiracist group, tweeted an image *celebrating* the Hamas paragliders who had descended on a Burning Man–type outdoor festival and raped and mutilated and gunned down hundreds of innocent ordinary people. Jewish students at seemingly progressive universities were harassed by angry mobs; posters of those 240 hostages—including the children—were ripped off walls and lampposts all over the world including, of all places, New York City and Los Angeles. Representative Rashida Tlaib, a member of the far-left-leaning Washington, DC, "Squad" that once symbolized hope for Jewish progressives wanting a more representative government, tweeted, "From the river to the sea, Palestine will be Free"—the thinly veiled call to abolish Israel and reclaim the entire land from the Jordan River to the Mediterranean Sea. (I now routinely ask protestors if they know the true meaning of that chant, and they often do not.) Tlaib later claimed that this is a phrase that calls for freedom, human rights, and peaceful coexistence, but one has only to check the original written charter of Hamas to see that "from the river to the sea" is anything but peaceful. It reflects their stated mission to destroy Israel and those living there.

Now, instead of looking to the left and seeing the faces of people who Jews have fought alongside for decades in defense of minority and oppressed groups and against things like rape as a weapon of war, we see people who are calling Israelis and, by extension (consciously or not), all Jews oppressors, colonizers, apartheidists, and white supremacists.

I am *not* suggesting that the Israeli government is beyond reproach and not to be criticized. But the criticism of a government is not the same as denying a country's right to exist, and it is certainly not the same as extending equal vitriol for a government's actions to an entire group of people, many of whom do not reside there. And that of course also goes for Palestinians, who are not all responsible for the actions of their government, Hamas.

What we saw on October 8th was the activation of approximately thirty years of well-coordinated anti-Israel rhetoric and bias. Once again, that invisible thread of Jew hatred, that ever so subtle whisper of "it's the Jews," filled in convenient blanks of the October 7th conversation. In this moment of confusion and chaos that looks familiar and yet does not, people want to make sense of things. They want to point a finger. And there we are.

Israel became the *Jew* of the world.

Remember when I told you about how Yossi Klein Halevi said that Jews are always used to describe whatever the worst, most loathsome thing is in society at any given moment? *This* is what he was prophesying. These educated, reasonably open-minded individuals have looked at us Jews, taken the Rorschach test, and seen the worst of their own society: racism, colonization, and apartheid. And now, they could wash their hands of their own racist, colonialist, apartheidist guilt as Americans by calling for the violent dissolution of Israel, an entire country, founded and built as a safe place not only for the Jews but for anyone who chooses to live there.

Because before people would say, "Let's rid the world of the Jew and everything will be okay," the new polite society prefers, "Let's get rid of *the Jewish state*, and everything will be okay."

THE FOUR LAYERS OF ANTISEMITISM

NOA: Let me make this simple for you: All the antisemitism we just went through since the pharaohs in Egypt can be boiled down to four main layers. Not a single one has gone away, and more than one can be in play at any time:

1. **Peoplehood:** "Jews are weird, dirty, scheming, and threatening—they need to go."

2. **Religion:** "Jews are God killers and baby killers and/or not Christian or Muslim—they need to convert or go."

3. **Racial/Political:** "The Jewish *race* is inferior, revolting, and evil; they can't convert out of it—we can blame them for political gain . . . and they should go."

4. **Anti-Israel:** "Israel is all of the above. And it should go."

We have a lot more nuance to unpack in this conversation, because the conflation of Jews and Israel as a new form of antisemitism has been simmering as a long game since well before October 7th and 8th—since before Israel was even formed. But for now, suffice it to say that when it comes to antisemitism, we're currently taking it from both sides. The old iterations never went away—the swastikas on synagogues, the conspiracy theorist rantings, the violence for wearing a yarmulke—and in addition, we have this newest chapter: a deep resentment, if not hate, for Israel. Not criticism of Israel's politics in a nuanced cultural and historical context, not acknowledgment that not all Jews support all of its policies, and not recognition that there is more than one force creating today's issues in the Middle East. Rather, an obsessive, almost blinding vitriol for Israel that can only be explained as a proxy for the Jews.

I've been attuned to this new chapter of antisemitism for years, and, as I've already told you, I've testified in front of Congress about it. The first time was in 2022, at the Interparliamentary Task Force to Combat Online Antisemitism. I waved a red flag in front of senators, representatives, and ultimately the FBI that 73 percent to 84 percent of online antisemitism wasn't about space lasers or Jews replacing us. No, it was coming from the left in the form of blood libel against Israel. And neatly tucked into that anti-Israel hatred are the same antisemitic tropes we've heard since the 1500s. The same tropes that, when left unchecked, led to the most catastrophic persecution of the Jewish population.

14.

THE HOLOCAUST, PART I

The (Very Real) History

EMMANUEL: Fifteen million Jews.

NOA: That's right.

EMMANUEL: I haven't been able to shake what you said since I first heard it because it just blows my mind—there's only 15 million Jews in the world. If I would've guessed, I maybe would have said 300 million, or at least 200 million. I mean, America's population is roughly 336 million, so surely 30 percent of that is Jewish. But no, only 7.5 million Jews are here, a little more than 2 percent. Is that because of the Holocaust?

NOA: That is because of the Holocaust.

EMMANUEL: I looked it up—the population of Jews in Europe went from 9.5 million in 1933 to 3.5 million in 1950. That's just absolutely crazy.

NOA: That's mass extermination. A Holocaust.

EMMANUEL: In May 2021, I went to New York as part of an MTV series on antisemitism and was privileged to have a conversation with a woman named Tova Friedman, a Holocaust survivor who was five years old when she was rounded up onto a cattle car to a concentration camp, and ultimately sent to a gas chamber. She would have been executed had it not malfunctioned.

NOA: What a miracle. At some concentration camps, or huge industrial complexes the Nazis built solely for assembly-line annihilation and/or enslavement of the Jews, the German soldiers would tell the Jews coming off the trains that they were going to shower, to be "disinfected." They would undress and the Nazis would pack them into large, empty rooms disguised as showers. They'd need to put their hands up in the air so the soldiers could cram in as many people as possible because the Nazis were looking for the most efficient way to kill the Jews. Initially, they piped in carbon monoxide to suffocate them, but that took too long, so they eventually discovered that Zyklon B, a form of cyanide that the Nazis had originally purchased to fumigate the soldiers' and prisoners' barracks to rid them of vermin, was more effective. Once the Jews were gassed, their naked bodies were ransacked for valuables like gold dental fillings and jewelry. The women's hair would be shaved off so the Germans could sell it as raw material for textiles, and they'd be bulldozed into a mass grave or burned in huge ovens called crematoriums. At the height of Jews being rounded up across Europe and deported in 1943 and 1944, as many as six thousand Jews were gassed at Auschwitz every single day. And that was just one camp out of many.

EMMANUEL: The level of dehumanization is incomprehensible to me. Tova told me that when she got off the cattle car that had transported her to Auschwitz, she was immediately separated from her mother and sent into the line with the other children as the adults formed a line of their own. The lines that would lead them to their death. By the time she had gotten to the front of the line, her name was no longer Tova; she would simply go by a number tattooed on her arm: *A27633*. She showed me the tattoo when we met, and that image has never left my mind.

NOA: I want everyone hearing this to know that Emmanuel knows that number by heart. That's how meaningful it is to him, and I thank you, Emmanuel, for that.

The Nazis kept meticulous records of everyone they murdered and used those tattoos to brand each of their prisoners—children, the elderly, everyone—upon arriving at some camps, including Auschwitz, the largest of the camps where more than one million people died. It was in Poland. You can visit it today, which confuses some people—*why would you want to do that?* Partly to bear witness, to honor the people who died there or whose families were decimated. But mostly, to remember so that the story of what happened there is never, ever lost. And more than that, so we can continue to understand and internalize *how* it happened. How it was a series of subtle, almost imperceptible incidents that eventually added up to this catastrophic moment in our global history; how individually, these incremental events didn't seem as though they would result in the murder of millions; and how many of the same political, economic, and social stepping stones that led to the Holocaust are once again being followed today.

EMMANUEL: I will forever remember looking out at the Hudson River with her and, staring at the Statue of Liberty. She said to me, "Promise me you'll forever tell my story. Because I won't be here to tell it much longer." And it's an honor to carry that burden, if you will, of always remembering Tova and the atrocities that she saw during her life. So that's what leads me to this chapter, the responsibility of remembering. Because I made that promise to her.

NOA: Almost every Jewish family has a story like that. I didn't talk about my grandmother Dina Tishby in my first book much, but she is my direct connection to the Holocaust. She was a glamorous and vivacious woman who kept her hair meticulously curled and her nails painted bright red. She escaped Poland before the Holocaust, but she had an older sister, Gita, who was not as lucky.

I was able to piece together what had happened to Gita through family whispers. The adults did their best to keep the story from us kids, but as children do, we heard it all. Gita, her husband, and her two young children were rounded up by the Nazis one morning, along with the rest of their village. Instead of sending them to the death camps, the soldiers just shot them all, then and there. Somehow the bullets missed Gita, and so she hid—under the bodies of her dead husband, children, and everyone she knew. She stayed like that for the entire day before pulling herself out and disappearing into the night, eventually finding her way to Israel. We never saw Gita much, because she would often be hiding in kitchen cupboards, screaming in search of her dead children. She'd survived in body but was forever broken in spirit.

EMMANUEL: Wow, I am so, so sorry, that is devastating . . . this type of pain and horror is truly unimaginable. When I hear stories like that, it really makes me understand why there is so much fear and anxiety in the hearts of my Jewish brothers and sisters today.

What shook me to the core was when Tova said, "The most brilliant minds of our world made the Holocaust." The greatest scientists, the greatest teachers, the greatest musicians. I asked this of Tova, but let me ask you, too, Noa—do you feel as though a Holocaust could occur again?

NOA: I *know* a Holocaust could occur again.

EMMANUEL: Is that just irrational fear? Like, slavery ain't happening again in America, I'll tell you that right now. Even after George Floyd got killed, I mean, there will unfortunately be another Black man getting unjustly killed by a cop. But slavery? No shot. So why do you and other Jews think a Holocaust could happen again?

NOA: To start, because Jews have been part of an ongoing cycle of persecution and extermination for as long as we have existed. There is a pattern, and that pattern has never changed. It's why we were so shaken by October 7th. It wasn't solely because so many Jews had been mutilated, raped, and slaughtered; it was also because it was part of a larger chain of events: anti-Jewish scapegoating, followed by an anti-Jewish movement, followed by anti-Jewish violence.

Similarly, the Holocaust was not an isolated event. In fact, that's the disservice that some Holocaust educations do for young people—they lead them to believe that the Jews woke up one morning, were rounded up, and killed; as though it came out of nowhere. No, the Holocaust was the result of *years* of persecuting Jews in Germany and other parts of Europe in a slowly escalating way. There was a subtle shift in language, insinuating that it was the Jews—as *some* of the bank owners and *some* of the members of the government—who were to blame for Germany's loss of World War I, tanking economy, weak leadership, unpleasant state of international affairs, and struggling national identity. Stereotypes and caricatures depicting them as godless, greedy, and conniving chipped away at their humanity. Eventually, over time, people—very smart, very educated people—started believing that Jews were, in fact, to blame for Germany's—and much of Eastern Europe's—economic downfall, and that they had to go. Those initial stages—the anger, the resentment, the generalizations, the blame—are not so different from what I've been seeing happen around the world now when it comes to the Jews and Israel.

I don't believe that the next Holocaust will look exactly the same as it did in the 1930s and '40s. There won't necessarily be cattle cars and gas chambers. But the run-up has looked exactly the same—the dehumanization and demonization of Jews. And now that there is a Jewish state that has been conflated with all Jews, it's been woven in there, too. All over social media and Middle Eastern media you can find the same tropes such as Jews and Israel controlling the world; Jews and Israel as evil, cruel, and bloodthirsty; and Jews having allegiance only to themselves and Israel. There are also similar images to what was used in Europe in the 1930s, including the Jews and Israel with their tentacles wrapped around the White House and Jews and Israel as the puppet masters manipulating world leaders. This rhetoric is identical to the hatred that the Jewish people experienced before their massacre in Granada in 1066, the same hatred they experienced in Europe before the Rhineland Massacres in 1096 and the Black Death persecutions in the 1300s, in Spain before the Inquisition in the 1500s, in Russia and Poland before the pogroms in the 1800s and 1900s, and in Germany before the Holocaust. It all sets the stage for the same conclusion: Jews (and Israel) are a problem, and it's okay, if not beneficial, to get rid of them.

But I'm not here to prophesy what the next Holocaust will be so much as to instill in people the understanding that the Holocaust was not a freak accident or an outlier. When you look at it in the larger historical context, you can see how it was the result of that ongoing cycle of historical hatred and scapegoating. And people are already forgetting that it happened at all.

We Need to Talk About the Holocaust

NOA: In her bestselling memoir *Educated*, Tara Westover writes about setting foot in a classroom for the first time at the age of seventeen when she, incredibly, gets herself to Brigham Young University. Having been raised by survivalists in the mountains of Idaho, this was the first time she'd ever received a formal education. So, as a freshman, she has a pretty steep learning curve. She describes sitting in class one day, opening an art history textbook, and seeing a strange word— a word she hadn't ever heard before, nor did she have any idea what it meant. She raises her hand to say, "Excuse me, what is this word?"

It was "Holocaust."

When I first read that, it almost knocked me out of my chair. I couldn't understand how anyone could be on this planet for seventeen years and not have heard about one of the most horrific, world-changing events that had unfolded barely eighty years ago. That was only two generations ago—my *grandparents* (not my great-great-great-grandparents) were lucky enough to escape, though many others from my family perished. The fact that you met a Holocaust survivor is testament to the fact that this is not ancient history. Also, *six million* Jews and *eleven million* non-Jews had been exterminated in the largest, most extensive, genocide this planet had ever witnessed over the course of twelve years. This was not a tiny blip on the radar.

But as shocked as I was about Tara, that paled in comparison to the fact that young people who are actually receiving an education, who are growing up in our country's school systems, are just as in the dark as she was.

According to a 2023 survey conducted by *The Economist*, only half of American young adults (ages eighteen to twenty-nine) disagreed with the statement "The Holocaust is a myth."

An even more expansive 2020 survey conducted in all fifty states by the Claims Conference, a group committed to seeking justice for victims of the Holocaust, paints the same stark picture among American millennials and Gen Z:

- 63 percent did not know that six million Jews were murdered. (Thirty-six percent thought it was two million or fewer.)

- 48 percent could not name a single one of the more than forty thousand concentration camps and ghettos established during World War II. In fact, overall, there was virtually no awareness of concentration camps or ghettos.

And then there's this:

- 11 percent believe it was the Jews who caused the Holocaust.

As we speak, thirty-three states do not require Holocaust curricula in public schools because it might cause "discomfort, guilt, anguish, or any other form of psychological distress." For the record, these are the same reasons cited behind anti–critical race theory laws, or laws that forbid teaching students about institutionalized racism, such as Texas's 2021 House Bill 3979.

EMMANUEL: This is so infuriating. You know my book *Uncomfortable Conversations with a Black Boy* has been banned in some school districts in Florida. I'm serious—google it. When I found that out, I was shocked. My book isn't spewing any propaganda or pushing some hidden agenda, but our society thinks that forgetting is a better alternative than learning from previous mistakes. It's really just crazy to me.

NOA: It *is* crazy, and horrifying and maddening. As you of course know, that kind of erasure is not an accident. It is meant to erase any kind of responsibility that we need to take for terrible things that have happened in our history—and responsibility for making sure they don't happen again. That's why the erasure of our history and the denial of our genocide is terrifying. It's why our grief and fear has been unbearable in the weeks and months since the October 7th attack—because the beats have felt far too similar to 1930s Germany. It's why it cuts so deeply when someone demands to see proof of the Hamas massacre, when Jews are blamed for their own tragedy, and when university presidents will not condemn students calling for our genocide. It's the jeers at Jewish students on campus, the swastika graffiti in my friend's daughter's school, the chairs through restaurant windows, the impossible position of being both an "inferior race" and the "beneficiaries of white privilege," the suspicion, the denial, the finger-pointing. Because those are all steps down a very specific path.

It's the same exact path that led a modern, civilized nation to believe the worst about its Jews. To turn neighbor against neighbor. To attempt to eliminate an entire group of people. In broad daylight, under the watchful eye of the entire world.

And the culmination of all that was the murder of six million Jews.

How the Dominoes Fell

NOA: Documentaries, books, entire *series* of books, have been devoted to the Holocaust. I am attempting to do in one chapter what some teachers spend days, if not months, unraveling for students. So, we're going to call this . . . ambitious (because "crazy" is not so PC anymore). It is a highly condensed, highly expedient overview of more than twelve years of intricate historical events so that you can see at a glance-ish how one event organically begat the next until the conclusion of genocide. And not only the sequencing of those events but also the timeless nature of each individual step, because they are not unique to the first decades of the twentieth century. This chapter is not intended to be your only source of Holocaust education. It is, however, intended for you to read with a critical eye toward how and why many of these events are not just history. They are prophecy.

Pre-1933: The Making of a Nazi

Germany gets crushed. In 1918, World War I ends with the Central Powers (primarily Germany, Austria-Hungary, the Ottoman Empire, and Bulgaria) losing their bid to take over all of Europe, and the Allied Powers (primarily France, Great Britain, the Russian Empire, Italy, Japan, and the United States) winning for having stopped them. Millions of men have been wiped out because of new battle technologies (tanks, grenades, airplanes, submarines, long-range artillery, machine guns, poison gas).

In an attempt to pull themselves back together, the Germans form their very first democracy, called the Weimar Republic. Things start stumbling along again—that is until the Allies force Germany to sign the Treaty of Versailles, a punitive, humiliating agreement that, among other things, requires Germans to pay reparations to the Allied Powers—a huge blow to German wallets and pride. And then on top of *that*, in 1929, the Great Depression hits, the economy collapses completely, the personal savings of the middle class are wiped out, and unemployment is rampant. So, people were pissed. And they were pissed at the Weimar Republic.

I should mention at this point that the Jews had for *centuries* been enjoying a relatively comfortable and assimilated, mostly middle-class existence in Germany. They were significant contributors to the country's vibrant intellectual and artistic communities. They were patriotic citizens who had fought shoulder to shoulder with their German counterparts in World War I and had received medals for their wartime valor and military service. They were, as far as anyone could tell, fully integrated in German society.

Politics swing to the right. Before World War I, Germans were increasingly in favor of a democratic shift toward the left and away from the authoritarian emperor (the Kaiser). But after 1919 and the Treaty of Versailles, the Germans resented the political left for rolling over to the demands of the Allied Powers and making Germany the laughingstock of the world. Plus, the upper and middle classes were terrified of the creeping threat of Communism that was consuming Eastern Europe. A movement that was, incidentally, perceived as a Jewish-inspired, Jewish-led grab for world domination (or what Nazis called "Judeo-Bolshevism"). It was a claim that was *so* originally derived from, here we go again, *The Protocols of the Elders of Zion*, the invented claim by Russian secret police that Jews were plotting to take over the world. (I really hope they're getting royalties on that!)

The more palatable alternative? A swing to the right: radical nationalism. Less wishy-washy pluralistic democratic solutions, more solid authoritarian direction and fierce patriotism. And they found that in Adolf Hitler and his German Workers' Party, aka the National Socialist German Workers' Party, which would eventually become the Nazi Party.

The Jews are to blame. Meanwhile, the spreading antisemitic murmur is getting louder. The Germans still can't get comfortable with the fact that their military had been defeated—and the German army can't either. So military leaders start shifting the blame to the Weimar Republic and the Jews, socialists, and Communists.*

Around this time, the German Workers' Party, headed up by one Adolf Hiter, started publicly capitalizing on the suspicion that international Jewry was attempting to control Germany. More and more people started to see the new Weimar Republic administration as an instrument of exploitation created by democratic Jews who were a "parasite upon the nations" (literally a line from Hitler's book, *Mein Kampf*), while establishing a government that would allow them to be more powerful than other Germans and to execute their world-domination aspirations.

––––––––––

Making Germany great again. In 1920, to bring Hitler's vision of restoring Germany to its former empire-worthy superiority to life, the National Socialist German Workers' Party puts forth the 25-Point Program. In addition to twenty-two other points, it called for:

––––––––––

* In 1919, when testifying in front of a parliamentary committee about why things went south during the war, the former commander in chief of the German army, General Paul von Hindenburg, had some choice words. First, he blamed the government itself for caving and starting peace negotiations prematurely. Then he alluded to something more nefarious at play. He said the German forces could have won had they not been "stabbed in the back." It was a dog whistle, and one that perked up the ears of right-wing extremist and nationalist groups—including the German Workers' Party—who believed that this sabotage was the work of an international Jewish conspiracy, now known as the "stab-in-the-back myth."

1. German ultranationalism,
2. The abolition of the Treaty of Versailles, and
3. "None but members of the nation may be citizens of the state. None but those of German blood, whatever their creed may be. No Jew, therefore, may be a member of the nation."

To be fair, that teeny-tiny Jewish detail was sandwiched between seemingly great stuff like the demands for a healthy middle class, prohibiting child labor, and better education for everyone, regardless of social status. A classic case of "Sure, I don't agree with *all* their policies, but . . ." Because essentially, their mission statement was to boost German morale and global standing. And the way they were going to do that was by returning Germany to the master or Aryan race that Nazi Party founders believed Germans had belonged to since the beginning of humanity itself. With an assist from pseudo-scientific analysis, the Germans decided to promote the belief that their Aryan race was, indeed, superior and that its greatest threat to existence would be contamination from lesser "races" such as the Romany (formerly Gypsies), the Polish, and above all: Jews. (Plus, eventually, Black people, homosexuals, Communists, people with mental disabilities or illnesses, feminists, and Jehovah's Witnesses. They were inclusive like that.)

1933–1938: The Water's Getting Warmer: Insurrection, Dismantled Democracy, and Stripped Civil Rights

Adolf Hitler and the Nazis get a foot in the door. In 1933, Paul von Hindenburg, of "stab-in-the-back myth" notoriety, is now the president of Germany. Hindenburg names Hitler chancellor, or leader, of Germany, despite the fact that he'd been previously incarcerated for trying to lead an insurrection against the Weimar Republic.* The Nazi Party is now the controlling party of the government.

And then they get a lot *of power.* One month after Hitler is named chancellor, the German parliament (Reichstag) building is burned down. The Nazis suspect arson at the hands of the Communists, and the Nazis convince the German president to issue an emergency decree, now known as the Reichstag Fire Decree. This allowed the regime to arrest and detain *anyone* without specific charge, dissolve dissenting political organizations, and suppress publications. No criticism or nonconformity would be tolerated. A few months later, the Enabling Act—or the Law to Remedy the Distress of the People and the Reich—passed. Hitler could now enact laws, even those in violation of the Weimar Constitution, without approval of parliament or the president. German judges didn't challenge the law, seeing themselves as mere servants of the Reich. And besides, the provisions would expire after four years—what could go wrong? Under their watch, Germany became a police state.

In 1934, President Hindenburg dies, and Hitler succeeds him as president; then, two weeks later, he abolishes the office

---

* He wrote (or, technically, dictated) *Mein Kampf* while he was in jail. CliffsNotes version: "If, with the help of his Marxist creed, the Jew is victorious over the other peoples of the world, his crown will be the funeral wreath of humanity and this planet will, as it did thousands of years ago, move through the ether devoid of men."

of president, merges those powers with the ones he had as chancellor, and declares himself "Führer" of the Third Reich, or leader of the German empire—an authoritarian dictatorship that dealt a final blow to any remaining checks on his power. And he could do this *because he had already destroyed the legal and constitutional limits to his authority.* The first victims of systematic Nazi persecution were Hitler's political opponents, whom he sent to Dachau, the first-ever concentration camp, just outside Munich. The next target was the Jews.

———

Jewish dehumanization begins. This comes in the form of a series of laws the Nazis institute, which, again, does not happen overnight. Rather, they unfolded in waves, slowly but methodically isolating and excluding the Jews from German society. First, in 1933, Jewish professors, teachers, and students were forced to leave German schools, and Germans were instructed to boycott Jewish-owned businesses. Next, in 1935, the Nazis enacted the Nuremberg Race Laws, which stated that no Jew could be a full citizen of Germany, have political rights, or marry or engage in a sexual relationship with Germans (aka "race defilement"). Within three years, in 1938, the "Decree for the Reporting of Jewish-Owned Property" required Jews to register any property or assets—furniture, homes, life insurance, stocks, *anything*—valued at more than 5,000 reichsmarks (between $30,000 and $40,000 today). The German government then repossessed every last bit of it—seven billion reichsmarks' worth—as part of its state-sanctioned plundering justified by "Aryanization." It was just the first step toward completely pushing Jews out of the German economy, followed by Jews being assessed the maximum tax rate regardless of income.

Later in 1938, a new law required Jews to name their children from a government-approved list. Any Jew who did not already have a name from that list had to adopt an additional first name: "Israel" for men and "Sara" for women. And then, in September 1941, all Jews six years old and older were required to wear a yellow Star of David–shaped badge labeled with the word *Jude* (German for "Jew") when in public.

If you're wondering *Why didn't they just leave?*, that is a great question. Remember, German Jews thought of themselves as fully assimilated into the most advanced and enlightened society in the world. For many, it was as though they were Germans first and Jews second. They assumed this madness would soon pass, plus they had friends, neighbors, and communities— allies whom they thought would protect them. Eventually, as things progressively worsened, some Jews did make the decision to go, though with great sacrifice. My great-grandfather Paul Schorr was one of them. He sensed the impending danger and first moved his family from the German town of Cologne to Prague in Czechoslovakia, never imagining that Hitler would make it that far in his quest to take over Europe. When it was clear that the Nazis were going to do just that, he was able to secure extremely difficult-to-get visas to join a small Zionist community in what would become Israel.

No one in my family knows for sure what had to happen to convince the passport office to issue those visas, but we only had to fill in the blanks. After one of the men in charge commented on the beauty of Paul's seventeen-year-old daughter, my grandmother Hilda, he understood the steep price of the survival of his family. He brought Hilda back for a closed-door meeting. They came home with the visas.

Eventually, restrictions on Jewish movement tightened further, and escape was virtually impossible. And even if you could secure a visa, few countries were taking Jewish immigrants, much less the numbers needed to save Europe's Jews.*

The living conditions for the Jews who remained would continue to rapidly deteriorate. As their property was repossessed by the government, the Germans boycotted their businesses, and new laws made it increasingly difficult to secure employment, they experienced extreme poverty. It was not uncommon for several families to live in one apartment, lacking basic amenities like reliable plumbing or heating. Meanwhile, Aryans took over many of those Jewish-owned businesses and properties, and the German economy got a boost as the government continued to liquidate the Jews' personal property, which is potentially why some Germans had an easier time turning a blind eye.

---

* Two of the most glaring instances of this occurred in North America. Canada had one of the lowest records among developed nations, accepting only 5,000 Jews between 1933 and 1945. Apparently, when asked how many Jews should be admitted to Canada, a senior government official responded, "None is too many." But the most infamous example of the world turning its back on the Jews was in 1939. The *St. Louis*, a ship carrying 937 passengers—almost all of whom were Jewish refugees—had sailed from Germany to Cuba. But the Cuban government canceled their landing permits. The ship then sailed near the Florida coast, but the US government also would not allow them to land because the passengers didn't have immigration visas and had not passed a security screening. The ship was sent back to Europe. Great Britain, France, Belgium, and the Netherlands each stepped up to admit a percentage of the refugees. But many of them were not able to escape Europe again before Germany invaded a year later, and 254 of them died in the Holocaust.

Words turn to violence. After years of simmering resentment toward the Jews, followed by years of slowly singling them out and projecting that these poor, dirty people were dragging down German excellence, Germany was now a volatile tinderbox.

The spark came in 1938, when a Jewish seventeen-year-old named Herschel Grynszpan assassinated a German diplomat in Paris. (There were rumors that it was a lovers' spat.) The Nazis immediately framed it as an assault by "World Jewry" on the Third Reich and gave the party's paramilitary and Hitler Youth the green light to unleash widespread violence on Jewish communities throughout Germany and German-controlled territories. Dressed in civilian clothing so the effort didn't appear state-sanctioned, they looted and destroyed 7,500 Jewish-owned businesses, desecrated Jewish cemeteries, raped Jewish women, and murdered hundreds of people. They also set fire to hundreds of synagogues, which were allowed to burn through the night as local firefighters, under orders, looked on only to ensure that the fires didn't spread to German buildings. The event became known as Kristallnacht, "Night of Broken Glass."

The German government announced that it was the Jews themselves who were to blame.*

That night, thirty thousand men were rounded up and sent to the concentration camps the Nazis had been quietly building around Germany. The next phase had begun. Jews would be arrested and deported solely for being Jewish.

---

* But the real pièce de résistance was when the German government confiscated the insurance payouts to any Jews whose businesses or homes had been looted or destroyed. And not only that, the government imposed a fine of what would then have been about $400 million.

1939–1945: The Final Solution to the Jewish Question

By 1939, Germany had dusted itself off. The economy had started to pick up, thanks to Hitler's policies (and repossessed Jewish property and businesses), and the country was once again feeling strong enough to assert its dominance over the world. Hitler steamrolled through Poland with the mission of expanding Germany's empire and ridding the world of the Jews he was convinced were—or had conveniently blamed for—both staining German excellence and taking over the world. Amped up on Aryan nationalism and the covenant of hate against anyone who would ever dare to try to bring them down, the German people ate it up.

Their desperation had been soothed by larger-than-life leadership and the perfect villains, both carefully crafted through years of subtle, steady messaging about what was good (the Führer) and what was very much not (the Jews). And you either agreed, convinced yourself to agree out of self-preservation, or died.

That is the answer to how the Holocaust was possible. Years of calculated fake news with the Nazis feeding the public a steady diet of propaganda and the polished vision of the perfect nationalistic German dream was how the Nazis were able to go from merely expelling Jews from Germany and other parts of Europe to killing them methodically and entirely: "The Final Solution to the Jewish Question," as they called it. That is how they justified rounding up Jews for mass shootings in their villages after forcing them to dig their own graves beforehand. It's how they built a machine of roughly nine hundred concentration camps, cramming Jews into cattle cars on trains, and sending them to Bergen-Belsen, Treblinka, Auschwitz-Birkenau, and Sobibor. It's how the people who lived in the villages near the camps, covered in ash, air thick with the stench of the cremated bodies of the Jews who had been gassed, tortured, hanged, shot, or subjected to gruesome living-person medical experiments, could go about their everyday lives. It's how companies like Volkswagen, Deutsche Bank, and Bayer turned a blind eye to Jewish enslavement, either benefiting from their access to subjects for medical testing or "extermination through labor." It is how human beings could man every single one of these death conveyor belts, sending hundreds of thousands of children and the mothers who wouldn't leave them, pregnant women, and the disabled to their deaths. How they could concoct the basest, most inhumane, most incomprehensible uses for other human beings. And how they would do it, again and again, to the Jews of Czechoslovakia, Poland, Denmark, Norway, the Netherlands, Belgium, Luxembourg, France, Yugoslavia, Greece, Estonia, Lithuania, Latvia, the Soviet Union, Romania, Albania, Austria, and Hungary.

Two out of every three Jews murdered.

For a total of six million Jews.

But as Dara Horn, the brilliant author of *People Love Dead Jews,* has so correctly pointed out, six million Jews don't have to die for us to consider it to be a cataclysmic event. Or twelve hundred. Or even one. The insidiousness lies in the stepping stones. The dominoes. Because if we don't put an end to the spread of anti-Jewish hate on the internet; if we don't put an end to people chanting "From the river to the sea"; if we don't put an end to people spitting "Zionist bitch" at Jews (okay, at me); if we don't put an end to people tearing down posters of children kidnapped by a terrorist organization; if we don't put an end to people romanticizing another intifada; if we don't put an end to university presidents allowing the call for our genocide in the name of free speech, it will all happen again.

15.

THE HOLOCAUST, PART II
The (Very Real) Aftermath

EMMANUEL: You know Noa, a question I cannot get out of my mind is why didn't anyone do anything about what was happening? What about the German bystanders? It seems like it was maybe a similar dynamic to what happened with slavery; there were people for it and people against it, but ultimately most were complicit.

NOA: I think that's a really powerful parallel, and that's what was at play here, too. There were many Germans who bought into Hitler's antisemitism and agreed with his policies. And then there were Germans who, perhaps, didn't agree with the Jew hatred but loved that Hitler was strengthening the economy. Or they could get a job in the Nazi war machine, which came with a lot of clout.

And, even if you didn't agree—well, what did it matter? The Nazis could simply arrest you and send you to a concentration camp if you spoke out.

We should remember, though, that there were small groups of people who did fight back; some non-Jews helped Jews to hide or escape; and there was a Jewish resistance movement. A few brave souls, like Oskar Schindler and Raoul Wallenberg, went to extraordinary lengths that often cost them everything to protect Jews and other targeted people. But ultimately, the majority of people were willing to look away—even in the United States, which only got involved in the war because the Japanese, as part of the German coalition, had bombed Pearl Harbor.

Educators from the United States Holocaust Memorial Museum put it in a chillingly eloquent way: "The Holocaust happened because of millions of individual choices."

What If We Just Made It All Up?

EMMANUEL: How do you feel when some people imply, or overtly state, the Holocaust didn't really happen? I can't wrap my head around that because I can't understand how you could see the same photographs that I've seen or heard the stories of survivors—seen the tattoos on their arms!—and think, *Eh, I bet the Jews just made it up.*

NOA: It is some of the most stunning mental gymnastics out there. Holocaust denial and distortion, or believing the Holocaust is somehow up for debate, is just one more way for people to be antisemitic. As is Holocaust revisionism, which is a new form of that denial that says maybe the Holocaust just wasn't *that* bad. And every year, teachers hear from parents that they want their children excused from Holocaust instruction because it isn't their "belief" that the Holocaust happened.

In 2022, the UN released a report that found 10 percent of Holocaust-related posts on Facebook and 15 percent on Twitter contained denial or distortion content—as in, not that many Jews died, the Jews caused it to happen, or it didn't happen at all. The former president of Iran has dismissed the Holocaust as "Zionist propaganda." Poland has passed a bill outlawing anyone from blaming Poland (home of the largest concentration camp, Auschwitz, as well as Chelmno, an extermination camp) for any crimes committed during the Holocaust.

The burden of proof has always been on the Jews when it comes to their tragedies. When Hamas released GoPro footage of the rapes and murders its members committed on October 7th, the world *still* needed more evidence. The Israeli government had to hold private screenings of the footage for reporters in response to the public outcry that insufficient evidence of the brutality had been produced. The *New York Times* ran a deeply reported investigative piece corroborating Hamas's use of sexual violence as a weapon of war, including eyewitness accounts of rape and countless female bodies stripped from the waist down, their genitals often grotesquely mutilated. Yet people are still arguing that women were not raped and that the claim is nothing but propaganda. And then there's the all-too-common experience we have of scrolling through comments on social media (frequently on my own posts) and hearing from those who flat out deny that anything had happened, saying the Jews made it all up. Or worse, that the Jews did it to themselves.

The thing is, the Holocaust is literally undeniable. The Nazis kept meticulous records for most of the Final Solution, registering every inmate who had come into the camps and who had died. There are forty-six volumes of "Death Books" that include the names of the 68,864 registered camp prisoners who died

at Auschwitz between July 29, 1941, and December 31, 1943.*
And then there are all the letters, memos, blueprints, orders, bills,
speeches, train schedules, and statistical summaries generated
by the Nazis. When they were eventually put on trial for their
crimes, there were more than 3,000 *tons* of records. You know
who takes this the most seriously? Germany. The Germans did
some real soul-searching after this all went down and have made
it clear that they never want to be the shame of the world again.
You can barely walk a block without seeing a memorial or plaque
or some way of keeping what happened in public memory.

Feeling It in My Bones

NOA: Emmanuel, you'd asked me in an earlier conversation
about trauma response and how that plays into the way we
react to things that people say or that happen to us, even if they
weren't intended to be hurtful. I think this is a really good place
to unpack more of that. Of course, now we're talking about
the trauma response itself and not who is responsible for that
response, but it's related to the Holocaust conversation.

We now know that there is very real biological trauma that
can be passed down through the generations. Of course, it's not
specific to Holocaust survivors and their descendants, but researchers at the Icahn School of Medicine at Mount Sinai in
New York have looked at this particular community to study
what exactly that looks like. And they found that the stress response from trauma can physiologically alter the formation of
both sperm and egg in a way that passes on the trauma response

---

* You can access these records online through the United States Holocaust Memorial Museum Database of Survivor and Victim Names.

to subsequent generations, called epigenetic trauma. And researchers think it could be the body's way of preparing offspring for challenges similar to the ones their parents (and their parents) faced, which is nothing short of incredible. But they've also found that it can make us, the offspring, more vulnerable to things like anxiety and the posttraumatic stress disorder (PTSD) that soldiers experience after being in active combat.

EMMANUEL: I hear you on that. The Black community experiences the same exact thing, what researchers call "racial battle fatigue." It's basically the result of always feeling like you're in danger or that you have to be on high alert, so you start suffering from anxiety, headaches, and high blood pressure. One in five Black Americans will experience an anxiety disorder at some point in their life, and as many as 14 percent have PTSD.

NOA: It's a tragic way to have to make a point, but exactly. Both our communities know what it's like to feel like the other shoe could drop at any moment. Which is why when we hear generalizations about "the Jews," or worse, when we hear the stories that emerged from the massacre of October 7th, we feel fear on a *cellular* level.

A couple of months after October 7th, I went to Israel to bear witness. I visited the site of the massacre in southern Israel and walked through burned and shattered homes. I met with families of the hostages who were taken on that day and with hostages who had returned from Hamas captivity. And I met with those who had survived the Hamas attacks. One of whom was twenty-seven-year-old Noam Ben-David. Noam went to the Nova music festival with her boyfriend, David, to make art, dance, and spread love. As the sun rose and the party peaked, the scene quickly shifted to hysteria as screams of warnings spread that armed men were attacking. Noam, her boyfriend, and four-teen others hid in a large trash container. Sixteen of them piled one on top of the other, doing their best to conceal themselves in garbage. David stood guard so that he could warn others of what was happening and attempt to alert rescue teams to their location. Hamas terrorists shot him, then sprayed the garbage container with gunfire. Noam was shot in the hip and had to muffle her breathing and her pain, buried under the bodies of her friends, covered in their blood, to survive. She did not know that only three others from the sixteen were still alive, until Israeli soldiers rescued her about an hour later. Noam, like my grand-mother's older sister, Gita, had to pull herself out from under-neath the dead bodies of the people she loved. It was the exact same story that horrified me as a child, and it was now being told to me, once again, as an adult. This horror happened to us again.

So, you see, when we hear the stories from eighty years ago, they are not theoretical to us because *we are those stories*. We are the descendants of the Jews hiding in closets and under dead bodies in Jerusalem, Cordoba, Fez, Baghdad, Warsaw, and Berlin. This is still very, very real to us.

Never Again

EMMANUEL: "When I was hiding under a blanket next to a corpse is when I felt safest." The horror of what you're telling me reminds me of the words that caused my heart to break as my jaw was left open. It was the most gut-wrenching thing that Tova shared with me. She felt safest when she was hiding in the morgue, along with corpses, to escape from the German soldiers following the malfunctioning of the gas chambers.

Hey, can I ask you a potentially insensitive question?

NOA: It's what we're here to do.

EMMANUEL: I'm asking this because, like everyone, I personally have experienced significant tragedy, and I feel as though that tragedy, what I've gone through, has helped propel me into the person I am today. It has made me into a more well-rounded individual; it has made me more empathetic; and it has made me into just a better overall human being. Because I had to suffer into that.

Is it unfair to say that the tragedy of the Holocaust is what helped shape the mental fortitude of the current Jewish population? Is it maybe what propelled them to reach higher highs than they may have reached if they wouldn't have suffered?

NOA: The Holocaust didn't need to happen for Jews to be resilient and strong. But I do also recognize how, to some extent, my struggles made me who I am. And that seems very likely to be true for the Jewish people, too, because we're not just talking about the Holocaust; we're talking about thousands of years of this sh— . . . stuff. Thousands of years of being squeezed out, of having to figure it out in the face of discrimination, of having to survive. *Okay, so if we can't do this, let's do that. Let's reinvent.* Jewish suffering is not new. You remember the joke about what every Jewish holiday is based on? "They tried to kill us; it didn't work out; let's eat."

I've also learned about something fascinating from my sister and niece, who both studied psychology—it's called post-traumatic growth (PTG), which was a theory developed in the mid-1990s by two psychologists. Basically, there's something else at play besides resilience when people who experience trauma not only survive but thrive. Researchers have found that people with PTG show an increased ability to appreciate life, form relationships, recognize new possibilities, and get stronger. If that doesn't describe the Jews, a tiny group of people who have consistently been pulverized by the biggest, baddest empires in the world only to go on to create, build, invent, and inspire—I don't know what does.

EMMANUEL: A friend of mine who studied engineering once told me that when you build a skyscraper, you have to dig the foundation hundreds of feet deep in order for it to be structurally sound. What you're saying reminds me of being in New York and looking up at these skyscrapers and realizing there was a lesson there—that you have to experience those depths and dig that deep if you want to achieve that height.

NOA: There's a similar lesson in Sacred Geometry, or the ancient spiritual belief that God used consistent geometric shapes when creating the Universe and everything in it. It's the idea of "as above, so below." As tall as the tree is above the ground, as deep are the roots. The world is balanced and exists in both the darkness and the light.

———

EMMANUEL: When you think about the fact that there are only fifteen million Jews in the world, and huge swaths of generations were either wiped out or not born, what's the first thing that comes to mind? Are you more saddened, or impressed by what they've been able to accomplish?

NOA: It's true that there would have been a lot more of us if six million hadn't been murdered. But even if the Holocaust hadn't happened, there would still be only about thirty-five million of us, and that's only 0.4 percent of the world's population. Our strength has never been in our numbers. I'm obviously saddened about the family I could have had and don't. But I'm more impressed. How much the Jews have rebuilt since then is extraordinary, considering what we've been through. It goes to show that something in Jewish life *works*. It's not magic. It's not genetics. It's that Talmudic mandate to be a light in the world—learning, practicing, teaching.

There's another very important reason we've been able to thrive in modern times, which is because of the safety and security that is afforded us by the existence of Israel, which officially became a country after the Holocaust. Israel was formally birthed when the international community finally realized that Jews needed a haven in the world where they could self-govern and be free of anti-Jewish hate, and where they could bring any other Jews who needed safety. But now that place that's been such a beacon of hope for us is under the exact same double-standard scrutiny that we Jews have been subjected to for as long as we can remember. It's being made an example of, a scapegoat on an international scale.

You know, there's a reason why we didn't talk about the Holocaust first in this book. It's true that Hitler and the Nazis are synonymous with the most obvious and extreme example of anti-Jew oppression, but they do not *define* Jewish people's experience with antisemitism. And they certainly do not define the Jewish experience period.

In fact, to truly understand what we as Jews continue to struggle with, the place to focus is not 1933 Germany. It is now, in the 2020s, in Israel.

16.

HOW THIS BOOK ALMOST DIDN'T HAPPEN

NOA: Emmanuel, up until now you've been driving this conversation and asking the questions. If it's okay with you, I'd like to take a turn for a moment because I think this is as good a time as any to talk about how this book almost didn't come to pass.

EMMANUEL: Ah, you mean the interview.

NOA: I mean the interview. And now we are *both* extremely uncomfortable.

EMMANUEL: I think maybe we start with a little background: When I approached Noa about writing this book, it was fifteen months before the Hamas attacks on October 7th, 2023. And prior to that, I had been friends with many Jewish people and educating myself about their struggle with antisemitism for years. I care about marginalized communities and oppressed groups, and the unheard outcry of Jewish suffering really bothered me. So as soon as I learned of the attacks, my thoughts went immediately to my Jewish friends. I checked in on the Noas and Amy Schumers and Montana Tuckers and my agents. My first instinct was to focus on the micro, on their individual experiences and pain, versus the macro or the bigger picture of what was unfolding.

But about a week later, I got a DM from an acquaintance and she was *disgusted* with me. Disgusted. I was just sitting on my couch on a Sunday, watching football, and there was a message from her saying, "How could you say that about the war? How could you be so malicious and harmful?" All I could think was, *What did I say?!* I was genuinely confused; it was like being accused of a crime you didn't even know was committed. Then I realized she was referring to the clip I posted of my Instagram Live with Noa, where I asked her what I could do to support my Jewish friends.

Now, I'm a fervent believer that if you're going to be mad at me, be upset about something I did, not something you *think* I did. So, I sent her that clip and asked, "What in here is malicious?" She proceeded to tell me about how her great-grandparents lived in Palestine and were run off their land by Israelis, how the Israelis are colonizers, and how nobody is checking on Palestinians as they're being attacked by Israel. She said, "How could you, as this person who seeks truth and as a Black person, sit there and support the Jewish community?"

At this point, truth be told, I had an internal struggle. Because now I'm in a bind—I love my Jewish friends, but I also love the truth. And here was this woman whose intelligence I respect, and whom I respect as an individual, and now she is disgusted with me.

I realized that I didn't know enough about the history of Palestine to respond. I was reminded of Chuck Klosterman's book *But What If We're Wrong?*, which basically says that to believe everything is right about history is asinine. It would be crazy and ill advised to assume that there is only one correct account of history. And I agree with that; that's why I live my life challenging those "truths," and it's why I set out on an exploratory journey of every perspective in this situation.

NOA: That's when you came to me and asked if I'd be a part of your *Uncomfortable Conversations* YouTube series. I thought, of course, what a perfect invitation; I'll share what had happened and why it was so completely devastating and terrifying to the global Jewish community. You told me that you'd also be interviewing, in a different episode, a historian and Middle East expert to explain how we got to where we were at, which I thought was a great idea as well. I came to your studio, we did the interview, I cried a lot, and went on my way. Then you sent me the trailer and, Emmanuel, I was devastated. You had edited me into a trailer for the interview not with an expert, but with a Palestinian woman who is a well-known anti-Israel activist and who, on October 7th, while bodies were still bleeding, said that the number of dead Israeli women, children, and men is "bean counting." She rejected the description of the atrocities as "barbarism" and appeared to defend the actions of Hamas, a designated terrorist organization.

My devastation was not because she was Palestinian—I have always been outspoken when it comes to being both pro-Israeli, pro-Palestinian, and anti-Hamas. And I don't believe all Palestinians represent the actions of Hamas, just as all Israelis don't represent the actions of their government. I was devastated because the subtext of that interview was clear: "To get the other side of the story."

This was *one week* after October 7th; entire families had been burned in their homes, parents hugging their children as they were asphyxiated; women mass raped and mutilated, babies murdered in their cribs; the dead paraded through the streets of Gaza; hundreds of innocent civilians stolen from their homes and taken hostage; and Jews around the world experiencing unspeakable generational trauma. At that point, Israel hadn't taken a single military action against Hamas. I get that you wanted to hear another side of the story, but Emmanuel, *what other side of the story?*

I know that you have nothing but love in your heart and that this was not coming from an antagonistic place. But as a Jewish woman, it was an all-too-familiar repeat of our experiences being diminished, denied, or even erased. And more than that, it felt like you were bending to a very dangerous and increasingly popular idea that a lot of people have right now—that there's no such thing as right and wrong anymore, that "everybody has a valid perspective," "you do you," and "this is my truth." The "whataboutisms" and justifications. I will absolutely agree that Israel isn't perfect and can always do better, as all countries can. I will also agree that innocent Palestinians in Gaza have suffered tremendously and now have little hope. However, when it comes to the Hamas massacre of innocent Israeli civilians, when it comes to the jihadi culture of Hamas (and ISIS and Hezbollah and Al Qaeda), there is *only* wrong. Definitively. No context required. *There was no other conceivable side.*

To be brutally honest, it felt like you were covering yourself with your followers by having both of us on. Putting me on a split screen with a woman who insisted on calling the members of Hamas who had raped women and burned babies "militants" rather than terrorists. It was too much for me. And the book collaboration ended.

EMMANUEL: Well, it hadn't ended just yet, at least not in my mind. The tension continued to rise because as I recall, you really, really did not want me to release my episode with her, but I knew I would feel guilty if I didn't. It was not about covering myself with my followers, so much as it was about covering my own conscience, making sure I was proud of who I was when I lay my head to rest at night. I am not Jewish, and I am not Palestinian, I am human, and I felt it was my responsibility to hear all the hearts that were hurting. To some, there may not be two sides to the story, but there was pain and hurt on both sides. I wanted to lend my ears and my empathy to that. I also felt compelled to speak after being called out by my friend on Instagram and seeing posts from the Black community at large. Posts insisting that the war didn't start on October 7th, posts insisting that Jewish people were colonizers and oppressors. Because of this internal calling to have the conversation with a Palestinian, I was unwavering, ignoring several of your earnest pleas for me not to sit with her once you recognized who I would be sitting with. I proceeded to air the episode—then I felt the book collaboration ended.

NOA: It's true; I walked away from the collaboration. I stopped replying to your messages; I felt like I couldn't trust you, and I went dark. I was in a dark place, trying to hold my own pain and the pain of my friends and family and country while also going on every media outlet that would have me to convey to the world what it was that we, the Jewish community and the people of Israel, were going through.

To me, it was as if, five days after George Floyd's murder, I would have had a Blue Lives Matter person on my platform, just to get the other side of the story. As if to say there had to be a *reason* why George Floyd was murdered, something *he* must have done. But there was no reason other than racism. Just like there was no other reason behind Hamas's brutality other than the intention to slaughter Jews and destroy Israel. So yes, I suppose you could say there is another side to the story, but that other side is denying my right to live, which is why I am not as accepting of it as some might want me to be.

EMMANUEL: The reason I didn't—and don't—think this is similar to the George Floyd aftermath is because when he was murdered, there was consensus in how people responded. It was almost unequivocally, "This is wrong." At least among the groups and friends whom I respect. But after October 7th, there wasn't consensus. Your point of view, Noa, about why this conflict happened in the first place was not what I was hearing from other people I was engaging with—and I don't rock with bad people. I also couldn't wrap my head around how some of the folks who follow me could see your post and say, "Oh my God, I love her; she's brilliant!" while others were like, "This woman is spreading blood libel!" On the exact same post.

NOA: By the way, that accusation itself is antisemitic; it's a term pulled directly from the early Christians. Remember? That centuries-old slur that refers to Jews using the blood of non-Jewish, usually Christian, children for our rituals? The very same one that European imperialists brought to Muslim countries in the 1800s?

And do you want to know why this response is divided, Emmanuel? Do you want to know why there's a "but"? Why our suffering can't just be our suffering? Why there has to be a justified cause for our murders?

Can you find me a reason other than "because it's Jews"?

EMMANUEL: I don't agree that it's that simple—people don't love Black people. No, I think there's controversy here because there's a group of people who feel as though their land was taken from them. And people sympathize with that.

NOA: But show me a massacre of *any* other group of people that made you think, "I wonder if they deserved it." If someone tries to assert that George Floyd or Breonna Taylor or Eric Garner had died because there was any reason aside from police negligence, because George Floyd or Eric Garner were resisting arrest or Breonna Taylor's boyfriend shot first, they would be immediately shut down and called racist. You cannot in good conscience believe that they were murdered for any other reason than because they were Black.

Well, those twelve hundred people, many of them children, were murdered by Hamas because they were Jewish or Israeli. The murderers were carrying out the word of their charter, which explicitly states their mission to destroy Israel and eliminate the Jews. But here we are, litigating *history* and whether these people had it coming. That lack of consensus, that need to question, that tiny voice that's compelled you—and many others—to wonder whether there is more to this story other than it just being a tragedy, is—to a *T*—the product of antisemitism.

That's why I decided to resume the collaboration because, at the end of the day, our having this bigger dialogue about what it means to be a Jew right now was more important than how I was feeling at that moment. I felt like we had a responsibility, to both the Jewish and the Black communities, to see it through. To show people what it looks like to have an uncomfortable conversation and make it out the other side, as in, the only way out is through. Which, to me, includes publicly sharing this painful moment we had and how we overcame it.

EMMANUEL: Exactly right. Although the book fell apart for a moment, we each stepped away and took some time to process. But ultimately I think we recognized each other's heart, and I really think we both realized where respect and love exist, disagreement can't triumph. And we're still talking about it. I don't necessarily regret interviewing a Palestinian person. I felt, and still feel, a responsibility for making sure all people feel heard. I just hate that it caused you pain, which was, of course, not my intention and is what temporarily derailed the process of writing this book. You know I actually had to check myself into a hotel to retreat from the whole situation because it got so emotionally intense for me. The turmoil of knowing I was going to hurt you, yet feeling so compelled to do what I knew I needed to do that I had to ignore that pain really sucked. Remember I sent you a text and said, "If our friendship is at stake, I won't air the conversation." Your response let me know that, regardless of my decision or the pain it may have caused you, you still cared for me. I'll never forget what you said: "Of course we're still friends; nothing is in jeopardy. But I'll need your continued support in these tough times." It looks like we both held up our end of the bargain.

17.

THE Z WORD

NOA: Zionism.

EMMANUEL: Dare I say this is my favorite conversation in the book? Mainly because I believe this is the crux of the tension in Israel. As an outsider, one who has spent hours upon hours talking to Palestinians and Jews, Zionists and anti-Zionists, I feel like this one word is the root of all the tension.

NOA: Let's make it clear—when I brought up this word for the first time, you asked me not to use it.

EMMANUEL: That's because whenever I see it used online, it always comes with controversy—people yelling at each other over it, cursing one another out over it, saying someone is or isn't a Zionist. It just seems like such a contentious word, and that word is often quickly followed by hate. The only times I've ever heard it used without that kind of controversy was either in *The Matrix* or in the Old Testament as Mount Zion. My most vivid memory of the word is of you on the Berkeley campus being called a freaking idiot by some student protestor because you stated that you were a Zionist (except he chose a different F-word). I'm not going to lie: I'm scared of where this conversation may go . . . but let's go there.

NOA: Are you sure you're ready to learn what exactly "Zionism" means? Because this could be a "You can't handle the truth" moment.

EMMANUEL: We're here now.

NOA: Zionism is the Jewish people's right to have self-determination and self-governance on parts of their ancestral land.

That's it. It's Israel's right to exist.

What, How, and Why Zionism

EMMANUEL: Hmmm, that's it? Okay, well then, I've got a lot of questions: When did Zionism begin? Is it a new idea? Didn't Israel always exist because it was the birthplace of Judaism? Why did Jews feel like they needed a self-determined state?

NOA: Okay, pump the brakes and let's take it one step at a time:

> Zionism the *idea* is as old as the Jews. *Zion* is one of seventy biblical names used to describe Jerusalem, sort of like Jerusalem's middle name. So "Zionism" in this context is the desire to return to Jerusalem, our ancestral land. It's a prayer and an idea that we've been carrying around with us since the First Temple in Jerusalem was destroyed by the Babylonians in 586 BCE and the Jews were exiled to Egypt and taken in captivity to Babylon, where Iraq is

now. Ever since, on Passover, we read the Haggadah—the special book that tells the ancient saga of the Jews' exodus from their enslavement in Egypt—and at the end of the reading we say, "L'Shana Haba'ah B'Yerushalayim"—"Next year in Jerusalem." I told you, we don't forget much.

Zionism the *movement* started in the 1800s. After thousands of years of being discriminated against, persecuted, and oppressed throughout Europe and the Middle East, rounded up in ghettos, pogromed, slaughtered, purged from pretty much every community, and generally tossed around like a political football, Jews started getting the idea that there was no safe haven for them. They eventually realized that if they wanted to be secure for generations to come, then they were going to have to create that safe haven for themselves and *re*-create the Jewish state. Just as the Chinese people have China, the Germans have Germany, the Japanese have Japan, so too the Jews should have their country if they want to, you know, survive. As we've established, Judaism is *not just* a religion, but an ethno-religion, an ethnic group, a people, and a people who have a state.

So, by the 1800s, the notion of returning to Israel seemed less like a pipe dream or theoretical concept and more like a plan. And thus Zionism, or the necessity for Jewish self-governance in our Jewish ancestral home, was born. But, like all good sagas, this one didn't happen overnight.

It was Theodor Herzl who helped put all the pieces together in the late nineteenth century. Ironically, this Austro-Hungarian Jewish writer initially believed that religious and cultural assimilation is what would save the Jews. He thought that if we could just "blend in" more, even convert to Christianity, we could assimilate our Jewishness away, and antisemitism would cease to exist.

But in 1895, he watched the Dreyfus Affair go down in person as a journalist—quick refresher: this was when a Jewish French artillery officer was falsely convicted of spying for the Germans, publicly stripped of his military insignia in front of a crowd screaming "Death to Judas, death to the Jew!" acquitted, and then continuously harassed. After which Herzl had a crystal-clear realization: a Jew in non-Jewish clothing was still, and would always be, a Jew. He also saw the writing on the soon-to-be-swastika'd wall and correctly intuited that antisemitism in Europe was going to get worse and that assimilation was, in fact, impossible. So Herzl did a complete one-eighty and concluded that if Jews wanted to make it to their next Passover, then they needed to return to their ancestral homeland and reestablish their own state. That land at the time was an underdeveloped region on the fringes of the Ottoman Empire.

Initially, the idea was not well received. The literary and journalistic establishment in Europe dismissed these radical ideas as silly and even desperate. The Jews, well, they were spread out all over the world—on almost every continent—many of them finding it difficult just to survive, much less hatch a plan for founding an entirely new nation and *moving* there. And the ones who were in any position to rally for such a thing wrote it off as too progressive. So, Theo did what all great visionaries do: he told a good story.

Herzl wrote about a new utopian state built on liberal values, including full, equal rights for men and women from all races, religions, and ethnicities. He described a socialist economic system that included a dash of capitalism to ensure its self-reliance. He championed free education, separation of church and state, maternity pay, overtime pay, and making stewardship of the environment a priority. His slogan? "You are my brother." Keep in mind, Emmanuel, this book was written in 1902, more than sixty years before American counterculture spread from the corner of Haight and Ashbury.

Herzl called for representatives of Jewish communities from all over the globe to gather in Basel, Switzerland, to discuss the future of the Jews and define what exactly Zionism and the Jewish state could look like. Incredibly, 208 delegates from seventeen countries did just that, arguing and debating for three days. Eventually, they agreed to call for the following:

- the establishment of a home for the Jewish people in the Land of Israel,
- the encouragement of aliyah (or migration) to Israel and reconnecting the Jews who had dispersed in the diaspora,
- a strengthening of a Jewish national identity, and
- taking next steps to obtain the proper approval to form this state.

Zionism is one of the most successful progressive movements in world history, literally progressing Jews from persecution to self-determination. It was only a matter of time after Herzl introduced these ideas that Jews came to understand that Zionism needed to be Plan A because there was no Plan B. And that was never clearer than after almost a third of the world's Jewish population was wiped out in the Holocaust.

EMMANUEL: This is interesting. So, if Zionism is Jewish people's right to have a country—what's the counter? What are people who are not Zionist, or anti-Zionist, a proponent of?

NOA: Well, that is a whole other story. And it depends on who you ask. But to keep it as simple as possible for this particular conversation: anti-Zionism is the rejection of Jewish nationhood. That can look a few different ways: Sometimes it's refuting Israel's right to exist. Sometimes it's denying the historical or spiritual connection that Jews have with the Land of Israel. Sometimes it's going so far as to demonize Israel in a way that reduces the people who live there and/or all Jews to certain stereotypes, such as being pervasively militant, or lapdogs of the West. It is *not*, however, criticism of the policies or actions of the Israeli government.

To be clear: This is currently very touchy territory for a lot of people, Jews and non-Jews. But I feel very comfortable saying that if someone checks any of the above anti-Zionist boxes, then whether they know it or not, they're dipping their toe into antisemitic waters.

EMMANUEL: Here's where I notice the real issue lies, with people who say they are anti-Zionist though not antisemitic. People feel as though Jews did not find a barren land, and in an effort to create Zionism, Palestinians, who occupied the land, were kicked out. Zionism sounds peaceful and civil when told from the Jewish perspective, but what about the perspective of the person whose home, town, city, and region now had to deal with the influx of people in search of a self-governed Jewish state? There are parallels being drawn by the Black community between what they believe Jewish people did historically to the Palestinians and what white Americans did to the Native Americans. What do you think about that?

NOA: You're bringing up a lot of important points, and I want to give them all the time and space they need. So let me begin with your point about comparing the creation of Israel to what Americans did to the Native Americans, because that's the narrative that's been purposefully programmed into society over the last thirty years or so. But it is *not* analogous. That narrative does a few things really well: It erases the hard evidence that supports the archaeologically and historically well-attested fact that the Land of Israel dates back to biblical times, that the Jewish people are indigenous to that land, and that they have had a continued presence there. It also erases the accuracy of what historically happened in that region before and around the establishment of Israel. And it certainly erases the fact that Israel was there as an independent nation before anything else.

Whose Land Is It Anyway?

NOA: One of my favorite things that antisemites will say to me, or any other Jew, is: "Go back to where you came from." Because that would, of course, be Israel. And yet, in the same breath, we're being told that that's not the case. So, we're going to take that stunning double standard by the horns and we're going to talk about none other than—drum roll—Jesus.

EMMANUEL: I see where you're going with this.

NOA: Every December, billions of people around the globe celebrate the birthday of a Jewish man who was born in Bethlehem over two thousand years ago. And at the same time, many people are trying to tell me that the Jews weren't there before 1948, the year Israel was officially founded. To say this is frustrating is the understatement of the millennium.

EMMANUEL: It's ironic you say that. I was just home for Thanksgiving and while at Thanksgiving dinner someone who goes to my church in Dallas came up to me and said, "I have an issue with your content. You know that Jesus was born in Palestine, right?" I looked at him confused, because unless he skipped the Sunday school lesson that I went to, we both know that Jesus was born in Bethlehem—a manger in Bethlehem, to be exact. But he was implying that the area in which Jesus was born is currently a Palestinian town, thus Jesus was born in Palestine. This conundrum actually stumped me for a second, but then I thought of it like this: The American football team the St. Louis Rams moved to Los Angeles in 2016, becoming the Los Angeles Rams. But Kurt Warner, one of the greatest quarterbacks for St. Louis, would not say that he played for the Los Angeles Rams. Because that's not what team it was when he played. Though he played for the Rams, and though the Rams had actually been the Los Angeles Rams before moving to St. Louis, Kurt played for the St. Louis Rams, and to say he played for the LA Rams would simply be inaccurate. So, are people saying that Jesus was Palestinian because the land he was born on is, in fact, Palestine?

NOA: Let the record show that I am taking a very deep breath. The answer is unequivocally No. Jesus was not born in Palestine. Before there was Palestine, there was Israel. Which is where Jesus was born.

You know what; let's take a little historical road trip. We're going to, once again, condense thousands of years of geography, archaeology, and science and my entire first book's worth of information and make it perfectly bite-size. No sweat; here we go:

1800 to 970 BCE: The Old Testament describes the borders of what would later become the ancient Kingdom of

Israel: ranging from approximately modern-day Lebanon in the north, to the Mediterranean Sea in the west, to Jordan in the east, to the Negev desert in the south. Most scholars agree that at that time, the land was sparsely populated with a sprinkling of Canaanites—indigenous tribes living in organized agricultural communities and small city-states. By around 2000 BCE, Abraham and Sarah move there following God's Google Map directions from Ur.

Around 1030 BCE, the country became a sovereign Jewish kingdom, referred to in the Hebrew Bible as the United Monarchy. King David enters the scene, his wife gives birth to the future King Solomon, who then went on to build the First Temple in Jerusalem. So now we're up to about 970 BCE.

722 to 167 BCE: The First Kingdom of Israel falls. First to the Assyrians, then to King Nebuchadnezzar and the Babylonians, then to Cyrus the Great and the Persian Empire. Jew status is shaky, as most of them have been exiled. But Cyrus, being great, allows some Jews to return to Jerusalem—referred to as the Return to Zion—and build the Second Temple of Jerusalem. Next come two more Greats, Alexander and Antiochus, both of whom were more about chillin' than they were about killin', at least when it came to the Jews. Antiochus's son, on the other hand, Antiochus IV Epiphanes (aka "the Madman"), wanted everyone to worship Zeus and overtook the Temple. The Jews said, "Hard pass," retook the Temple in rebellion, and were miraculously able to keep the temple flames burning for eight nights. (Happy Hanukah, everyone!)

167 BCE to 33 CE: The Jews reestablish the Jewish state and their national sovereignty—at least for a couple hundred years. Which is long enough for a particularly noteworthy individual from Bethlehem to roam the land preaching peace, love, and humility.

So: Jesus, not Palestinian. Jews, indigenous to Israel.

EMMANUEL: Got it. You know, one of my favorite phrases is that lies are often decorated in truths. What are the truths that would "decorate" the idea that Jesus was a Palestinian?

NOA: That would be a matter of semantics. The town where Jesus was born is currently under Palestinian control à la the Los Angeles Rams. What's also causing a lot of confusion is that people don't understand the origin of the name "Palestine" to begin with:

In 63 CE, the Romans invade, the Jews rebel, Emperor Nero sends the general Vespasian, who is later succeeded by his son Titus, to crush the uprising. In 70 CE, the Romans burn the Second Temple and either kill, exile, or enslave *almost* every Jew. You see, the Romans hated the Jews so much—to the extent that scholars generally recognize this as fact—that after the Jews (unsuccessfully) revolted and prompted the third and final Jewish–Roman war between 132 and 136 CE, the Romans wanted to punish them beyond laying waste to Judea (which they also did). So they changed the administrative name of Judea to "Palaestina" in order to sever the Jews in name from their historical homeland—possibly history's first case of Jewish gaslighting! This new namesake was a nod to the Philistines, who had been living nearby on the Mediterranean coast, and who researchers have concluded, using DNA, were most likely Greeks (and of no relation to modern-day

Palestinians). Why the Philistines of all people? Because they were the Israelites' greatest enemies in the Bible.

EMMANUEL: Wait—so the Romans came up with the name Palestine?

NOA: Yep. Words matter! From then on, that geographical area was referred to in history as Palestine. But there was no distinct ethnic group known as Palestinians at that time. That's because the Arabs who lived there after the birth of the Islamic Empire— about six centuries after the Romans bulldozed through the area—were, like most of the Middle East during the run-up to Israel's creation, a collection of cities, towns, and tribes. They were a part of the larger Muslim or pan-Arabic community. The term *Palestinian* was used to describe anyone who lived in the area—Arabs of Palestine, Jews of Palestine, Christians of Palestine. It's like saying "Noa Tishby of Los Angeles" and "Emmanuel Acho of Los Angeles"—same geographical location, but not a distinct ethnicity. The first person to self-describe Palestine's Arabs as "Palestinians" was Khalil Beidas in 1898, and Palestinian as a national identity emerged in the late nineteenth century.

But we're getting ahead of ourselves, especially if you want to see how exactly Israel as a country started taking shape.

324 to 638 CE: The Eastern Romans get a rebrand as the "Byzantines," Emperor Constantine converts the entire Roman Empire to Christianity, and well, you pretty much know how that went for the Jews.

638 to 1099 CE: Six years after the death of the Prophet Muhammad, waves of Muslim conquests came through the area as part of their mission to create the Muslim Empire, or the Caliphate. Muslim leaders didn't slaughter the Jews or force them to convert—which was a great change of pace for the Jews. But Jews, and Christians, were considered second-class citizens called *dhimmis*, or "protected persons." They weren't allowed to ride camels or horses; they couldn't testify in court against Muslims; they were not allowed to bear arms; they had to pay additional taxes for being non-Muslim; and their houses had to be lower than their neighbors'.

1099 to 1917 CE: We're going to warp through eight hundred years here: After the Caliphate, the land was controlled by the European Crusaders (death to almost all non-Christians, enslavement of the rest), the Mamluks, non-Arabic mixed-origin slaves who converted to Islam (death to Jews, forced conversions to Islam), and the Turks (death to Jews, enslavement, forced conversions to Islam, or exile). So now we're up to the Ottoman Empire and the year 1516 CE. The Jews get pretty battered along the way, but they are still hanging in and hanging around. In fact, by the late nineteenth century, they're beginning to make their way *back* to the Land of Israel from Europe, North Africa, and other parts of the Middle East where they've been subjected to endless bouts of violence. The Zionist dream looks like it could finally become a reality . . . and then the Brits show up.

1917 to 1947: This is where things start sounding like a political thriller:

Thomas Edward Lawrence, better known as Lawrence of Arabia (yes, that one), had been sent to the Middle East for an archaeological expedition on behalf of the British Museum. While there, he is rerouted by both the museum and the British government to make up-to-date maps of a region referred to in the Bible as the "Wilderness of Zin." Spoiler Alert: It was to help plot their favorite pastime, empire building, because taking control of the territory was the first thing on their to-do list after they were finished driving out the Turks.

When Lawrence gets to Aqaba, Jordan, he befriends some of the locals, most notably the Amir of Mecca's son, Prince Faisal (an Arab Muslim), and one of the leaders of the Zionist movement/soon-to-be Israel's first president, Dr. Chaim Weizmann (a Russian Jew). Lawrence learned all about the Arab desire for independence from the Turks, as well as the Jews' desire to return to their homeland—an idea that some of the Arabs agreed to as well. He sympathized with these groups, certainly more so than the greedy, warmongering, imperialist Brits. He wanted to help the Arabs fight as a unified front for their autonomy against the Ottoman Empire, and he wanted to help the Jewish pioneers, who he had seen purchasing sparsely populated plots of land in nowheresville from local Arabs, Turks, and Christians.*

The Arab and Jewish leaders of the time go on to sign an agreement—conditional, and perhaps a little optimistic, but an agreement—acknowledging that both peoples should have sovereignty in the region: the Arabs in Syria

---

* In a letter Lawrence wrote in 1909, he said: "The sooner the Jews farm it all, the better: Their colonies are bright spots in a desert." Semantic note: a colony (or group of people of one nationality or ethnicity living in a foreign city or country) does not make you a colon*ist*.

and the Hedjaz desert (present-day Saudi Arabia), and the Jews in their ancestral land of Israel.

To really seal the deal, about a month before Great Britain captured Jerusalem from the Ottoman Army in 1917, the British foreign secretary Arthur James Lord Balfour wrote a letter, later known as the Balfour Declaration, to Lionel Walter Rothschild, the unofficial leader of the British Jewish community. In it, Balfour promises to "establish" (more like reestablish) an independent "national home for the Jewish people." And it was to be in the former Ottoman province of Palestine, so named by the Romans. Remember that F-you to the Jews?

Then in November of 1918, the Allies win World War I. The Brits keep their word to the Arabs and the Jews; both of these indigenous groups get their land back from the colonial empire; and we've all been best friends ever since.

Yeah. As if. The Brits and the French, and to some extent the Russians, royally . . . forked us all after the war was over.

It turned out that for two years, a secret treaty was in the works between the UK and France to divvy up the Ottoman Empire with a few scraps going to Russia for helping the Allies run the Turks out of town. This treaty, called the Sykes-Picot Agreement, ultimately allocated the land that was *supposed* to go to the Arabs and the Jews (per the Balfour Declaration) to the British, in what became known as the British Mandate for Palestine. The borders closely resembled Israel's borders today, and it was called "Palestina EY," the abbreviation of the Hebrew term for the Land of Israel, Eretz Yisrael. It would be ruled by British law and run by the high commissioner reporting to the secretary of state for the colonies in the British government. Which, so we're totally clear, *is* colonizing—or the taking over of a place by a group that is not indigenous to that place in order to exploit the land and its inhabitants for the service of the empire. In theory, the mandate was supposed to uphold the Balfour Declaration. But in reality, the British constantly vacillated in their support of the Zionist movement, restricting Jewish immigration and ultimately pissing off *both* Arabs and Jews in the process. In short: the Jews and the Arabs got nothing except the fond regard of His Royal Highness.

1947 to 1948: But that all changed when, in the aftermath of the Holocaust, the UN recognized the imperative of a safe place for Jews to live. With the Brits bowing out of the Middle East (more on this in a moment), the real estate could finally be granted back to both groups as promised. The United Nations Partition Plan (Resolution 181) parceled out the land to create a Jewish state and an Arab state.

The Jews, who had reclaimed their indigenous land, had also *de*colonized it from the Brits, just like India, Malaysia, and Nigeria would eventually do. The next step was to give this new-not-new homeland a name. It shouldn't be called "Judea" because it had to be clear that one need not be a Jew in order to live there. "Zion" was also ruled out because a person didn't have to live there in order to be a Zion*ist*. That left "Israel," an inclusive notion of a place mentioned approximately two thousand times in the Old Testament and was befitting a nation of people who had suffered the darkest whims of humanity.

Because Israel means: "One who wrestles with God and prevails."

The Arab world said no. And not only did they say no, but many Arab countries promised that should Israel be created, they would go to war in order to wipe the new Jewish state off the map.

18.

PEACE, LOVE, AND HUMMUS

EMMANUEL: Is this an atypical reaction to the perception or reality that someone is trying to take land that you believe belongs to you? Historically, when someone attempts to take what you believe is yours, isn't fighting back a normal response? I know if someone came to my house in West Hollywood and started taking and claiming stuff, I wouldn't just gladly let them have it.

NOA: But it wasn't *their* house; it wasn't a state that was owned by anybody. It was inhabited by Christians, Muslims, and Jews and colonized by a series of conquerors and crusaders for two thousand years.

Here's the thing; critics of Israel like to assert that it was all peace, love, and hummus in the Middle East until Israel was created. But the reality is that there had historically been tense relations between the Jewish and Muslim communities—and it often had less to do with Zionism and a lot more to do with Judaism. Remember, Jews were second-class citizens under the Muslim Caliphate, and they faced forced conversions and persecution under the Muslim Mamluks and Turks. Yes, when Zionist immigration started to pick up in the 1880s, there were local fallouts over things like grazing rights and land titles, but when more empire-building Europeans started showing up around 1900 with their anti-Jewish laundry list, these conflicts took on a different flavor. What went from skirmishes among neighbors became "the greedy, devious Jews are bent on world domination." That perception was forever fused with Zionism.

And things only got messier. After winning World War I in 1918, the Brits and the French waltzed into the region and quickly got to work arbitrarily dividing things up into countries—Iraq, Saudi Arabia, Jordan. In doing so, they randomly mashed together widespread constellations of villages, towns, and nomadic tribes. These newly minted governments lacked a cohesive structure and weren't always accepted as legitimate, and with this new non-organization organization, they struggled for resources.

But they did seem to have something in common: They weren't so hot on the Jews. Namely their growing numbers in Palestine, their desire to re-create their homeland, and their potential as an economic power in the region. David Ben-Gurion, a Polish-born Jew who would become Israel's first prime minister and minister of defense, recognized this growing tension and saw it as an opportunity to extend the olive branch to Arab leaders, hoping their partnership and goodwill could bring prosperity to *everyone*. But in 1933, during a conversation with Musa Alami, one of the most prominent Arab leaders at the time, he was told "[I] would prefer the land to remain poor and desolate even for another hundred years, until Arabs themselves were capable of developing it and making it flower." Okey-dokey.

The new Jewish villages and kibbutzim, built on legally purchased plots of land, began suffering from a string of attacks from local Arabs. In fact, there were so many assaults on these young Zionist outposts by neighboring villages throughout the years that they collectively called them *meoraot* or "the Incidents." There were incidents in 1920, 1921, and 1929, plus the longest-lasting stretch of violence, the Arab Revolt, from 1936 to 1939. It was, essentially, a constant barrage of robberies, sniper attacks, and massacres.

One particularly anti-Zionist Arab who was at the center of this Jewish-Arab tension and violence was the Muslim leader Haj Amin Al-Husseini. He organized and incited this string of attacks that ultimately killed hundreds of Jews. And as Grand Mufti of Jerusalem—and eventually of all of Palestine—a position he was appointed to by the British, he made clear to anyone who would listen that he was not going to let Zionism fly. He was also, it turns out, a big fan of Hitler's. In 1941, Al-Husseini traveled to Germany to meet with der Führer, hoping to get him to agree to a treaty in which Germany would pledge to help remove the proposed Jewish homeland in Palestine. Hitler declined to make anything official, but he *did* say that he would "continue the struggle [against the Jews] until the complete destruction of Jewish-Communist European empire."

But the Nazis kept Al-Husseini close because it turned out he was great at mobilizing Muslims for their effort, especially after Al-Husseini publicly declared that "Jews are the bitterest enemies of Islam."* When the Axis Powers lose the

---

* When Israel apprehended Adolf Eichmann in 1960, a Saudi newspaper headline read, "Capture of Eichmann, Who Had the Honor of Killing Five Million Jews."

war, Al-Husseini, wanted by the British as a Nazi collaborator, flees to Switzerland, gets handed over to the French, escapes house arrest, and makes his way back to Egypt. He returns to the Middle East just in time to reject the UN's two-state plan proposed in 1947. What a mensch.[*]

So, that was the temperature of things when the UN agreed to divide the land into two states and the State of Israel was formed in 1948. Coupled with the fact that there had been a fair share of Jew-on-Arab and Jew-on-British violence because they were sick and tired of Arab hostility and British meddling. It was anything but warm and fuzzy between the Arabs and Jews, which is why the War of Independence actually started *before* Israel declared its statehood. It happened in two phases:

The first phase was in 1947, the day after the UN resolution passed and local Arab militias started a civil war.

The second phase came the minute Israel was officially established on May 14, 1948, when Israel got a surprise housewarming and was attacked by all of her neighbors and a few of their friends: Syria, Jordan, Egypt, and Iraq, with the help of Saudi Arabia, Lebanon, the Arab Liberation Army (a militia formed by the Arab League), and a few battalions of Muslim Brotherhood volunteers from Egypt.

After a little over a year of fighting, the people of Israel, resolute to not be decimated again, won this war they didn't want or start. The Arabs signed a *temporary* truce, and Israel now controlled not only the area that the UN had set aside for them but also even more of the land that would have originally

---

[*] Al-Husseini would eventually, in 1959, send a "secret" memorandum to the leaders of all Arab states calling for Arab unity against "Jewish aggression and imperialism" and denouncing the partition of Palestine.

gone to the Arabs, including West Jerusalem, the Galilee, and more of the Negev desert.

Then the Arab countries surrounding Israel took advantage of the unrest and snapped up what could have been part of that *new* Arab state: the Gaza Strip went to Egypt, and the West Bank and much of Jerusalem—including the Old City—went to Jordan, and a thin strip on the Sea of Galilee was seized by Syria. There was also a lingering refugee issue.

———

NOA: While Israel refers to this first war as the War of Independence, the Arabs call it the *Nakba*, Arabic for "the Catastrophe" and a reference to the 700,000 to 750,000 Arabs forced to vacate their homes. Before and during the 1948 war, Arab leaders ordered them to leave, and many others fled out of fear of the impending war.* And some got pushed out violently; it was war, though not an ethnic cleansing as dark corners of the internet and media would have you believe. About 150,000 Arabs stayed, automatically becoming Israeli citizens. Ultimately, though, there were still hundreds of thousands of Arab refugees.

After the war, those same countries encouraging the mass exodus of Arabs from Israel did not welcome these refugees with open arms or offer an apology for starting the war in the first place. Rather, these Arab nations, namely Lebanon, Syria, and Jordan, swept them into refugee camps instead. That

———

*The Iraqi prime minister Nuri Said declared, "We will smash the country with our guns and obliterate every place the Jews seek shelter in. The Arabs should conduct their wives and children to safe areas until the fighting has died down."

refugee status is passed down through the generations, meaning if you are born in these countries to refugee parents, you too are considered a refugee and not a citizen. Which is why you see images of Palestinian refugee camps now, even though it has been more than seventy-five years since the war.*

EMMANUEL: Given that the ripple effect of Zionism for the Arab and Palestinian people was displacement and refugee camps, can you blame Palestinian people who have an adverse reaction to the concept of Zionism?

NOA: I totally understand how Palestinian people who were displaced would have an adverse reaction to Zionism and to the creation of Israel. That I understand. And what ultimately breaks my heart is how much they have had to suffer because they are ultimately the pawns of a game, the collateral damage of men with deep pockets and a single-minded fixation on vengeance, which has played out again and again. Even now, Hamas admits to having "successfully" sacrificed Gaza in the name of perpetual war to overthrow Israel. In November 2023, Khalil al-Hayya, a senior Hamas official, told the *New York Times* from his home in Qatar, not Gaza, that "This battle was not because we wanted fuel or laborers. It did not seek to improve the situation in Gaza. This battle is to completely overthrow the situation."

---

* A much less discussed by-product of the war is that after Israel's victory, Arab countries such as Iraq, Yemen, and Morocco have expelled (or "strongly encouraged to leave" with harassments, vandalism, and assaults) approximately 850,000 Jews. Is anyone insisting on their right to return or calling for those countries to be dismantled? Not even as a joke.

It's been this way since 1948, with Israel wanting to, you know, *exist* in the Middle East, and the Arabs not having any of it.

In 1967, Egypt, Jordan, and Syria failed to once more destroy Israel in what is now called the Six-Day War. Israel wins and—while defending itself—takes the Golan Heights from Syria, East Jerusalem—including the Kotel, Judaism's holiest site—and the West Bank from Jordan, and the Sinai Peninsula and Gaza Strip from Egypt. In 1973, Israel fights the Yom Kippur War against Egypt, Syria, and many other Arab countries that have attacked. Israel barely wins.

There have been some successful steps toward peace. There was a peace treaty with Egypt in 1979, where Israel gave back the Sinai Peninsula, and another peace treaty with Jordan in 1994.

In 1993, Israeli and Palestinian representatives agreed to come to the table to talk peace. But seven years of negotiations fell apart when the Palestinian leader Yasser Arafat refused to sign the final deal in 2000 that would have given the Palestinians a state. His hangup? To this day, nobody knows. Even Bill Clinton says it still keeps him up at night. And with that fatal blow to the peacemaking process, Arafat sentences the region to ongoing bloodshed.*

On September 15, 2020, Israel signed a breakthrough peace treaty with the United Arab Emirates, Bahrain, and Morocco called the Abraham Accord, essentially a public acknowledgment of a regional alliance against Iran. But other

---

* While also quietly siphoning billions of dollars from the Palestinian cause. His net worth at the time of his death was an estimated $4.2 billion to $6.5 billion.

than that, with the rest of the region, it has been the same rinse-and-repeat cycle of attempts at peace and war.

Which brings us to where we are now. So, as it turns out, Zionism has everything to do with why we're sitting here, doing what we're doing. Because we can't talk about Zionism without talking about antisemitism.

19.

THE NEW FACE OF ANTISEMITISM

EMMANUEL: Okay, now that we've hashed out Zionism, what does it mean when someone says they are anti-Zionist?

NOA: People will give you all kinds of answers, but to me, it's very simple: Zionism is the Jewish people's right to have self-determination and a state to govern, and anti-Zionism is denying that right.

I want to go back to that antisemitic layer cake we talked about earlier, that layer-by-layer accumulation of Jewish hate that's been building, compounding, and shape-shifting for thousands of years. Remember how none of those ideas has gone away? Instead, they've continued to inform assumptions about Jewish people—that they're greedy, morally corrupt, calculating, dangerous. Even when antisemitism is not at a full boil like it was in Nazi Germany, these ideas are there, seeping into how people view Jews. So, when something problematic is happening in the world, those assumptions are right there within arm's reach and are often used to blame the Jews. It happened in the Middle Ages when Jews were scapegoated for the bubonic plague; in 1900s Russia, where economic and political upheaval was pegged on the Jews; in 1950s America, where the threat of Communism was chalked up to the Jews, and so on.

It's the same exact cycle, every single time.

And now the world has Israel to blame. Because seamlessly, without skipping a beat since 1948, Israel became the Jew of the world. That's how antisemitism works: find what is most evil to you (racism, oppression, colonization, apartheid) and blame it on the Jews—or on the Jewish state. It's so insidious because people think that they are calling to take down a country when they are calling to take down a people.

When you look more closely at the language and criticism of Israel since its founding in 1948, you see the same classic tropes at play: Israel is a globalist manipulator; Israel is a bloodthirsty warmonger; Israel is an immoral society; Israel is the sole cause of all problems that exist in the world. So now you have Jewish stereotypes being applied to Israel, and Israel stereotypes being applied to Jews. But I think we all can reasonably agree on this: People are not always their government, and a government is not always its people. This is not about criticizing policies, politics, or politicians. *That* is totally valid; I have dabbled in that myself many times over.

EMMANUEL: Hold on, let me write that one down; I love that: People are not always their government, and a government is not always its people.

NOA: Of course not. But when you combine the general population's lack of understanding about what exactly Zionism is, their uncertainty about how exactly Israel came to be and what it represents for Jewish people, as well as any unconscious biases they might have about the Jews, then you have a recipe for a new brand of antisemitism: anti-Zionism.

Never mind that Israel is, in fact, a refugee state that was literally decolonized from Britain. Or that a majority of Israeli Jews are people of color, many of whom are from families that were ethnically cleansed from other parts of the Middle East. Or that Jews originate from the Land of Israel, derive our religion and our practices from the land, and—despite centuries of exile and displacement—have always kept an unbroken presence there. Or that it is not an apartheid, defined as a minority ruling over the majority and segregated based on race, nor is it an exclusively Jewish state, because Israeli Arabs are about 20 percent of the population and have held positions in the Knesset, Israel's parliament, since the first elections in 1949.

We can all agree that we don't love every US government policy, yet people aren't seriously calling to dismantle the United States, or Australia, or Canada, or literally any other country or state. People are, however, trying to dismantle Israel. Israel is the only country in the world whose right to exist is being questioned. It's the only country that has a Wikipedia page dedicated to that question, as in: "The Legitimacy of the State of Israel."

Jews and Israel are consistently held to a double standard. That's how you end up with American activists screaming "From the river to the sea, Palestine will be free," calling for Israel—where more than seven million Jews and two million Arabs currently live—to be dismantled and the Jews there driven out. That's how we end up with Greta Thunberg, the personification of all that is good and pure and cool, chanting "crush Zionism" on the streets of Sweden. Hamas showed us on

October 7th exactly what "crushing Zionism" looks like. That's how you end up with a disproportionate obsession with and vitriol against the world's single Jewish state.

All I can say is that if you find yourself on the same side of an argument as David Duke, the Iranian government, and ISIS, then I think you ought to reflect on how you got there in the first place.

So, let's do that right now; let's see how we got into this mess in the first place. Because when we do, you're going to see one very unsettling truth: all the finger-pointing, name-calling, animosity, and violence directed toward Israel and Zionism has never been just about a land dispute.

It Was Never Just About Land

NOA: From the moment Jews began nurturing the idea of a Jewish state, anti-Zionist rhetoric has spread around the globe. That's not coincidental, and it's definitely not because there's an innate problem with Israel. The fact is: Israel has been, and continues to be, the world's most convenient scapegoat, complete with reinforcement from almost every single layer of the antisemitism layer cake and each of their centuries-old tropes.

Here are the biggest perpetrators:

- *The Arab Countries*: These would be the nations in Israel's vicinity—Iraq, Syria, Egypt, Lebanon, Yemen, Jordan—the ones who said that should an Israeli state ever emerge, they would not only deny its existence but also make every effort to eradicate it. Why? You don't have to look much further than the fact that the creation of Israel, a liberal democracy, was mutually beneficial for the West—governments with whom Middle Eastern dictatorships were at odds. Does that make a band of terrorized pogrom and Holocaust survivors and the generations that followed the colonist puppets of the United States and Europe? No. But did it mean there was the potential for an emerging Jewish democracy in an oppressive neighborhood that gave all its citizens equal rights and the ability to vote in fair elections? You bet. Add over one hundred years of Europe's exported antisemitism into the mix, and this led to the anti-Jewish rhetoric that not only should Israel not exist but the Jews should be systematically and wholesale cleansed from the region.

- *The Soviets*: After hundreds of years of Jewish torment in the Russian Empire and later the Soviet Union, it should come as somewhat of a surprise that the Soviet Union applauded the creation of a Jewish state. Granted, in 1948, some of that enthusiasm was because Israel was socialist-leaning and the USSR thought it could be persuaded to convert to Communism—a big middle finger to the West. But it was not to be.

  The final straw came in 1953 with the "doctors' plot," when Soviet dictator Joseph Stalin accused nine doctors—six of whom were Jewish—of conspiring against the state and plotting to murder Soviet leaders. The Soviet press spread the word that all the doctors had confessed their guilt. But there was never a trial because 1) Stalin died, and 2) it turned out that, well, the doctors had all been tortured to falsely confess. So the doctors, excluding the two who had died as a result of that torture, were exonerated. But the proceedings had already publicly reinforced the national notion of the calculating, bloodthirsty Jew. It didn't help that in protest of the doctors' plot, an anti-Soviet group lobbed a bomb into the Russian consulate in Tel Aviv, and Israel-Soviet relations got . . . frosty. Soon after, Soviet state media was flooded with anti-Zionist propaganda. With images of bloated, hook-nosed Jewish bankers and world-consuming serpents embossed with the Star of David, anti-Zionism became interchangeable with antisemitism.* So now you have the 1950s and beyond being saturated with the Russian rhetoric that Israel is a corrupt imperialist and is also threatening world peace.† These Russian-generated images and ideas weaseled their way through the world, and eventually to the United Nations.

- *The UN*: In 1975, the idea of the Jews being the "chosen people" comes back to haunt them once again. The United Nations subcommission had previously been tasked with drafting a resolution on the "elimination of all forms of racial discrimination." So, the Soviets, wanting to make a mockery of this initiative, got creative and argued that Judaism's concept of being "chosen" promoted racial superiority. They then added to

---

* British political theorist Alan Johnson observed, "What 'the Jew' once was in older antisemitism—uniquely malevolent, full of blood lust, all-controlling, the hidden hand, tricksy, always acting in bad faith, the obstacle to a better, purer, more spiritual world, uniquely deserving of punishment, and so on—the Jewish state now is . . ."
† It was a play right out of Hitler's book—a "Big Lie," or the strategy of introducing an idea so overblown and over-the-top that people would never think that such a thing could be fabricated. And so they accept these lies as truth.

the resolution: "Zionism is a form of racism and racial discrimination."

Resolution 3379, and its declaration that Zionism was racism, *passed*. Thankfully, in 1991, it was called out for what it was and revoked,* but there's no time travel function that allows you to strike such things from the collective memory.

Although the UN voted to create Israel, it has historically dropped the ball when it comes to shutting down antisemitism† and has consistently held Israel to a double standard. According to UN Watch, a Geneva-based nongovernmental organization: "The numbers alone reveal the UN's irrational obsession with one nation. Even those who deem Israel deserving of criticism cannot dispute that this amounts to an extreme case of selective prosecution." For example, between 2006 and 2023, the Human Rights Council issued sixteen condemnatory resolutions to North Korea, fourteen to Iran, and zero to China. To Israel? 103.

In 2023, it took the UN almost eight weeks to denounce Hamas's use of sexual violence on October 7th, despite many eyewitnesses, physical evidence, and confessions by members of Hamas. It wasn't lost on Jews and anyone else paying attention that the UN had swiftly, and crucially, called attention to the use of sexual

---

* In 1991, US ambassador to the United Nations Daniel Patrick Moynihan declared that because of the 1975 Soviet Resolution 3379, "a great evil has been loosed upon the world" and that "the abomination of antisemitism has been given the appearance of international sanction."

† In the early 1960s, the Communist and Arab voting bloc barred a United States–Brazil proposal from including a condemnation of antisemitism from the UN's International Convention on the Elimination of All Forms of Racial Discrimination.

violence as a tool of war in Sudan right around the same time. The subtext would be *The Jews had it coming* had it not been for the actual text: UN workers *participating* in the October 7th attacks.*

- *BDS*: Welcome to my favorite–least favorite topic: BDS.

EMMANUEL: Should I know what this is? It sounds familiar.

NOA: If you haven't been on a college campus in the last twenty or so years, you might have missed this movement, the lies it has spread, and the damage it has done to understanding the Israel-Palestine issue, but I'll catch you up: BDS is the acronym for Boycott, Divestment, Sanctions, meaning the campaign supports all of the above against Israel—divesting investments away from Israel, boycotting Israeli products and academia, not doing business with Israeli companies, and placing economic sanctions on Israel. On its website, its official statement is this:

> Boycott, Divestment, Sanctions (BDS) is a Palestinian-led movement for freedom, justice, and equality. BDS upholds the simple principle that Palestinians are entitled to the same rights as the rest of humanity.

---

* In January 2024, Israeli intelligence provided the US government with a dossier connecting at least twelve employees of the UN's Relief and Works Agency (UNRWA) with the October 7th attacks, including supplying ammunition and coordinating logistics. The allegations were credible enough for the UN to terminate the contracts of ten of these employees (the remaining two had since died), and for the US—along with the UK, Germany, Australia, Canada, the Netherlands, Italy, Switzerland, and Finland—to suspend aid from UNRWA. As of March 2024, the investigation is ongoing.

Which, at first glance, sounds definitively great. I, and most Israelis, support this idea. It is a politically correct, highly sympathetic message, which is likely why the movement has gained support from some members of the US House of Representatives, including Representative Rashida Tlaib (D-MI), Representative Ilhan Omar (D-MN), and Representative Alexandria Ocasio-Cortez (D-NY), among many individuals who identify as liberal. The movement has gained particularly widespread support among college students who want their universities—and the US government—to boycott Israel in support of this aim.

But here's the thing: It's bunk. It is a bunch of whitewashed antisemitism hiding behind a sympathetic message. When you dig deeper into the ideas of the BDS leadership, their agenda is clear: Israel should not exist. Take it from BDS's cofounder, Omar Barghouti, who has said such things as:

Definitely, most definitely, we oppose a Jewish state in any part of Palestine. No Palestinian, rational Palestinian, not a sell-out Palestinian, would ever accept a Jewish state in Palestine.

[Palestinians have a right to] resistance by any means, including armed resistance. [Jews] aren't indigenous just because you say you are . . .

BDS also regularly demonizes Israel and the Jews, even on its website, calling them colonialists and apartheidists. And if you still have any doubts about the character or aims of BDS, just look at the groups they've allowed to sit on their national commitee: Hamas, Palestinian Islamic Jihad, and the Popular Front for the Liberation of Palestine. All designated terrorist groups, all groups whose stated aim is to eradicate Israel.

The reasoning for all of this becomes clear when you look at the roots of BDS. The concept of boycotting Jews in Israel didn't start after Israel was formed. It started *before*. Three years, to be exact. BDS's ideas mirror those of the Arab League, whose very first collective action in 1945, three months after the end of World War II, three months after much of Europe's decimated Jewry realized that Israel was their only safe haven, was to encourage all Arab states to boycott Jews. Not Israel, the emerging political entity and its policies—no, there was no Israel or policies. Just Jews. Their official declaration stated, "Jewish products and manufactured goods shall be considered undesirable to the Arab countries." Remember, this is just a few years after the Nazi boycott on Jewish businesses as part of the run-up to the Holocaust.

Some of these countries eventually went on to pressure thousands of companies around the world to not do business with Israel, and in 2005 BDS was created and headed up by the aforementioned Omar Barghouti. And now you have a growing number of progressive college students who are okay with companies based in China (TikTok) but not in Israel (SodaStream), or buying products allegedly made in sweatshops (Shein, Uniqlo, Adidas, Gap, Urban Outfitters) but not by Israeli companies (Sabra hummus). But more alarming is the recycled Soviet rhetoric that BDS—along with their partners in antisemitism, Students for Justice in Palestine (SJP)—is spreading, particularly on college campuses. They are insinuating that Israel, Zionism, *and therefore Jews* are synonymous with evil, and the world will be a much better place if only Israel ceased to exist.

- *The Alt Right*: Anti-Zionism as thinly veiled anti-semitism comes in handy in alt-right circles, too. Take the 2005 international conference that neo-Nazi politician David Duke was associated with called "Zionism as the Biggest Threat to Modern Civilization." Talk about cutting to the chase. The sentiment then was the same as it is now: Zionists are the Jews controlling the world, and Zionism is the fruits of Jews' nefarious evildoing.

- *The Social Justice Warriors*: Here's the deal: there's no magic pill that prevents Jew hatred. We are all human, and because of that, even the most educated, seemingly open-minded individuals can be . . . antisemitically spiced—something that looks different for everyone. For some, way down deep beyond that desire to make the world a better place is guilt about the colonialist sins of their forefathers, or their participation in the white supremacist constructs embedded in American infrastructure. For others, it's taking a look around at what they like least in society and chalking it up to a scapegoat that's been served up on a silver platter: the white, affluent, too-powerful-for-their-own-good Jews. And some folks are taking power dynamics that they know—slavery, the slaughter of Native Americans, South African apartheid—and shoehorning the Israel-Palestine issue inside them, saying the Hamas attack was like a slave uprising, that the state of Israel is an apartheid state, or that the Palestinians are like the Native Americans being driven off their land by the colonizing Jews. None of it is a neat and tidy fit; none of it is parallel.

In all of the above scenarios, Israel is the laser focus. In all of this, Israel's right to exist comes into question. In all of this, the Jews are painted as the inhuman and inhumane tyrants.

- *The Religious Extremists*: People have gotten very comfortable saying that whereas the Nazis came for the Jews because they were Jews, Hamas came for Israel in the name of liberation. But nope, it's the other one, Jews dead. Just look at the original Hamas charter, which calls for:

    the complete destruction of Israel and the establishment of a theocratic state based on Islamic (Sharia) law,

    the need for holy war (jihad) to do that, and

    the eradication of the Jews.

Israel's issues with Hamas—and a number of other jihadist groups—are not about a map.

Yes, some of the conflict is owing to the ongoing litigation of what happened in 1948 or issues with policing or finally, after almost eighty years, mutually agreeing on borders. But most of this struggle has to do with one simple fact: militant jihadist groups see Israel and the Jews as an abomination.*

Despite what many on the left will claim, we are not deal-

---

* Even Golda Meir, Israel's first female prime minister, was talking about this back in the 1970s: "Our quarrel with the Arabs is not a quarrel for a piece of land; it's not for territory; it's not for anything concrete. They just refuse to believe that we have the right to exist at all."

ing with freedom fighters. We are not dealing with people who have been pushed to the point of violence because of unspeakable horrors that they have been subjected to at the hands of the Israelis. Sam Harris, the philosopher and neuroscientist, blew my mind with the clarity of his explanation on his *Making Sense* podcast:

> We imagine that people everywhere, at bottom, want the same things: They want to live safe and prosperous lives. They want clean drinking water and good schools for their kids. And we imagine that if whole groups of people start behaving in extraordinarily destructive ways, practicing suicidal terrorism against noncombatants, for instance, they must have been pushed into extremis by others. What could turn ordinary human beings into suicide bombers, and what could get vast numbers of their neighbors to celebrate them as martyrs, other than their entire society being oppressed and humiliated to the point of madness by some malign power?

Now, there are many things to be said in criticism of Israel, in particular its expansion of settlements on contested land. But Israel's behavior is not what explains the suicidal and genocidal inclinations of a group like Hamas. The Islamic doctrines of martyrdom and jihad do.

When your belief is that paradise is promised to those who die in order to conquer the world in the name of the one true faith, then killing innocent civilians, or using women and children as human shields, is not just a means to an end, it is justified. It is holy. To understand the consequences of these dogmatic beliefs—and that those who hold them surround the state of Israel in rocket's reach—is to understand the chilling existential threat that Israel faces.

EMMANUEL: How do you reconcile Palestinians who are not Hamas, but who are okay with the actions of Hamas because they are intentionally or inadvertently acting as their bodyguard? I obviously don't know anyone in Hamas, but some Palestinians feel as though Hamas is their only way of fighting against Jewish oppression.

NOA: Hamas is not acting as the Palestinian people's bodyguards. In fact, it is exactly the other way around. Hamas uses the Palestinian people as *their* bodyguards when they attack Israeli civilians and then embed themselves in the Palestinian civilian population, whether it's in the tunnels they've built directly beneath hospitals and other civilian infrastructure or hiding supplies and weapons in schools. So, if you are sympathetic to Hamas, we have a problem. The wider answer to that is a question I would pose back to any Palestinian and that is: What do *you* want? Because if you want to live side by side peacefully with Israel—let's talk. But if you want to throw me into the Mediterranean Sea—no thanks.

- *The Jews*: We've already talked about how centuries of internalized antisemitism has caused many Jews to absorb the criticisms of our community; that applies here, too. Because if you're already coming from a place of just wanting to fit in or low-key self-loathing, conscious or not, plus you identify as part of the American progressive Left—which many Jews do—then you're a lot more vulnerable to the suggestion that Israel somehow doesn't meet the criteria required in order to exist.

In addition to all the reasons I've given for why that argument does not stand, I'd also like to point out that it is literally impossible to be Jewish and not have any connection with Israel, and I'm not talking about borders or a dot on a map. I'm talking about the actual earth. Judaism, in and of itself, is an indigenous religion. Our holidays are synced to the moon cycle in Israel. The four species—*lulav, hadass, arava, etrog*—used to bless our sukkahs during Sukkot are native to Israel. The candles we light on Hanukah celebrate the oil that burned in the Second Temple in Israel. These rituals are inseparable from that land. Yes, it's a time-tested tradition for us Jews to doubt and question, but doubting the worthiness of Israel is a guilt we are not meant to carry.

20.

HOW TO NOT LOSE FRIENDS AND ALIENATE PEOPLE

EMMANUEL: Okay, okay, hold on, answer me this: Is it possible to disagree with Jewish people and their ideologies without being antisemitic? I feel like we're throwing that word around too loosely. For example, I'm cognizant of how frequently I throw around the word *racist*. Not everything makes everyone a racist. I remember I was asked to host *The Bachelor: After the Final Rose*, the season finale episode of one of America's top reality shows that's regularly viewed by seven million people. I was brought in to host that episode because the show had a Black bachelor for the first time in its twenty-year history. A Black man cast with twenty-five or so women, in search of his one true love. The woman that this Black man, Matt James, had chosen had previously taken photos at an antebellum plantation–themed ball dressed up in antebellum-era costume—meaning she was (consciously or not) celebrating pre-Abolition times. These photos surfaced during the airing of the season and were released prior to the episode I was hosting, so there was immense tension. Matt had already chosen to spend his life with her privately, but in this episode, the public would both find out that he had chosen her and see whether they had maintained their relationship since the photos came to light. The producers gave me the script of what I was to say when introducing the episode and the young woman, but any time I saw the word *racist*, I replaced it with *racially insensitive* or *racially ignorant*. I didn't think this woman was racist because of pictures she had taken when she was eighteen. I believe racism requires three things: power, privilege, and prejudice, and she didn't have all three. I believe she was racially ignorant, and as we've discussed, words matter.

I say this to say, I feel like we're throwing the word *antisemitism* around very loosely, as if any form of disagreement with Jewish people or Zionism makes you antisemitic. It's as if there's no grace for the individual who simply doesn't want war along with whatever else it takes for Zionism to exist. Can you simply be an anti-Zionist without being antisemitic?

NOA: If by anti-Zionist you mean being critical of Israel's policies, then of course you're not an antisemite. I am a great example of how one can be a staunch Zionist and still criticize the Israeli government's politics, as one does in a healthy democracy. In January 2023, Israel's new right-wing government, headed by longtime prime minister Benjamin Netanyahu, brought to a vote a series of proposed laws to overhaul the judicial system. These laws were extreme and some of them, if passed, would have weakened Israel's democracy. In response, millions of Israelis took to the streets in protest. At the time, I was Israel's Special Envoy for Combatting Antisemitism and Delegitimization, which, while an unpaid position, still technically made me a government employee. After carefully weighing my options,

I decided to publicly speak out against the overhaul, first in an op-ed in the Israeli media, then on HBO's *Real Time with Bill Maher*. I fiercely condemned these policies—not the country of Israel, not the people of Israel—and predicted that they would not pass (they have not). For that, I was removed from my position. But I don't think you'll find anyone who would call me an anti-Zionist or an antisemite.

But if by anti-Zionist you mean wanting to eliminate or dismantle the world's only Jewish state, then yeah, that's problematic. Denying Israel's right to exist *is* antisemitic. You can protest against Israel; you can be frustrated with—or outright resent—Israel's decisions. You can raise all the "what abouts" regarding all the issues you have with Israel, past and present—because just like other countries, there *are* issues with Israel, past and present. However, there are twenty-three countries where Islam is the official state religion and thirteen where Christianity is the official state religion and only one Jewish state. Why target that state in particular?

You see, when it comes to Israel, the Jews are in an impossible situation. We are damned if we do have a state, and we are certainly damned if we don't. It's pretty telling that many Jews feel safer in Israel—where almost every year, hundreds if not thousands of rockets are fired by Hamas, Hezbollah, and other militant groups—than anywhere else in the world. The bottom line is that anti-Zionism is a movement to deny Israel's right to exist, and Israel is the only country in the world where that's up for debate. So, you cannot deny that the Jewish people have a right to secure and self-govern a Jewish homeland or advocate for the dismantlement of that secure homeland and consider yourself a tolerant, non-antisemitic person. Israel cannot be the only country that is not allowed to exist.

EMMANUEL: Are there ways someone can check themselves or their arguments to see if they're potentially coming from an antisemitic place?

NOA: Absolutely. I think that starts with *all* people, Jews and non-Jews, having a better understanding of how criticism of Israel can easily become antisemitic. Reading this chapter is a great start.

Another good barometer is to consider whether your criticism:

1. is an indictment of all Jews,
2. capitalizes on stereotyping tropes, or
3. lays blame for an entire issue solely on Israel.

Take these examples:

"Israel is the root of instability in the Middle East." Antisemitic: it solely blames Israel for the region's problems.

"Israel and Palestine's struggle to find resolution is destabilizing to the Middle East." Not antisemitic: it's a zoomed-out, objective assessment of the situation that neither demonizes Israel nor holds it to a double standard.

"Zionism is racism." Antisemitic: both false and a sweeping generalization of beliefs held by an entire group.

"Zionism has had oppressive consequences for Palestinians." Not antisemitic: again, objectively true and drawing attention to these consequences and not inaccurately demonizing the actions of an entire group.

One more solid tool for gauging whether your criticism of Israel is antisemitic is applying the criteria created by Natan Sharansky, a human rights activist who spent nine years in a Soviet prison, having been convicted of treason and spying for the United States as a result of his advocacy for Soviet Jews trying to immigrate to Israel. He was also only the fourth non-American to receive the US Presidential Medal of Freedom. He created a standard to separate legitimate criticism of Israeli policies from antisemitism, and this framework was adopted by the US Department of State in 2010. It is called the 3D Test: Demonization, Double Standards, Delegitimization. If a person or an organization criticizes Israel (which is totally a valid and a legitimate thing to do!) but expresses any or all of the above Ds, then they've found themselves on the wrong side of the antisemitic boundary.

Here's how it works in practice:

Demonization: This can look a few different ways: making blanket statements that generalize all Israelis and/or Jews; demonizing Israelis/the Jews with descriptions such as "murderous" or "Nazis"; or using one-dimensional caricatures of Israel/Israelis/Jews, such as being cruel, power-hungry, barbaric, or bloodthirsty.

Double Standards: Simply put: people judge Jews by one standard and the rest of the world by another. Pakistan is the perfect parallel: There's virtually no difference between the creation stories of these two countries—both were decolonized from the United Kingdom, and both were created as safe havens for persecuted groups—Middle Eastern Jews and South Asian Muslims. Both engaged in land disputes, and both control religious sites of other religions.

They were even established a few months apart as part of the Partition—both countries even use this term—of larger British colonies. Why not boycott Pakistan and call for its dismantlement? Where are the protests demanding justice and liberation for the Punjabis? *That* is the double standard, and it's one of the biggest antisemitic tells of anti-Zionism.

Delegitimization: Denying Israel's right to exist, rejecting the United Nations' legal basis for the creation of the state, and/or refuting that Israel is the historic homeland of the Jewish people all serve to undermine Israel's right to exist. These matters are not opinions; they are facts.

The Canary in the Coal Mine

NOA: The other reason why it's crucial to talk about all of these issues is because where there is lack of information, there is *dis*-information. Because disinformation and conspiracy theories are always at the ready to fill in the blanks for people. And we already know how easy it has become to believe the worst about the Jews and Israel.

Earlier I mentioned the dangerous trend that there is no longer one truth, rather that truth is subjective or whatever you "feel" like it is. Well, if you come to believe that less than 0.2 percent of the world's population—the Jews—are working against you or controlling the world in some significant way, then you are likely to believe *anything*. It's a very short leap from that framework of reality to not trusting our very real institutions anymore: media, science, government. That seed of doubt is what we saw driving a wedge between Americans in the wake of COVID-19, what politicians are preying on since the 2020 election, and it's what we're seeing on college campuses right now. These students have gotten so swept up in disinformation from both a torrent of unchecked social media exposure and antisemitism-soaked campus activism that they are sitting ducks for alternative realities. That Hamas, again, a *terrorist* organization that purposefully and systematically killed babies, mutilated women, and burned entire families alive, is the solution to the Israel-Palestine problem, for one. Or that Osama bin Laden's antisemitism-laced "Letter to the American People" had some "good points." Or that the politicians in Washington, DC, are too establishment, so let's just take the whole system down and see what happens. This is not only bad for Jews, it's also bad for democracy.

It reminds me of a metaphor that's been making the rounds, which is that Jews are the canary in the coal mine for a society's health. Meaning when a society can't protect its Jews, it's a sign that there's a sickness starting to spread. That tightening noose around the Jews' necks is symptomatic of a larger, more pervasive issue, whether it's economic turmoil, political upheaval, violent social clashes, or international chaos. Everything that's happening right now to the Jews and Israel by proxy is nothing short of a cancer diagnosis for our society.

And if we're going to stand a chance to fix things, then we're going to need allies.

Part III

WE

21.

SOUL FOOD SHABBAT

NOA: You know, Emmanuel, I've got something I want to get off my chest. I, along with many of the Jewish people I've spoken to, feel like the Black community has slowly turned their backs on the Jewish community. It's one of the main reasons I wanted to do this book with you, to rebuild the bridge between us.

We Jews have been vocal allies for Black people, and our ties run deep. I don't have to remind you—Jews helped found the National Association for the Advancement of Colored People (NAACP); Julius Rosenwald (a Jew) dedicated much of his philanthropy to the improvement of education for Black students, constructing about five thousand schools in the South, and extending fellowship grants to Black artists and writers, including Maya Angelou, W. E. B. Du Bois, and Langston Hughes. Fifty percent of the white civil rights workers who went to the South, including the Freedom Riders, were Jews; and Rabbi Abraham Joshua Heschel marched on the front line with Dr. Martin Luther King Jr. in Selma, Alabama.

And we felt the love in return. At a fundraising dinner

shortly before his assassination, Dr. King shut down someone disparaging Zionists with "Don't talk like that! When people criticize Zionists, they mean Jews. You're talking antisemitism." Bayard Rustin, one of Dr. King's organizers and the architect of the March on Washington, started the Black Americans movement to support Israel because of how it was being demonized by the UN.

But our shared history started way before that; it goes all the way back to our stories in the Bible that became part of the Christian movement in Africa two thousand years ago. The Queen of Sheba visited Solomon in Jerusalem (the first Black-Israel summit!). Theodore Herzl's vision that formed the foundation of Israel was a call for equal rights and the condemnation of slavery and colonialism. Moses, Zion, enslavement—these things are all in our origin stories in some way.

So, the KKK and David Duke can spout off about Jews being the Devil—because I don't expect anything from them—but when there's silence, or worse, animosity and hate from the Black community, it cuts deep. And it feels like lately, a lot of the hate has come from Black men—Kanye West, after promising to go "death con 3" on Jewish people, stated that he'd rather his kids learn about Hanukah than Kwanzaa because "at least it will come with some financial engineering"; Kyrie Irving promoted a movie that denies the Holocaust happened; Dave Chappelle amplified the stereotype about Jews controlling Hollywood. Not to mention the fact that October 7th was a fracturing moment between the Black and Jewish communities—we needed help, and we felt shoved into the "oppressor" box. Hamas's unspeakable violence was categorized as justified resistance.

Did we occasionally abandon our post of allyship along the path? Did our dynamic change after the Jews were granted their "white permits"? Without question. I can't blame the

Black community for feeling like we haven't always been there to do the work. Yet this feels different. It wasn't just animosity or a cold shoulder, it was outright attacks. And it hurts.

But what's sad and enraging and alarming to me is that the vacuum of our allyship created a space for all those antisemitic tropes to seep in. This moment we're in is just the activation of thirty, forty years of intentional external sabotage. You can trace a straight line to so much of this from a 1960s propaganda campaign to destabilize the West and further vilify the Jews, not unlike the Russian meddling in the 2016 election. What was one of the most unstable things happening then in the United States? The struggle for Black freedom. International bad actors planting the seeds of antisemitism and antagonism toward Israel in that movement is how you ended up with Jews being accused of a conspiracy to control Africa's mineral wealth (they do not); Louis Farrakhan, the head of the Nation of Islam and the most famous antisemite in America, out there saying the Jews are the Devil and the architects of the Atlantic slave trade (we were not); the Black Hebrew Israelites accusing us of not being real Jews (we very much are); BLM Chicago cele-brating Hamas paragliders; and the Black community drawing parallels between the Palestinians and slavery.*

We *all* became losing pawns in that long game, and now here we are. So yeah, I'm upset, and frankly, I don't know where we go from here—but I want to move forward.

---

* For more background about this 1960s disinformation campaign, I highly recommend reading Dumisani Washington's book *Zionism and the Black Church*, which lays out the corroborated connection between the Soviet Union, Yasser Arafat—a confirmed KGB operative—and the Palestine Liberation Organization (PLO). Arafat's meetings with young American civil rights leaders in the 1960s coupled with this initiative was a watershed moment in the Black community's perception of Israel and the Jews, as well as ongoing demonization of Israel and the Jews.

EMMANUEL: This is why it was so important for me to write this book with you, because I did see the anger of the Black community toward the Jewish community and the pain that existed in both groups. Especially in industries I'm a part of, whether sports or entertainment, so I wanted to try and bridge that gap, if you will. Kanye, Kyrie, and others were saying ignorant and hurtful things, and I didn't want the Jewish community to think they represent all Black people.

But I'm honestly not surprised about the friction that exists between our communities, because while our groups do have many things in common, and while I do think we ultimately have a long-standing bond that can be healed and restored, we have one very innate, very crucial difference: our relationship with America. When I was standing on the edge of the Hudson River looking out at the Statue of Liberty with Tova Friedman, the Holocaust survivor, she told me with great relief in her voice that she saw that statue as a symbol of her freedom. The same can't be said by Black people. James Baldwin put this so powerfully when he said: "The Jewish travail occurred across the sea and America rescued him from the house of bondage. But America is the house of bondage for the Negro, and no country can rescue him. What happens to the Negro here happens to him because he is an American."

I hear you that there have been people trying to mess with our communities and pitting us against one another—because they always have and they always will. Larger powers win when the minorities are too busy duking it out with each other to pay attention to the bigger picture. But I don't think that friction is only because of "external sabotage," I think it's because of us.

It's because, at the end of the day, Black people are still those kids on the playground watching Jewish people get to have their extra recess while we need to go back inside for the math test. Sure, some of you tried to get us some extra time, too, but ultimately, that wasn't up to you, it was up to the teacher—and you were in her class. It may not seem "fair," but it's a natural human reaction. And it really clicked for me one day when I read something else that Baldwin had written: "And if one blames the Jew for having become a white American, one may perfectly well, if one is black, be speaking out of nothing more than envy."

I'm not saying that envy or resentment is right, but it sure as heck is real. As long as Jewish people get to benefit from appearing white while Black people have to suffer for being Black, there will always be resentment. Because the same thing that grants you all access—your skin color—is what grants us pain and punishment in perpetuity.

That white permit that some of you possess isn't always harmless to us. Sometimes, even though the Jewish community may not necessarily mean to, we're hurt by it. Kinda like when I try to squeeze myself into my 5'2" friend's bathroom. It's not a space meant for my 6'2", 240-pound self, so I end up knocking over her little trinkets and plants and towels, even though I'm definitely not trying to make a mess.

I think the best, most recent and public example of this is when Jamie Foxx had to issue an apology because so many people in the Jewish community made the situation about them.

NOA: What do you mean?

EMMANUEL: In the summer of 2023, Jamie posted on Instagram: "They killed this dude named Jesus . . . What do you think they'll do to you???! #fakefriends #fakelove." And then Jennifer Aniston liked the post. After which the Jewish community immediately attacked both Jamie, for blaming the Jews for killing Jesus and being antisemitic, and Jennifer, for supporting antisemitism. So, Jennifer goes on Instagram and denounces antisemitism and hate of any kind, which implied that Jamie was being antisemitic. So, then Jamie Foxx has to issue an apology to the Jewish community.

The thing is, what Jamie said in his post is an expression that a lot of Black people use, and it only means that you can't trust everybody in your circle. And it's not referencing the Jews, it's referencing Judas, one of Jesus's twelve closest friends who betrayed him. There was no antisemitism at play. But here you had what seemed, to me, like Jewish people looking for pain where it didn't exist.

NOA: What I do understand—and I think you maybe now have a clearer idea of why Jamie's post *appeared* to be antisemitic. And Jamie's Instagram isn't a private conversation with like-minded friends; it's a public display for over seventeen million people from very different walks of life. So even though the Black community may have been familiar with this expression and this reference, I don't believe many people in the white or Jewish community were or are. So no, in this case, I don't think people were looking for pain that didn't exist; I think people felt real pain, real fear, and real betrayal—even if it wasn't intended.

But also, yeah, we made it about ourselves. Because that's what human beings do. And it's what a group of people who have been consistently hurt and left to clean up the mess on their own do. But this time, it also caused pain to someone in your community.

EMMANUEL: I hear you about that hurt and fear; I know it's real. But innocent Black people—like Jamie Foxx—should not have to prove that they're not antisemitic; maybe they're just . . . not.

NOA: Jews feel the same exact way! We don't want to have to always prove that we're not nefarious, power-hungry goblins; maybe we're just . . . not.

EMMANUEL: That's fair; I really think the only way we can alleviate these misunderstandings is through conversation and dialogue, sitting back and listening. Listening to somebody who doesn't look like you. The way we're doing right now—because we are not each other's real opponents.

NOA: That's right. Because you know what the old patriarchy would *love* for us to do? To be alienated from each other, so they can continue to divide and conquer. Who wins when people hate the Jews? Or Black people? Or Asian people? Or queer people? Short answer: the people who promote fascism. Extremism. Hate.

EMMANUEL: Ya know, I think of it like this: When I played football for the University of Texas, our biggest, fiercest rivals were the Oklahoma Sooners. Every time we'd play our big annual game against each other, the Red River Rivalry, it would be at a stadium in Dallas because that was halfway between our schools—that's how intense that match-up was, because if the stadium were an inch closer to one school over the other, there'd be pandemonium. You'd also walk into that stadium, and it would be split right down the middle—Texas Longhorn white and burnt orange on one side, and Oklahoma Sooner crimson and white on the other. So, could you imagine what the Longhorn fans would feel if they walked in and saw all the players in burnt orange out there on the field just tackling themselves while the Sooners were out there scoring touchdowns?

That's what it feels like the Black and Jewish communities are doing right now—we're tackling one another while the real opponent wins. We should be walking out of that tunnel, arms locked, ready to do battle against our shared opponents—against hate, against marginalization, against oppression. People need to ask themselves who they're out there fighting against because it shouldn't be Black versus white, or white versus Black, or Black versus Jew, or Jew versus Black—it should just be good versus evil, love versus hate.

So yeah, we've been yelling at each other from across the field, or worse, attacking each other as though we're the opponents. But we've bled together, cried together, marched together, sat in together, sweat together.

NOA: That reminds me of the moment I had after I'd walked away from this project. I realized that if I directed my anger and resentment at you, then our communities would never be able to move beyond that either. And that the biggest, most pressing issue we need to address is how to bring them back together. I also knew that through sharing the exact experience we had, of overcoming disagreement and hurt, we can embody what it is we are talking about.

EMMANUEL: Amen, amen, and amen. And I'm forever grateful that you made that decision. You know, Noa, this all makes me think about an event you invited me to a few months back, "Soul Food Shabbat." Now, if there's one thing I will always go for when I want a "cheat" meal, it's soul food—fried chicken, candied yams, mac 'n' cheese, and corn bread. I'm getting hungry right now just thinking about it. So, combining that with an opportunity to learn more about the Jewish culture and form

new relationships with people who see the world in different—
but also many of the same—ways as me was speaking my love
language fluently.

If we're going to get where we need to go, then we're going
to need a lot more Soul Food Shabbats.

22.

BE A MENSCH
Show Up as an Ally

EMMANUEL: Talking about allyship was by far my favorite conversation in my first book because it's about coming together. We've had a lot of intense conversations leading up to now, but ultimately, this book was birthed from me trying to be an ally. This book was birthed from a desire to lend my heart and my hand to a community I am not a part of. I define "allyship" as finding a need and filling it. What are the needs of the hurting and how can I help fill those gaps? The biggest need that I see as an outsider is ending antisemitism. Do you believe that is even possible?

NOA: Let's put it this way: There's only one thing that's hung in there as long as the Jews and that's antisemitism. So, my intention isn't necessarily to "end" antisemitism so much as make it go out of style. We're not going to get rid of it completely, but we *can* learn how to manage it, both in our day-to-day lives and in the larger systems. If enough people can recognize the unconscious biases and preconceived notions they're carrying around about the Jews—even, or especially, the "positive" ones—antisemitism can be less dangerous.

EMMANUEL: More than anything, I want people to think about what it could look like if we all collectively decide to commit to being allies for one another. Allyship doesn't mean quitting your job to become a full-time social justice crusader. It means doing what's in your power, at that moment, to do. I tell people all the time—I haven't been at one protest or on one march. Instead of going outside, I went inside, into a studio. My voice has been my sword; that is the weapon I can use to wage war against hate. Everybody has their own weapons; they just have to fight the way they know how.

NOA: *Precisely.* Ultimately—and I cannot say this enough—so go us, so go you, especially if you're a member of a marginalized group. Or as Rabbi Jonathan Sacks put it: "The hate that begins with Jews never ends with the Jews." You only have to look at the Nazis, who broadened their scope of hate to include Black people, people with disabilities, and queer people.

EMMANUEL: One time while I was in college, my strength coach opened his hand and commanded that I strike it with my open palm. He then instructed me to make a fist with that same hand and strike his palm again. His point: five fingers held separately would make a marginal impact compared to a closed fist, when all five fingers are brought together in unison. In the same way, marginalized and oppressed communities can make a much greater impact when they come together.

If we are only focused on ourselves, then hate will continue to prevail. Oppression will continue to prevail. There is so much collective strength that we gain when we choose to fight together. So, let's wage war on that oppression together, because we can accomplish so much more as a team than as individuals.

Show Up!

NOA: You said earlier that being an ally is as simple as finding a need and filling it—which I would agree with, and it's refreshingly simple, especially for someone who wants to do the right thing but isn't ready to take on the injustices of the entire world.

EMMANUEL: It really isn't any more complicated than that. One of my favorite allyship stories from my own life was when I started my *Uncomfortable Conversations* series. It was very much a DIY project—I found a wedding videographer to help me shoot the episode and my best friend, Mo, was my producer. That was my entire team; and I was in charge of putting music behind it. So, I googled, found the perfect song, and uploaded the episode to YouTube. Cue huge red "X" on my screen—because using the song was copyright infringement.

A few days later, I was talking to my friend Nick Hetherington—and remember, I launched the series in the aftermath of George Floyd's murder, so this was around that time—and he said, "I'm so sorry for what's going on in your community; is there anything I can do to help?" To which I said, "Nick, I need some music." He'd worked for a TV network, so I figured he'd know how to navigate this type of thing. And sure enough, he sent me a whole catalog of music that I'd be able to use. The song I chose is the same one that plays in every one of my episodes; it's the one that over one hundred million people have heard when they tune in; and it's the one that ultimately filled the room in Los Angeles after W. Kamau Bell announced, "And the Emmy Award goes to . . . Emmanuel Acho and *Uncomfortable Conversations with a Black Man.*"

I don't know if Nick ever attended a protest or read an antiracism book, but it didn't matter—he showed up as an ally in a way that he could. That seemingly small gesture from him, something he had the power to do, turned out to be the exact thing that I needed, figuratively and literally, at that moment. It's also helped elevate racial dialogue that's since been heard by tens of millions of people.

It's the same thing as me seeing that you and your community were hurting and asking if I could amplify your message on my platform. It cost me no money; it didn't take more than an hour; and I won't speak for you, but I hope it made you feel heard.

NOA: That is a beautiful story, Emmanuel, and yes, of course, I felt heard. Your reaching out to ask how I was and what I needed was being an ally. Every time I get something as simple as a text message from one of my non-Jewish friends checking in on me, that's being an ally. Whenever I'm scrolling through my social media feed and stumble upon a non-Jewish person publicly speaking out against Hamas and standing up for the Jews (thank you, Meghan McCain, Ritchie Torres, Daniel-Ryan Spaulding, Sarah Idan, Malynda Hale, Caroline D'Amore, Bassem Eid, Mosab Hassan Yousef—to name a few), I feel that allyship.

You see, we are not asking people to hide us in their attics; we are not those people anymore. *We're asking them to come out of hiding for us.* Each one of these acts contributes in ways that might feel small but add up to big changes—but I'd argue that the easiest place to start is figuring out how to simply speak up.

Speak Up!

EMMANUEL: I'd be remiss if I didn't overtly state that while being an ally doesn't mean you have to march or paint a sign or grab a microphone, it does mean that you can't just be silent.

NOA: I couldn't agree more. There is no greater feeling, or more powerful antidote to antisemitism, than having a friend or friends who want to be out there kicking butt on your behalf. Especially when your community is feeling exhausted and demoralized.

Here are some things someone could do right now:

Adopt the IHRA Definition of Antisemitism: The International Holocaust Remembrance Alliance provides a working definition of antisemitism that you can bring to your school, your boss, your roommates, your chanting circle; whoever, whatever, wherever. It will give everyone a clear-cut framework for understanding whether or not something is antisemitic—because as we know, it's tricky sometimes!

Revisit Natan Sharansky's 3Ds: Demonization, Double Standards, Delegitimization. Use these benchmarks for keeping an eye on your own language, regardless of whether it's about the Jews. (The Ds aren't good for anyone.) Or if someone else says something that checks any of these boxes, then it's time to have a little chat. Let's use it in a sentence: "Hey, university presidents, it's a delegitimizing double standard when you say that calling for the genocide of Jews does not constitute hate speech since I'm pretty sure calling for the lynching of Black people or gunning down of Asian people would." See? Easy!

EMMANUEL: I'll add a couple:

1. *Do your homework.* As allies, we are responsible for educating ourselves about people's experiences and not the other way around. And when it comes to this particular syllabus, I think it requires two kinds of learning: intellectual and experiential. You not only have to do the reading (or listening) to intellectually understand a person's history or experience but also walk alongside them in that experience. You could tell me what it's like to be a parent, or I could babysit your kids for a weekend and understand firsthand what that's like. Both are important and both together are what maximizes our learning.

   I would also add, if your life doesn't look diverse enough, go out of your way to add some diversity to it. My friend Montana Tucker, a proud Jewish performer, invited me to a Jewish event at the Grove, an outdoor shopping mall in West Hollywood. I knew nothing about the event besides it being a celebration of Judaism and that Montana would be there, but I showed up. I figured there was no better way to learn about a culture than to immerse myself in that culture. Jewish hip-hop was playing (I didn't know that existed), and I got to meet one of the oldest Holocaust survivors.

2. Ask your Jewish friends or colleagues to be invited for Shabbat. First of all, you'll have a great time and learn a lot. Second of all, they'll love that you're asking. Don't worry about them saying no—I've yet to have anyone say no; only ask me when I'm coming back.

NOA: Say no? We would never!

EMMANUEL: And make sure you go if asked! It's so easy for us to say no; so much more convenient and so much less scary. But this is how you learn, and this is how you create more connection and compassion.

NOA: Yes! And I should also clarify here that Shabbat is *fun!* It's joyful, not some solemn, boring affair. At its center is a moment to look back on what probably felt like a really long week and be grateful that we can all have some well-deserved rest. Even if you're joining a bare-minimum-Shabbat type of Jew, at the very least you're going to have something good for dinner.

Okay, my turn again. And these next ones are for the Jews:

1. *Go analog, not digital.* Most of the recommendations in this chapter are geared toward non-Jews who want to become better allies, but I hear all the time from Jewish people asking me, "How do I become a better pro-Jewish activist?" And I always say, "You don't. Don't worry about being some online activist

you might not be called to be. But rather, just like Judaism is all about being in life, go be in life!" Making a real change happens when people know people, not just online but old-school IRL. And each one of us can impact our own community if we just reach across the aisle. So, stop worrying about your social media life and focus on your *actual* social life. Ignore the comments on your feed and invite your non-Jewish friends or colleagues for a holiday meal or to partake in your practices and rituals. Because, like Emmanuel just said, that kind of exposure and real-life education is so powerful. Plus, if you're the one to give someone their first challah or matzoh ball soup, they're always going to have a special place in their heart for you.

2. *Loud and proud, baby, loud and proud.* And probably the most important point I would make here is: Stop hiding! We have tried that for generations and it never works. We have tried to fit in or to be something that we are not for forever, and that software needs to be updated. Being Jewish is such an honor and has so much to teach us, who are we to hide it? One of my key mantras comes from the greatest of them all, Dolly Parton. She said that in life one needs to "find out who you are, then do it on purpose." So go learn about who you are and then do it on purpose! Be loud and proud of your Jewish identity. Learn the stories, enjoy the holidays, find your personal connection to this ancient tribe, and embrace it. When real inner pride takes over our community and shines outward, then antisemitism

will be shoved in humanity's dusty back seat again, where it belongs.

EMMANUEL: I've said it before and I'll say it again: proximity breeds care, and distance breeds fear. The closer you are to people or the more exposure you have to them, their culture, and their community, the more you can understand their pain. And the more empathy you have, the better ally you can be.

If more people are having uncomfortable—and also respectful, open-minded, and open-hearted—conversations with one another, then they will also be strengthening their relationships. When we do more listening, and when we keep the volume of our exchanges at a reasonable level, there grows more healing than hurt.

NOA: So, what you're saying is that we all benefit from people getting curious, asking more uncomfortable questions, and doing more listening?

EMMANUEL: Precisely.

Conclusion

TODAY IS WHERE YOUR BOOK BEGINS, THE REST IS STILL UNWRITTEN

NOA: A few months ago, I was at my friend Sarah's house. Her eight-year-old daughter, Marion, and my son, Ari, were off playing while Sarah and I caught up on life. Eventually, we all sat down to eat dinner, when out of nowhere Sarah's daughter asked:

"Why are we here?"

Sarah and I exchanged looks as if to say, *Um, how does one even answer that?!* But then my son chimed in with, "Yeah, what's our *purpose*?" Sarah and I were both surprised and delighted with the deep turn this conversation with two eight-year-olds was taking. I looked at them and said: "Well, these are great questions, kids. These are questions that a lot of adults ask themselves all the time."

Ari barely missed a beat before responding, "Well, Imi,* I know what *your* purpose in life is."

"Oh yeah, what's that?"

"Your purpose in life is to tell the story of the Jewish people."

My sudden tears nearly made me choke on the butternut squash, I was so completely floored. Ari saw me. He gets me. He sees my purpose.

And I agreed.

Emmanuel, remember that night, the evening of October 7th, when you saw that I was on Instagram Live?

EMMANUEL: I don't think I could ever forget.

NOA: That broadcast that you first saw, the one that seemed like chaos—because it was, because I was trying to piece together what was happening in the early-morning hours in Israel— what you don't know is that throughout the entire time I was on, my Instagram Live screen kept filling up with messages that people were sending me. Messages from people under attack, asking me for help. "Please, Noa, they're getting into the kibbutz." "I'm in Kfar Aza, please send someone." "I'm in Sderot, there are terrorists everywhere." On and on it went, people begging: "Please help us." I kept trying to figure out what was happening and how I could possibly help all these people, sitting in Los Angeles while Israel was being attacked. All I knew was that whatever was going on was so deeply horrific, and that people were feeling so intensely desperate, that their only hope rested on a message sent over Instagram to someone halfway across the world.

---

* A combination of "Ima" (Hebrew for "Mom") and "Mommy"; by far the most adorable name in the history of names.

After hours of being live and as the sun rose in Los Angeles, I turned off my phone and got a couple hours of rest. But I didn't post that Live recording to my feed. When you don't post a Live, it disappears. Into the ether. And I've never shaken the thought that some of those people sending me messages most likely didn't survive the massacre. That they had disappeared with their messages.

These people—I would never know their names—but they asked for my help. At that moment, I was unable to help them. So, I'm doing this for them, in their memory. And I'm also doing it for every single Jew who lives in fear that it could just as easily have been them—to remind them that *we are all survivors*.

If I were to tell you that there was a tiny group of people who existed thousands of years ago, and every few decades the largest empires in the world would intentionally try and kill them; and if I told you that that same group survived not once, not twice, not three times, but over and over and over again, and then *thrived*—a rational person would say that it is statistically impossible. That it makes zero sense. But that is the Jewish people. Their persistence, not to mention their achievements, in the thick of turbulence and trauma is nothing short of miraculous. Every single Jew you meet is a survivor.

That is where my strength comes from—because I live in constant gratitude and awe of the fact that my existence is the product of the greatest suffering and the greatest strength. And now my son is part of that incredible lineage, and his children, and their children, God willing. So, I am not taking any of this lying down—but I can't fight alone.

I have felt for so long that I've been screaming into the wind, talking to the walls and plants and the five people who would listen to me. But now the world has changed, and people are ready to hear what I have to say. What we all have to say. And I feel like *you* heard it without even knowing me, like you heard the same ancient whisper of a people and knew something had to be done.

What you and I both understand is that our history does not have to be our future. In the Mishnah, a part of our oral Torah, it says: יופצ תושרהו הנותנ בוטבו סלועה ןודנ לכהו יפל בור השעמה לכה (Mishnah, Avot 3.15), "All is foreseen, and freedom of choice is granted. The world is judged with goodness, but in accordance with the amount of people's positive deeds." Meaning, the future is predicted, but it is ultimately shaped by our choices and, mostly, our deeds. So, it is everyone's commandment to go forth and make the future. Write the rest of the story.

EMMANUEL: One of the most powerful things a pastor reminded me of is that the Scripture says "Blessed are the peacemakers." Not the peace*keepers*, the peace*makers*. In order to make peace, you have to go out and find that war. Find the suffering. Find the hurting. Find the conflict. And I agree, Noa, that you can't fight alone. The wars waged against hate and antisemitism, against discrimination and racism—those battles can't be waged on your own. We need each other, and everyone listening in, everyone reading, to not just lend your eyes and ears but also your hearts. Don't just read this book; we need you to move. We need you to act. This conversation is so much more than a dialogue; it's a blueprint—it's a plan of action.

During a football game, just before the ball is snapped and the players move into action, they huddle up in a circle. And in that huddle, the quarterback announces the play. While each player hears the entirety of the play call, the different words said during the call are giving each player a different implicit set of instructions, depending on the position they play for their team.

See, family, this book is that huddle. Noa and I are the quarterbacks and we're giving people the play, laying out what has to happen if our hope for society can become a reality. I realize that this huddle is composed of people who don't look alike; who don't share the same race, gender, or religion; who may actually have very little in common. But we are all on the same team, coming together to infuse peace into society.

Just like you don't go to a football game to watch a bunch of players stand around in a huddle—that would be silly and stupid and a waste of time—to read this book and do nothing would be silly and stupid and a waste of time. You go to see what happens after that huddle, to watch with exhilaration as unlimited possibility—and a little bit of magic—unfolds in real time when the pieces of the whole are working together in sync. That's the precipice that we're standing on right now.

Reading this book is just the first step. Now we're breaking the huddle, and every single one of you has a different responsibility based on your role on our collective team. Our jobs may each look different, but our objective is the same. And I guarantee you that if we can start thinking like a team, we can win like one, too.

Director's Cut

OCTOBER 7TH

EMMANUEL: There are certain dates that will be entrenched in my mind forever—December 25th (Jesus's birthday), November 10th (my birthday), September 11th, and now October 7th. Those are the dates I will always remember; dates of birth and dates of death.

When the events of October 7th occurred, my world stopped. And since then, I've had an overwhelming desire to understand what happened—something that I know many people share. We had to talk about it, and we still do, which is why we're including here the conversation I had with Noa just one week later, on October 15th. It is unedited; it is raw; and it is just as powerful today as it was then.

EMMANUEL: Welcome to another episode of *Uncomfortable Conversations with Emmanuel Acho*.

Though our world is at war, may we never lose our appetite for humanity. Real hurt, real pain, real people. I'm joined now by Israeli-born Noa Tishby—daughter, mother, author. A woman who's dedicated her life to serving the Jewish people and community, Israel, a land that she loves.

Noa, what are you feeling right now?

NOA: It's been the worst week of my life and the worst week of the entire world Jewish community and Western civilization, should people understand what's going on. It's everyone's worst nightmares. Generational trauma re-created.

It's like all the horror stories that the Jewish community has heard about—of mothers slaughtered in front of their children, children being burnt alive, handcuffed behind their backs, families burned in their homes. I mean, horror stories that we've been raised with are happening in reality. And not just that they're happening; they're filmed and presented to the world.

So, what's happening right now is going to take decades to heal, if at all.

EMMANUEL: How is ... how is your family? Because obviously you have family over there. How are they?

NOA: Every single person I know knows people that were slaughtered in the most brutal way. My nieces and nephews are going to, like, double, triple, quadruple funerals every day. They know multiple families that have been affected by this.

EMMANUEL: How'd we get here?

NOA: On Saturday morning, 6:30 in the morning, Israel time, 8:30 p.m. Friday night on the West Coast, Israel was surprised by a terrorist attack by the terrorist organization Hamas, which took over Gaza—the Gaza Strip—in 2006. They started launching thousands of rockets, but that was actually hiding a ground-invasion operation. So, the numbers, the recent numbers that I heard is thirty-five hundred terrorists invaded Israel on trucks, on motorcycles, on paragliders—like gliding into Israel—armed to the teeth—and conquered, invaded all these towns, went one house to the next, and slaughtered every man, woman, and child that they could find.

EMMANUEL: This is the most Jews that have been slaughtered since the Holocaust—

NOA: —in one day, yeah.

EMMANUEL: How does hearing that make you feel? What is your response to that ugly reality?

NOA: You know, after the Holocaust, the Jewish community, we had a saying: "Never Again." We worked very hard to, you know, to rebuild the Jewish community. And we kept saying "never again."

And it happened again.

EMMANUEL: You feel like this is triggering that same emotional response?

NOA: A hundred percent. And it's not just me. There are fifteen million Jews in the world.

It's a very small number that people are not aware of. People think that there are a lot more Jews in the world. But the world, the Jewish community, is 0.2 percent of the world population.

Every single Jew around the world is having nightmares

right now. Every Jewish family has a story of persecution, extermination, expulsion, discrimination, murder. *Every* Jewish family.

EMMANUEL: What's been the hardest part for you through all of this? Is it communicating these events, even to your young son? Is it communicating them to loved ones? Like, is it trying to go to sleep at night with horror thoughts in your mind? What's been the hardest part?

NOA: I have not been sleeping through the night. You just—I've never experienced anything like that. Like you fall asleep and you just jump like *that* because you have these images of what actually went down.

I think, honestly, one of the worst things for me is the lack of understanding that the world has to what went down and the support that that barbaric terrorist organization is getting.

EMMANUEL: I've seen the sentiment from so many of my Jewish brothers and sisters that the Jewish community, they stood by the LGBTQ+ community; they stood by the Black community. What do you hope that other marginalized communities would do for and with the Jewish community right now?

NOA: This is a great question, and I don't want to be making anybody wrong or making anybody feel bad right now. Historically, we've been on the side of human rights. Rabbi Heschel marched with Martin Luther King on the bridge in Selma; literally front line. When the Freedom Riders were slaughtered, there were Jewish people in the Freedom Riders; the Jewish community has been there for oppressed communities throughout the generations.

In the past decades we have been feeling extraordinarily alone. You cannot say that you are a person that is supportive of human rights, women's rights, democracy, freedom of speech, LGBTQ+ rights, minorities, and stand with Hamas.

EMMANUEL: At this very moment, do you, as a Jewish woman, walk around scared?

NOA: It—it just pains me to say that. Yes. I tried not to, but I haven't left the house in a week.

EMMANUEL: Have you given yourself the opportunity to feel?

NOA: I try not to.

EMMANUEL: Why?

NOA: Because then I'll fall apart.

EMMANUEL: You have two groups communicating to the world, "Don't fall on the wrong side of history," but they're communicating to fall on different sides of history. How is someone like me supposed to adequately assess what side of history to fall on?

NOA: You don't have to love the Israeli government. You don't have to agree with every action of the Israeli government. The only thing is that Israel has the right to exist. That's literally the line.

EMMANUEL: Why do some argue that Zionism is racist; Zionism is oppressive; Zionism is colonialist; to be Zionist is to hate and oppress another group of people?

NOA: So, to ask the question, Why is Zionism oppression? I would ask, Why is there no Palestine? We've been dying to have a Palestine, for a very long time. The majority of Israel. At times we're like, *All right, let's just find a solution here.* There's this two-state solution—you guys mostly are living here. We live mostly there. Let's divide it. Every time, and I'm saying this as clear as day and, please don't take my word for it—look it up. Every time there's been an offer for a Palestinian state, they said no every time.

EMMANUEL: What do you feel when you hear the words "Free Palestine"?

NOA: Absolutely Free Palestine. Free Palestine from Hamas. Absolutely free Palestine.

Let me say one more thing, right? Gaza is not occupied by Israel. I'm going to say it again: Israel does not occupy Gaza.

When Hamas declared war on Israel on October 7th, they declared war, first of all, on themselves, because there's not going to be any more Hamas. That's number one. And number two—and that's the thing that people need to understand—they declared war on their own people.

Hamas is sacrificing Gaza and sacrificing Gazans.

EMMANUEL: So, is it possible to be pro-Palestinian and anti-Hamas?

NOA: Absolutely. There are a lot of people who are, by the way. It's also possible to be pro-Israeli and pro-Palestinian, which is what I am.

EMMANUEL: What do Palestinians want? Wouldn't that answer be freedom? What do we do in Gaza?

NOA: Absolutely. What do we do in Gaza? That's what Israel did in Gaza. *We're out. Here you go. The keys, you got the keys.* Israel left in Gaza greenhouses, houses, fields. You know what Hamas did to those greenhouses and fields and houses? They burnt them.

I'm not kidding. We want freedom for Palestinians, too. I can't say it in so many words, there were peace offerings given to the Palestinian people many times throughout history, and they kept saying no. Hamas burnt down the infrastructure that Israel left. Israel went, *Here are the keys. Get your freedom, enjoy, create.*

EMMANUEL: Then why view Israel as the oppressor?

NOA: Exactly.

EMMANUEL: I'm asking you—

NOA: It's a great question, Emmanuel.

It's that people need to come to terms and understand that they see the worst of Israel. Israel can almost do no right. With antisemitism, with anti-Jewish racism, it's a little bit more tricky because when you look at a Jew, you don't necessarily only look down at a Jew; you also look *up* at a Jew. So anti-Jewish racism also sounds like "The Jewish people, they have the control. They control Hollywood, they control the money. They control the banks."

When you walk around and you have that unchecked subconscious bias where you think, *Well, then the Jews control the world, they control the American media, they control the American government.* When you think that, you will believe the worst of Israel immediately.

So, when you hear, well, Israel's a colonialist state, obviously, and you have a subconscious bias about the Jewish people, you're gonna believe it.

EMMANUEL: What can someone who is unaffected—neither Jewish nor Palestinian—what can someone like me do in this moment to support someone like you?

NOA: So, the first thing is literally as simple as check in on your Jewish friends, be vocal on social media. Do not allow for this equivocation—you can't compare these sides at all.

EMMANUEL: And lastly, in your mind, how does this end?

NOA: I have no idea how this war ends. I really don't. But I can tell you this: In the Jewish community, we have been through such hell in the past and, sadly, we know how to get through this. So, I see already stories of unity and help and friendship and community all over the world that are helping the Jewish people and helping Israel.

The Jewish people are extraordinarily strong. We say this a lot, but it's true: *Am Yisrael Chai*, the people of Israel live. And we're going to keep living.

EMMANUEL: Well, Noa, thank you for your courage.

NOA: Thank you so much for having me. And thank you for speaking up. And thank you for being an ally.

EMMANUEL: Of course. Of course. It's an honor. It is.

And thank you all for tuning in to another episode of *Uncomfortable Conversations with Emmanuel Acho.* Remember, justice will not be served until those that are unaffected are as outraged as those that are affected. So do your part to seek and fight for and find justice.

We'll see you next time.

Acknowledgments

From Emmanuel

I think this is the part of the book where I'm supposed to say thank you to all of the instrumental people who helped me in creating *Uncomfortable Conversations with a Jew*. It's almost like an acceptance speech. Which, by the way, I've never really been good at giving because I didn't really win a lot growing up, but here goes nothing!

To you, yes, you, the reader. Thank *you*. This book, this project, the tense nights, and even the lost friendships were well worth it because you have chosen to at least take the first step toward making our world a better place. So thank you for sitting at this table with me and Noa to have this conversation.

Noa, there are not enough words, my friend. You are a world changer. I called you back in 2021 in hopes of writing a book together, and you immediately heard my heart and saw the vision. Your passion is unmatched, and your desire to speak with and for those who may not have the words or the energy is truly awe inspiring. Heck, ordering food with another person can be a challenge, and we wrote a *whole book* together! I can't believe we did it; I can't believe it actually happened, but I'm so glad it did. Thank you for never abandoning me, and thank you for never giving up on us and this project. I know things were not always easy, and I know I offended you at times, but I love you always, my friend, and I'm glad *you* know that.

Doris, your heart is as pure as gold, and our earth is better because your feet have traveled across it. Thank you for believing in me and Noa from the beginning, and thank you for going on this journey with us. Your vulnerability and emotions reminded me how important this book is; I'm grateful for you.

Rachel, standing ovation, my friend, standing ovation. You are one of the hardest workers I've ever met in my life, and your ability to help Noa and me make this project come to life so quickly was marvelous. Thanks for challenging me, for talking through things with me, for picking up at all . . . well, most hours of the day (I forget about the whole sleeping thing sometimes). You are a true warrior for good and justice, and I'm grateful to know you.

Meredith, you really have to stop letting me write books. I told you after the first one (in 2020) that I would not write another. . . . Well, it's 2024 and I've published four books now, oops. Thanks for tolerating me and my madness, as always.

Mo, I'm forever grateful for you. You've been there through every episode of the show and every page of the book. Before this was ever a book, when it was simply an idea, you helped complete my thoughts and finish my sentences. As I said before, maybe this book could have been written without you, but I don't want to imagine how. Thank you.

To my brother, Sam, you inspire me, encourage me, and motivate me. Everything I do, I try to do excellently because of you. You're my biggest inspiration, and I love you more than you know. Thanks for setting the bar so high; you've made me a better man and a better human.

Steph, your love for me doesn't go unnoticed. You've always wanted to see me win, and you were the first one to speak my current reality of life into existence. Thanks for believing in me before there was much to believe in.

Chichi, you're forever one of my favorite humans on the earth. When my life got chaotic, our conversations about nothing and everything all at the same time kept me sane. I can't imagine my life with you. You're the best.

Dad, I got my ability to communicate from you. The reason my words have resonated with so many is because of what I caught from you and was taught by you growing up. Thank you for the sacrifices you made for me, putting me in a position to try and change the world. You taught me how to work and how to sacrifice. You taught me how to deliver truth with grace and love. I am who I am because of you.

Mom, you're an angel walking the earth. If Dad taught me how to communicate, you taught me how to have compassion. Thanks for being my biggest cheerleader and biggest supporter. Thanks for always making sure that your youngest son felt loved and taken care of. I love you.

Lastly, I end this book with the way I started every episode of *Uncomfortable Conversations with a Black Man* and anything I do of significance. By thanking God. I've consistently referred to this season in my life as my "Esther moment" (Esther 4:14). I'm honored that God equipped and called me to be a messenger in this moment. Jesus's love for me has set the bar for the way in which I'm called to love people, and the way in which I'm called to love you, Reader.

I'm humbled to have been able to help write this book and facilitate this message, and I'm grateful that you chose to come on this journey with me and Noa.

Let's continue to change the world, together. Love y'all.

*If these acknowledgments sound strikingly similar to my acknowledgments at the end of my previous book, *Uncomfort-*

able Conversations with a Black Man, that's because they are. I still love my family, my friends, and Jesus, and I love you even more now because you read both books. Okay, bye for real this time.

From Noa

I love the acknowledgments section of a book. It's one of my favorite parts. It's a moment to peek behind the curtains into a broken fourth wall, to get an insight into an author circle and sometimes into who they are without any filters. In my first book, *Israel: A Simple Guide to the Most Misunderstood Country on Earth*, I basically thanked anyone and everyone I ever met. We are nothing without our community, and I wanted to use that opportunity to acknowledge the people who surrounded me. This time, since two people have to thank double the number of friends and family, I will keep it shorter. If you were acknowledged in my first book, consider yourself acknowledged again! I love you all just the same.

Emmanuel, your north compass is unparalleled. I was on the phone with you before we started working together, placing clean and folded clothes back in my closet, one of the most mundane and uninspiring acts of domestic life, when you uttered the words "*I want your community to know that relief is on the way.*" I remember where I was because I burst into tears, just like that, alone in my bedroom, standing in front of my closet. Profound and divine moments can occur in the simplest of places, and this was one of them. Thank you for being willing to put yourself on the line for what you believe in, and for pushing back and asking me the questions you know others might want to ask and either can't or won't. I am thrilled to have found my match in hard work, commitment, and drive to make the world a better place. You are my partner, my friend, and my family (*mishpocha*) for life, and you have an open invitation for Shabbat anytime.

Doris Cooper, thank you for believing in Emmanuel and me right from the start and for feeling so intimately that this was your book. Thank you for being eager to ask questions and learn deeply with us. I feel like we have all been on this journey together and are now coming out on the other side better and more compassionate than ever before. We are lucky to have you. Thank you, also, to the Simon Element team for supporting this book in ways great and small: Richard Rhorer, Katie McClimon, Jessica Preeg, Elizabeth Breeden, Nan Rittenhouse, Michael Nagin, Jackie Seow, Davina Mock, and Chris Artis. Thank you, Jonathan Karp, for believing in me again. I love this partnership of ours.

Rachel Holtzman, Emmanuel and I started this process without you, and on October 7th the earth fell from underneath us all and this book became not only important but crucial and beyond urgent. You are the fastest- and, yes, hardest-working human I have ever met, and you are the best book doula we could have asked for. Thank you for helping us birth this book; what an intense and powerful journey it was.

Becky Sweren, you are still and forever my spirit animal. Your instincts on this book were spot on. Thank you for knowing what I need before I even know I need it. I thank my lucky stars for our partnership as my literary agent, my creative soulmate, my protector, and my friend.

Lesley and Jeff Wolman, thank you for decades of love and support. You are my chosen family. I still couldn't have done it without you.

To my UTA team, Jacob Fenton, Geoff Suddleson, Marc

Peskin, Nancy Gates, and Ryan Hayden for making this *shid-doch* (another great Yiddish word!) and matching Emmanuel and me. To Cindi Berger, Justin Solar, Tracy Cole, Lori Lousaraian, thank you for hustling on behalf of us and this book, to Jonathan Lyons for all book legal work, and to Maya for helping us in anything and everything. To Ivan Solotaroff and Netta Geist for helping us keep the record straight, to Rabbis Sharon Brous and Jeremy Borovitz for keeping us in line with tradition, and to Pastor Dumisani Washington for additional perspective and knowledge. Jamie Black, thank you for working me hard and smart.

To my main squeezes RJ Richman and Yoav Davies, thank you for being as obsessed with the cause as I am. There is no one in the world I would rather work around the clock with, travel all over with, and laugh with. We have no nights, no holidays, and no weekends, and we love it. We are all equally cray, thank God we found each other.

To Oded for bursting into our lives and brightening them up, we both love you.

To my dad, Daniel, I wish you were here to watch and share this ride with me; my lord, you would have loved it so much. I know you are watching us, and I know you're proud. I want to just make sure you know that Ari loves music, math, and candy just as much as you did.

To my sisters, Mira, Michal, Iris, and Tomosh, I love you so much. You are my backbone and support system, and I can't imagine life without you.

To my mom, the now famous Safta Yael. I love and appreciate you and everything you taught me. If anyone thinks I am a strong woman, I huff and point to you. There is no one stronger, and I am honored I was able to learn so much just from being your child.

Thank you to the young men and women in the Israeli army defending the Jewish homeland for the entirety of the Jewish people and Western civilization. How you jumped into service made all our hearts explode with pride. May you forever be protected.

To my love, my heart, my soul, my eyes, Ari. This is all still for you. Being your mom is the greatest honor and greatest fun; it is the ride of my life. Thank you for still wanting kirbooli and for still thinking I am somewhat cool. I'll take both for as long as I can. Keep on marching to the beat of your own drum and having zero FOMO. I can't for the life of me get where you got this from. I love you so so much.

Thank you to Hashem, the universe, God, divine intervention. I am honored, blessed, and grateful.

And lastly, I hope that by the time this book comes out, this will be outdated and not needed, but here goes—BRING THEM HOME.

Thank you all for going on this ride with us, love and light. XO Noa

Appendix A

AN ANTISEMITIC APPENDIX

NOA: When we started this book, I made it clear that I don't believe in safe spaces; I believe in real spaces. I believe that none of us wins if we spend our precious energy trying not to offend one another rather than understanding why things are offensive. So, I don't want anyone to feel like they need to walk on eggshells around their Jewish friends. Believe me, we Jews know how to not take ourselves so seriously. Our relationship with humor goes all the way back to the Talmud, so we know a good joke when we see one.

But the laughing stops when the language is hurtful or dangerous. And it's safe to say that all of the phrases below fall in the "hard no" category. At best because they make us feel marginalized or tokenized. But at worst because they perpetuate the tropes that we've been talking about throughout this book, the ones that, when used often enough, start to chip away at Jews' humanity and make it easier to blame them for pretty much anything.

If you're not sure? Ask a friend or keep it to yourself. Or if you do happen to really step in it, an apology, without excuses, goes a long way! We're all still learning.

Dehumanizing Generalizations

NOA: Statements like these reinforce anti-Jewish tropes, such as "Jews control the media" or "All Jews believe X or Y." Bottom line: If a statement makes a generalization about all Jews, all Israelis, or all actions of Israel, then it is antisemitic.

"Jews control the media/banks/space lasers."

"Jews are cheap."

"Jews have a lot of money."

Take a cue from Dave Chappelle: anything beginning with "The Jews."

"Zionism is racism."

"Israelis are Nazis."

"Jews always stick together."

"Jews will always defend Israel over the United States."

"Israel is the worst human rights offender in the world."

"The Jews believe [insert Israeli governmental policy]."

Microaggressions

NOA: These statements also further anti-Jewish stereotypes but are often confused as compliments or even neutral observations.

"You're good with money."

"You're Jewish? You must love to [fill in the blank]."

"You don't look Jewish."

"You're not Jewish, you're white."

"You're not white, you're Jewish."

"You're my only Jewish friend."

"I mean you're not *Jewish* Jewish."

Denials

NOA: Refusing to acknowledge the lived experience of another group, or diminishing it, dehumanizes that group.

"I can't be antisemitic; I have Jewish friends."

"I can't be antisemitic because I'm an Arab/'Semite.'"

"As a minority, I understand how bad the Holocaust was for the Jews."

"Jews have had it bad, but not as bad as X or Y group."

"I think the Jews made up [pick a massacre]."

"The Jews must have deserved [pick a massacre]." (Try asking us how we're doing instead!)

Justifying Violence

NOA: This type of language emerges when someone or a group has internalized enough dehumanizing stereotypes about the Jews that they're only able to see them as a problem.

> "This issue would be solved/this situation would be better if Israel/the Jews were gone."

> "There is only one solution: intifada revolutions."

> "Globalize the intifada."

Highly Offensive Terms

NOA: In no context are these terms acceptable or funny, and, no, we don't "know what you're talking about."

> **Kike:** An ethnic slur for a Jewish person that is considered to be a form of hate speech.

> **Shyster:** While this isn't Jewish-specific, it means "unscrupulous" or "shady" and is often used in an antisemitic context.

> **Shylock:** A reference to Shakespeare's *Merchant of Venice* character who personified Jews as money-loving and conniving.

JAP or Jappy: "Jewish American Princess" (and some Canadians, too). This term was first used to describe upwardly mobile Jewish women and implies one is bitchy, whiny, materialistic, and helplessly dependent on Daddy's money until she finds a wealthy husband. Some Jewish women have "reclaimed" this term and use it to self-own for being high maintenance, but others argue that it still creates an unflattering characterization of women in general, as well as reinforces detrimental associations between Jews and money.

Hymie: Short for the common Jewish name "Hyman," this Jewish slur got a boost from Reverend Jesse Jackson in 1984 when he referred to Jews as "Hymies" and New York City as "Hymietown." He'd used these terms in a private conversation with a Black *Washington Post* reporter, Milton Coleman, assuming the references wouldn't be printed, but when another reporter wrote an article on Jackson's not-great relations with the American Jews, Coleman contributed the quote. Jackson initially denied the remarks, then accused the Jews of conspiring to defeat him.

Heeb: Short for *Hebrew*; if you're not a member of the tribe, this one's not for you.

Yid: Short for Yiddish; same deal.

Christ killer: We covered it in chapter 11. Enough already!

Appendix B

ASK ME ANYTHING: JEWISH EDITION

NOA: In the name of getting educated, getting informed, and becoming an ally—or at the very least, feeling a little more comfortable when you get invited to a bar mitzvah or your coworker says they keep kosher—I think it's time for a good ol' rapid-fire, nothing-off-limits Ask Me Anything. (Me as in Noa, an occasionally synagogue-going Jew.) We're talking all things Jewish—yarmulke, High Holidays, mezuzah—all the things you wondered about but were maybe too shy to ask . . . or had no idea how to pronounce. Just a little taste of each because different branches of Judaism sometimes have different interpretations (and a hair less sarcasm)—but you'll get the gist.

EMMANUEL: Let the record show I am rubbing my hands together in anticipation. I'll be honest, there is so much that I'm curious about. For example—and please don't judge me—I had no idea that "Shabbat" was the Hebrew word for Sabbath until, like, two months ago. I probably should've put two and two together given that they share the same letters and I've heard about the Sabbath my whole life, but yeah. That goes to show how many similarities people share in life but are completely ignorant about.

All right, walk me through these, then. Let's start with the word I just mentioned, Shabbat.

NOA: Shabbat, or Shabbos, as some Ashkenazi Jews will call it, is the Jewish day of rest. As in, God created the world in six days and on the seventh He rested. It lasts from sunset on Friday evening to sunset on Saturday.

As for how Jews observe Shabbat, it's a huge menu. I always tell my son that every family does Shabbat differently. Some barely notice it, some light Shabbat candles and maybe eat challah (it's one of the major challah moments as far as our rituals go), and some have a special meal that's meant to be a little slower and more meaningful than other nights of the week. People sometimes say prayers: Kiddush to bless the wine; Eshet Chayil or "Woman of Valor," where the woman of the household is blessed by her partner; and the blessing parents say over their children. And some Jews go to synagogue for services on Friday and/or Saturday. Since the Torah commands that we not "work" on Shabbat, some Jews interpret that as not driving, cooking, or using electronics and/or electricity. What I love so much about Shabbat is that, no matter how you observe it, it's a weekly reminder to pause, reflect, and connect with your community.

For extra credit, wish your friends "Shabbat shalom," or "a peaceful Shabbat," on Fridays!

EMMANUEL: I hear my Jewish friends talking about the High Holidays—I'm assuming that has to do with their holiness and not a trip to the dispensary.

NOA: LOL. So, the High Holidays are why the fall is basically a wash for us Jews. It's the Jewish holiday season. You could also call them the High Holy Days, which, no, has nothing (or less) to do with the dispensary than their being some of the most sacred days in our scripture. First up is Rosh Hashanah, which is our New Year's celebration. Since our calendar follows the lunar cycle, our year doesn't sync up with the Gregorian calendar. We also start the count of our years way before most of the world, so this book will actually be published in the year 5784.

Anyway, like any good New Year's, we celebrate, we reflect, we make resolutions. We also eat something sweet, such as apples and/or challah dipped in honey, to symbolize sweetness in the new year, or we have pomegranate so the year will be full of goodness—or at least full of antioxidants. Feel free to wish your friends a Happy New Year, a Sweet New Year, or go all out and text them a "Shana Tova!" Which means "a good year."

A little over a week after Rosh Hashanah comes Yom Kippur, the day of atonement. We apologize—to ourselves, to others, to the world—for any wrongdoings we have inflicted over the course of the previous year, and we do one of the hardest things any Jew could do: we fast from sundown to sundown. Which is why we say to one another, "Wishing you a meaningful fast" and not "Happy Yom Kippur." Of course, we break the fast with an epic feast, and it's on to the next two holidays.

First there's Sukkot, a seven-day-long celebration where we build huts, or sukkahs, to remember the ones the Jews lived in after escaping Egypt. It's a mitzvah or commandment to eat our meals in the sukkah as well as to invite our community to join us, so don't be shy about trying to score an invite. And then there's Simchat Torah, or literally rejoicing of the Torah. There's dancing and singing in celebration of this ancient scroll, and it also marks kicking off another year of reading the entire Torah, which is typically broken up into weekly portions on Shabbat (Saturday) mornings. The October 7th massacre happened on Simchat Torah, one of our holiest days, which will never be the same for the Jewish community.

EMMANUEL: How about keeping kosher? What does that mean? Do you?

NOA: I must say that no, I do not keep kosher. At least not all the time. Sometimes I'm "kosher style," and sometimes I enjoy a cheeseburger. But being kosher is not a deal-breaker when it comes to being Jewish. (At least according to some rabbis.)

Keeping kosher refers to a long (long) list of dietary rules, including things like not mixing meat and dairy in the same meal, as well as not eating certain animals (such as shellfish, birds of prey, and those that have split hooves, such as pigs), and of the animals that can be eaten, they must be killed in accordance with Jewish law, which is considered to be most humane. As for why people keep kosher, it's essentially one more thing that's required as part of our covenant as commanded by the Torah, so it's one more way for us to show our devotion to God.

There's also a wide range of kosher-keeping in between, such as those Jews who keep kosher at home but not outside the home. If a friend or coworker keeps kosher, and you want to be sure to include them in a snack or meal you're planning, don't be afraid to ask for suggestions or guidance!

EMMANUEL: Hit me with a few more that I've most likely missed.

NOA: Let's see. There's:

Yarmulke (ya-muh-kah): The head covering Jewish boys and men, and now some women, wear that symbolizes an awe of God. *Kippa* is the Hebrew word for the same item. Married Jewish women who are observant also cover their hair in public with a scarf, a headband, or a wig called a *sheitel*.

Mezuzah (muh-zu-zuh): You might have noticed in some Jewish homes or businesses a small, decorative case that's hung on the right side of the door frame of the entrance or room. This is a mezuzah, and inside is a little scroll with verses from Deuteronomy that remind Jews of their obligation to God—like your mom telling you to stay out of trouble every time you leave the house.

Bar/Bat Mitzvah: You mentioned that you grew up with a lot of Jewish kids, so this one's not totally new to you. But it's sometimes hard to tell what this is all about besides a blow-out party. Essentially, a bar or bat mitzvah is the celebration of a Jewish boy (age thirteen) or a Jewish girl (age twelve or thirteen) becoming responsible for their own actions and reaching the attainment of "religious majority," meaning they now have the right to read the Torah and recite blessings over it. The ceremony includes reading the Torah and giving a speech in front of your seventh-grade classmates while trying not to die of embarrassment. The preparation for the big day can also include a "mitzvah project," where the bar or bat mitzvah chooses a way to contribute to their community in a charitable, *tikkun olam* (world healing)–inspired way. As for those outrageous parties, they are by no means required, nor does every bar or bat mitzvah have one—although I enjoyed watching them in Adam Sandler's *You Are So Not Invited to My Bat Mitzvah*. No matter how this day looks for the bar or bat mitzvah, it's always appropriate to wish them and their families a hearty "Mazel tov!" or "Congratulations!"

Bris: Or more formally, *brit milah*. The Jewish ceremony where a baby boy is circumcised—which we don't have to get too deep into the whys of because now it's not solely a Jewish or even a religious practice. But it was part of God's original deal with Abraham for entering the covenant, so within the first ten days of a boy's birth, farewell, foreskin. A trained mohel (rhymes with *toil*) performs the ceremony, the new parents cry tears of exhaustion—er, happiness— and everybody eats. It's the same as if the doctor in the hospital performs the procedure, just with cheers and food. And not to worry, there's now a ceremony for girls to enter the covenant called *simchat bat*, which involves no scalpels but just as many bagels.

Tikkun Olam is a concept of repairing the world through our actions. This includes acts of kindness, good deeds, the adherence to God's commandments (also known as *mitzvot*, the plural of *mitzvah*), and righteous acts that make the world a more just place.

Tzedakah (se-dah-kah): A huge part of the Jewish culture is *tzedakah*, which loosely translates to charity. It is a mitzvah, or a mandate by Jewish law, to give to the less fortunate. It's a part of the Jewish tradition and culture, and many Jewish families include charitable donations as part of their annual financial planning. The Jews are only 2.4 percent of the US population, and yet the Jewish community is responsible for about 20 percent of all charitable contributions in America—something that has nothing to do with income. A 2017 report by Giving USA found that American Jews were the most philanthropic across all other faiths, with the average Jewish household averaging $2,526 that year (the next highest was Protestants, with an average of $1,749). Sixty percent of Jewish households earning less than $50,000 a year (yes, there are plenty of Jewish households earning less than $50,000 a year) made charitable donations, compared to 46 percent of non-Jewish households in the same income bracket.

Shiva (shih-va): If you have a Jewish friend and someone in their family passes, you might hear that they'll be "sitting shiva." This is probably one of the most beautiful Jewish traditions as well as the most practical solution to a very primal problem. Sitting shiva, or the formal mourning period that lasts for seven days after someone is buried, is the built-in guarantee that those experiencing the deepest grief will not only not be left alone right after losing a loved one but also that they will never go hungry. Family and friends drop in, bring trays of food, reminisce about the departed, and even laugh. The loveliest thing you can do for a Jewish friend is go visit and sit shiva with them.

Chai: Not like the drink, like "Hi," but with that good back-of-the-throat *cccchhh*. We Jews are a mystical people, and in Hebrew, each letter has a numerical value. When you combine the letter for 8 and the letter for 10, you get the word *chai*, which means life. As in, "L'chaim!" Our toast that means "To Life!" So, the number 18 is a special one and represents good luck, which is why when giving monetary gifts or donations, Jews will frequently give in multiples of 18. A nice little knowledge nugget for the next time you're invited to a Jewish wedding, baby naming, bris, or bar/bat mitzvah.

And a Bisl of Yiddish

NOA: I also couldn't get through this chapter without giving you a taste of some of my favorite Yiddish expressions. Yiddish is the marriage of convenience among German dialects and Hebrew, with words from Romance and Slavic languages sprinkled in. Scholars are still working to agree on how exactly these languages fused together, if only because the migratory paths of Jews escaping violence across Europe are many and tangled. But what we do know is that as this community moved and regrouped, so did their shared language. However, as a result of the Holocaust, when 85 percent of the Jews killed were Yiddish speakers, Yiddish has been classified by UNESCO as an endangered language. But there are many, many words that have been warmly embraced in our English lexicon. To use them is to love them:

> **Bisl** (bissel): From the German *bisen*, which means "bite," as in "a little bit." "A whole shot of tequila? No, just pour me a *bisl*."

> **Chutzpah** (choots-pah): Guts or confidence. "These days it takes real chutzpah to stand up against antisemitism."

Farshteyst (far-shtayst): Despite not being as widely known as some of these others, this one might be my fave. It means "ya know what I mean?" or "you got that?" But in a backhanded way. "Emmanuel, just *look* at these young NFL boys thinking they invented the wheel! *Farshteyst?*"

Kvetch: To complain. "I made my sister a challah and all she did was kvetch that it was too dry."

Mensch (mench): An honorable or decent person. "Emmanuel Acho, what a mensch."

Mishegoss (mih-suh-gahs): Insanity, craziness, or silliness. "Emmanuel, when we're done with all this book *mishegoss*, let's treat ourselves to more than a bisl of tequila."

Mishpocha (mish-poo-cha): Family, also used for close friends. "Emmanuel, we're not just friends, we're *mishpocha*."

Nosh: A snack or nibble—verb or noun. "The first thing I'm going to do when I'm done writing this chapter is put together a little nosh."

Pulkes (pool-kes): Adorably chubby baby thighs—and also, chicken drumstick. Pretty much the nicest thing you can say to a parent about their child. "I want to eat those *pulkes!*"

Putz: Quite literally, a penis—but really, a fool or jerk. *See also* schmuck. "He ghosted you? What a *schmuck*. Only a *putz* couldn't see how amazing you are."

Schlep: To carry something heavy or a long hard trip; usually accompanied by kvetching. "The only reason I'd schlep all the way out to her house through LA traffic is because she knows how to make a mean chicken soup."

Schmutz (shmootz): A little bit of dirt or food, usually on one's face. "Come here and let me clean that schmutz off your mouth." (Proceeds to lick finger and wipe with saliva.)

Tchotchke (choch-kah or kee): A trinket or little object with no function. See also: the contents of at least one shelf in every bubbe's, or Jewish grandmother's, home.

Tuches (tuh-chus): Butt, bootie, backside, bum.

Yenta: A gossip, a busybody. "Of course she had all the good scoop; she's such a yenta."

Zaftig: A voluptuous, curvy woman with the most beautiful body you've ever seen. "What I wouldn't give to have a tuches like the one on that zaftig goddess."

EMMANUEL: Ya know, the only thing I would change about this conversation is when it occurred in my life. I wish this was a conversation I could've had in middle school. This would have allowed me to be a much more well-rounded human. To know more, and to love people better. Noa, I'm forever grateful for you, for your heart, your bravery, but most important, your friendship.

NOA: I mean, we just did in about twenty chapters what ten different books would have done in hundreds of pages each. This was no small task, and I couldn't have asked for a better partner. Thank you for getting curious, getting intense, and, of course, getting uncomfortable.

Recommendations

FOR MORE INSIGHT into and information about the Jewish experience, Israel, and the Middle East, check out these resources:

Read

Letters to My Palestinian Neighbor by Yossi Klein Halevi. An empathetic assessment of Palestinian suffering and paths to reconciliation through the eyes of an Israeli.

Start-up Nation by Dan Senor and Saul Singer. Analysis of how and why Israel has inspired so much innovation, including the world's highest density of tech start-ups.

The Genius of Israel by Dan Senor and Saul Singer. A look at the unique qualities about Israel, its culture, and the policies that have allowed it to thrive.

Here All Along by Sarah Hurwitz. Michelle Obama's former head speechwriter and self-described "lapsed Jew" reflects on her surprising reconnection with Judaism.

Anything and everything written or recorded by Rabbi Jonathan Sacks, formerly Britain's Chief Rabbi and one of the most prominent spiritual advisors in the world. He shares wisdom for how to heal the world through a uniquely Jewish lens.

Anything and everything by Benny Morris. An Israeli historian and professor who provides multiple points of view on major Middle Eastern historical events.

Rise and Kill First by Ronen Bergman. If you want real-life thriller stories of the Israeli Mossad, this is your book.

Israel by me, Noa Tishby. (What can I say? I like this one.) Everything you ever wanted to know about the past, present, and future of Israel in one readable, digestible place.

Follow on Social Media

A Wider Frame. Jewish world news.

Eve Barlow. Scottish journalist and proud Zionist.

IsraelCC. Israel on Campus Coalition for college students.

Michael Rapaport. Comedian, Zionist, and host of the *I Am Rapaport* podcast; go for the humor, stay for the Jewish world news coverage.

Brett Gelman. Actor, Zionist, and host of the *Gelmania* podcast; also Jewish world news with a side of levity.

Debra Messing. Actor and huge-hearted advocate for Israel.

Hen Mazzig. Israeli and senior fellow of the Tel Aviv Institute, a minority group advocacy organization.

The True Adventures. An eighty-nine-year-old Holocaust survivor and his partner espousing peace, love, and understanding.

Blake Flayton. Writer and cohost of the *We Should All Be Zionists* podcast.

Jews of NY. Jewish life in New York and around the world.

Lizzy Savetsky. Pop culture with a stylish splash of Zionism.

Notes

A Word from Noa

xvii *dating back to Alexandria, Egypt*: https://jcpa.org/article/the
      -egyptian-beginning-of-anti-semitism's-long-history/.

xviii *whether Hitler and Osama bin Laden*: https://www.isdglobal
      .org/wp-content/uploads/2021/08/HateScape_v5.pdf.

xviii *biggest spike in anti-Jewish rhetoric*: https://www.npr.org/2022
      /11/30/1139971241/anti-semitism-is-on-the-rise
      -and-not-just-among-high-profile-figures.

xviii *sympathizing with bin Laden*: https://www.cnn.com/2023/11
      /16/tech/tiktok-osama-bin-laden-letter-to-america/index
      .html.

xix   *religion-based attacks*: https://www.whitehouse.gov/briefing
      -room/speeches-remarks/2023/05/25/remarks-of-second
      -gentleman-douglas-emhoff-at-the-launch-of-the-u-s
      -national-strategy-to-counter-antisemitism/.

xxi   *C-SPAN*: https://www.c-span.org/video/?c5093458/noa-tish
      by-full.

2: The Name Game: Who (or What) on Earth *Is* a Jew?

12   *oldest surviving monotheistic religion*: https://www.britannica
      .com/story/which-religion-is-the-oldest.

13   *region of West Asia*: https://janes.scholasticahq.com/article
      /2450-numbers-34-2-12-the-boundaries-of-the-land-of
      -canaan-and-the-empire-of-necho/attachment/6391.pdf.

13   *Quran as, well, Israel*: Noa Tishby, *Israel: A Simple Guide to the
      Most Misunderstood Country on Earth* (New York: Free Press,
      2021), 4.

13 *2,700-year-old seal:* https://www.cnn.com/2015/12/03/middle
    east/king-hezekiah-royal-seal/index.html.

14 *existed somewhere between*: https://www.biblicalarchaeology.org
    /daily/ancient-cultures/ancient-israel/does-the-merneptah
    -stele-contain-the-first-mention-of-israel/.

15 *Rabbi Jeremy Borovitz*: Director of Jewish Learning for Hillel
    Deutschland in Berlin.

19 *Rabbi Sharon Brous*: Founder and Senior Rabbi of Ikar, a Jewish
    community rooted in Los Angeles.

3: The Culture Club

27 *"They tried to kill us, we won, let's eat"*: https://www.abc.net.au
    /news/2004-05-10/comedian-alan-king-dies-at-76-in-new
    -york/1972974?pfmredir=sm&pfm=sm.

30 *(compulsory education!)*: https://www.pbs.org/newshour/economy
    /the-chosen-few-a-new-explanati.

30 *lick it off*: https://www.ynet.co.il/articles/1,7340,L-3946766,00
    .html.

30 *"this-life-focused religion"*: https://www.youtube.com/watch?v=
    _ao4u1FuIOM&ab_channel=JewishLearningInstitute.

30 *"in some other life"*: https://www.youtube.com/watch?v=_ao4u1
    FuIOM&ab_channel=JewishLearningInstitute.

4: The Jewish . . . Race?

34 *(formerly known as Gypsy)*: https://encyclopedia.ushmm.org
    /content/en/article/aryan-1.

35 *social, not biological, construct*: https://www.ncbi.nlm.nih.gov
    /pmc/articles/PMC3543766.

6: You're Not White Enough

42 *Lady Liberty's doorstep*: https://nationalhumanitiescenter.org
    /tserve/twenty/tkeyinfo/jewishexp.htm#:~:text=Be
    tween1900and1924%2C%20another,formed%20about%20
    3%EF%BF%BD%20percent.

42 *accepting lower wages*: https://siepr.stanford.edu/news/what
    -history-tells-us-about-assimilation-immigrants.

43   *criminals and charity abusers*: Thomas C. Leonard, *Illiberal Re-
      formers: Race, Eugenics and American Economics in the Progressive
      Era* (Princeton, NJ: Princeton University Press, 2016).

43   *tween of a global power*: Richard L. McCormick, *The Party Pe-
      riod and Public Policy: American Politics from the Age of Jackson to
      the Progressive Era* (New York: Oxford University Press, 1986),
      281; and James F. Smith, *A Nation that Welcomes Immigrants?:
      An Historical Examination of United States Immigration Policy*
      (Sacramento, CA: U.C. Davis Journal of International Law and
      Policy, 1995).

43   *"socially unfit traits"*: https://www.salon.com/2014/03/23/hitlers
      _favorite_american_biological_fascism_in_the_shadow_of
      _new_york_city/.

43   *"White gene pool"*: https://www.washingtonpost.com/dc-md-va
      /2023/01/24/geneticists-eugenics-apology/.

43   *to the bank*: https://www.salon.com/2014/03/23/hitlers_favorite
      _american_biological_fascism_in_the_shadow_of_new_york
      _city/.

44   *on his scale*: https://www.tabletmag.com/sections/history
      /articles/jewish-whiteness-blackness-tudor-parfitt.

44   *and Black origins*: https://www.tabletmag.com/sections/history
      /articles/jewish-whiteness-blackness-tudor-parfitt.

44   *quite an impression*: https://www.jewishvirtuallibrary.org/quot
      -the-international-jew-quot; and https://reformjudaism.org
      /blog/henry-fords-apology.

44   *"as my inspiration"*: https://www.bridgemi.com/michigan
      -government/henry-ford-and-jews-story-dearborn-didnt
      -want-told.

45   *cake or death*: https://www.youtube.com/watch?v=PVH0gZO
      5lq0.

46   *"to do it"*: https://forward.com/culture/450247/mccarthy-was
      -anti-communist-was-he-also-anti-semitic/.

46   *otherwise humiliated*: https://jwa.org/teach/livingthelegacy
      /jewish-radicalism-and-red-scare-introductory-essay; and June
      Melby Benowitz, "Jewish Organisations' Response to Com-
      munism and to Senator McCarthy (review)," *American Jew-
      ish History* 94, no. 3 (2008): 264–66, https://doi.org/10.1353
      /ajh.0.0073.

7: You're Too White

49 *those two positions*: https://www.theatlantic.com/politics/archive /2016/12/are-jews-white/509453/.

52 *in 1995*: https://www.theatlantic.com/politics/archive/2016/12 /are-jews-white/509453/.

52 388 *percent*: https://www.adl.org/resources/press-release/adl -records-dramatic-increase-us-antisemitic-incidents -following-oct-7.

52 *"historic levels"*: https://www.bbc.com/news/world-us-canada -67281042.

8: The Mythical Me: Where Truth Ends and Stereotypes Begin

58 *Exodus 34:29*: https://biblehub.com/exodus/34-29.htm.

59 *"grew horns"*: https://www.myjewishlearning.com/article/anti -semitic-stereotypes-of-the-jewish-body/.

59 *Hebrew would have avoided*: https://www.thetorah.com/article /moses-shining-or-horned-face.

59 *mega horn-bearer himself*: https://www.degruyter.com/document /doi/10.1515/9783110671773-004/html?lang=en.

59 *Jew crew*: https://www.amazon.co.uk/Devil-Jews-Medieval -Conception-Anti-Semitism/dp/0827602278.

59 *Jews and Their Lies*: https://www.degruyter.com/document /doi/10.1515/9783110671773-004/html?lang=en.

60 *as the thirteenth century*: https://www.nybooks.com/online/2016 /06/06/the-first-anti-jewish-caricature/.

60 *Jews as capitalist infiltrators*: https://dh.scu.edu/exhibits /exhibits/show/the-cold-war--2022-/soviet-union-propaganda /1970s-propaganda/anti-semitism-in-the-soviet-un.

62 *about 1.1 percent*: https://economictimes.indiatimes.com/news /company/corporate-trends/christians-hold-largest-percentage -of-global-wealth-report/articleshow/45886471.cms.

62 *worldwide wealth*: https://economictimes.indiatimes.com/news /company/corporate-trends/christians-hold-largest-percentage -of-global-wealth-report/articleshow/45886471.cms.

9: The Math Ain't Mathing: Jews, Money, and Power

63   *borrowed was verboten*: https://www.myjewishlearning.com /article/jewish-moneylending/.

64   *Talmudic Sages cosigned*: https://www.myjewishlearning.com /article/jewish-moneylending/.

64   *less honorable connotation*: https://www.jewishhistory.org/the -rothschilds/.

64   *the nobleman killed him*: https://www.jewishhistory.org/the -rothschilds/.

64   *to pay increasing taxes*: https://www.myjewishlearning.com /article/jewish-moneylending/.

64   *they were literate*: https://www.myjewishlearning.com/article /jewish-moneylending/; and https://www.pbs.org/newshour /economy/the-chosen-few-a-new-explanati#:~:text=A%20 popular%20view%20contends%20that,moneylending%20 during%20the%20Middle%20Ages.

64   *political and economic turmoil*: https://academic.oup.com /restud/article/87/1/289/5280103.

65   *motor of European capitalism*: https://themarginaliareview .com/jewish-moneylending-questioning-paradigms-shattering -myths/.

65   *between 1933 and 1939*: https://www.smithsonianmag.com /arts-culture/why-scholars-still-debate-whether-or-not -shakespeares-merchant-venice-anti-semitic-180958867/; and https://www.nytimes.com/1993/04/04/theater/theater-shy lock-and-nazi-propaganda.html.

69   *slaughtered in Russian and Ukrainian pogroms*: https://www .timesofisrael.com/20-years-before-the-holocaust-pogroms -killed-100000-jews-then-were-forgotten/.

71   *emerging professions like law*: https://www.rollingstone.com /tv-movies/tv-movie-features/jews-in-hollywood-kanye-west -dave-chappelle-rabbi-explains-1234645366/.

71   *"unsuitable" for white Christians*: https://www.rollingstone.com /tv-movies/tv-movie-features/jews-in-hollywood-kanye-west -dave-chappelle-rabbi-explains-1234645366/.

71   *to get mixed up with*: https://www.rollingstone.com/tv-movies /tv-movie-features/jews-in-hollywood-kanye-west-dave -chappelle-rabbi-explains-1234645366/.

71 *slowly but surely built their own*: https://jewishunpacked.com /how-american-jews-built-hollywood/.

71 *and Universal*: https://www.rollingstone.com/tv-movies/tv-movie -features/jews-in-hollywood-kanye-west-dave-chappelle -rabbi-explains-1234645366/.

71 *(George Burns)*: https://www.rollingstone.com/tv-movies/tv-movie -features/jews-in-hollywood-kanye-west-dave-chappelle -rabbi-explains-1234645366/.

72 *Communist witch hunts*: https://www.britannica.com/topic /Hollywood-Ten.

73 *and the media*: chrome-extension://efaidnbmnnnibpcajpcglcle findmkaj/https://antisemitism.org.uk/wp-content/uploads /2020/07/Antisemitic-imagery-May-2020.pdf.

73 *believe in some part to be true*: https://www.washingtonpost. com/dc-md-va/2023/01/12/antisemitism-anti-defamation -league-survey/.

74 *"get what they want"*: https://www.washingtonpost.com/dc-md -va/2023/01/12/antisemitism-anti-defamation-league -survey/.

11: Did the Jews Kill Jesus?

87 *JC's death*: https://www.npr.org/2011/03/04/134264425/Pope -Jews-Are-Not-Responsible-For-Killing-Jesus; and https:// www.washingtonpost.com/national/on-faith/vatican-ii-the -beginning-of-the-end-of-catholic-anti-semitism/2012 /10/25/f2a2356e-1ee2-11e2-8817-41b9a7aaabc7_story .html.

12: The Antisemitism Layer Cake

89 *space lasers*: https://nymag.com/intelligencer/article/marjorie -taylor-greene-qanon-wildfires-space-laser-rothschild -execute.html.

91 *back in 1879*: https://www.britannica.com/topic/anti-Semitism.

91 *(spoken in Ethiopia)*: https://www.adl.org/spelling-antisemitism -vs-anti-semitism.

93 *which historian you ask*: https://www.biblicalarchaeology.org /daily/biblical-topics/exodus/exodus-fact-or-fiction/.

93   *secret rituals*: https://jewishstudies.washington.edu/who-are
-jews-jewish-history-origins-antisemitism/.

94   *they themselves were Jewish*: https://jewishstudies.washington
.edu/who-are-jews-jewish-history-origins-antisemitism/.

94   *propaganda in the West*: https://jewishstudies.washington.edu
/who-are-jews-jewish-history-origins-antisemitism/.

94   *throughout the Roman Empire*: https://jewishstudies.washington
.edu/who-are-jews-jewish-history-origins-antisemitism/.

94   *ad nauseam from then on*: https://www.britannica.com/event
/First-Jewish-Revolt.

94   *religion of the Roman Empire*: chrome-extension://efaidnbmnnni
bpcajpcglclefindmkaj/https://www.adl.org/sites/default/files
/brief-history-of-antisemitism.pdf.

95   *531 CE*: http://vlib.iue.it/carrie/texts/carrie_books/seaver/text
.html; and https://www.adl.org/sites/default/files/brief-history
-of-antisemitism.pdf.

95   *economic opportunities for Jews*: https://yivoencyclopedia.org
/article.aspx/Economic_Life.

95   *assaults on Jewish communities*: https://www.haaretz.com
/jewish/2014-05-27/ty-article/this-day-massacre-in-mainz
/0000017f-e712-df2c-a1ff-ff53c2230000.

95   *through to the Holocaust*: https://www.jewishvirtuallibrary.org
/the-crusades.

96   *celebration of Passover*: https://www.thenation.com/article/archive
/the-origins-of-blood-libel/.

96   *patron saint for the city*: https://www.thenation.com/article
/archive/the-origins-of-blood-libel/.

96   *unfortunate or tragic event*: https://www.thenation.com/article
/archive/the-origins-of-blood-libel/.

96   *"by historical evidence"*: https://www.thenation.com/article
/archive/the-origins-of-blood-libel/.

97   *rejecting and killing Christ*: Robert Michael, *A History of Catholic Antisemitism: The Dark Side of the Church* (New York: Pal-
grave Macmillan, 2011), 51.

97   *lived in the first place*: chrome-extension://efaidnbmnnnibp
cajpcglclefindmkaj/https://files.eric.ed.gov/fulltext
/EJ1169250.pdf.

97   *destroy Christianity*: https://www.jewishvirtuallibrary.org/the
-black-death.

97   *frequent handwashing*: https://www.ncbi.nlm.nih.gov/pmc/articles/PMC9632745/.

97   *burnt alive*: https://www.jewishvirtuallibrary.org/the-black-death.

97   *for Jesus's death*: https://www.washingtonpost.com/national/on-faith/vatican-ii-the-beginning-of-the-end-of-catholic-anti-semitism/2012/10/25/f2a2356e-1ee2-11e2-8817-41b9a7aaabc7_story.html.

98   *expulsions for Jews*: https://www.jewishvirtuallibrary.org/the-spanish-expulsion-1492.

98   *buying political support*: https://www.npr.org/2019/03/07/700901834/minnesota-congresswoman-ignites-debate-on-israel-and-anti-semitism; and https://www.cbsnews.com/minnesota/news/ilhan-omar-twitter-anti-semitism-aipac-its-all-about-the-benjamins/.

98   *"hypnotized the world"*: https://www.cbsnews.com/minnesota/news/ilhan-omar-twitter-anti-semitism-aipac-its-all-about-the-benjamins/.

99   *for one Adolf Hitler*: https://www.britannica.com/biography/Karl-Lueger.

100 *part of the world*: https://aish.com/catherine-the-great-and-the-jews-5-facts/.

100 *Order of Expulsion*: https://aish.com/catherine-the-great-and-the-jews-5-facts/.

100 *Jewish life in Russia*: https://jewoughtaknow.com/assassination-of-czar-alexander-ii.

100 *Pale of Settlement*: https://kids.britannica.com/students/article/Jewish-Pale-of-Settlement/332366#:~:text=Ascending%20to%20the%20throne%20in,the%20boundaries%20of%20the%20Pale.

100 *And it was so*: https://www.juf.org/news/campaign.aspx?id=443567.

101 *all-controlling global cabal*: https://www.adl.org/sites/default/files/brief-history-of-antisemitism.pdf.

101 *through Jewish villages*: https://www.adl.org/sites/default/files/brief-history-of-antisemitism.pdf; and https://encyclopedia.ushmm.org/content/en/article/pogroms.

101 *children had been murdered*: https://www.adl.org/sites/default/files/brief-history-of-antisemitism.pdf.

101 *interest in Zionism*: https://jewoughtaknow.com/assassination

-of-czar-alexander-ii; and https://aish.com/catherine-the great
-and-the-jews-5-facts/.

102 *Babylon in 586 BCE*: https://medium.com/@Ksantini/the-list
-of-crimes-committed-by-muslims-against-jews-since-the
-7th-century-0ff1a8eb0ad0.

102 *"ritual murders" took the blame*: https://slate.com/news-and
-politics/2001/10/the-roots-of-arab-anti-semitism.html.

102 *advancement and modernization*: https://rpl.hds.harvard.edu
/faq/young-turks.

103 *made matters worse*: https://encyclopedia.1914-1918-online
.net/article/post-war_economies_germany#:~:text=In%20
quantitative%20terms%2C%20the%20economic,levels%20
for%20the%20first%20time.

103 *conspiring to take over the world*: https://slate.com/news-and
-politics/2001/10/the-roots-of-arab-anti-semitism.html.

107 *and/or oneself*: https://irows.ucr.edu/cd/courses/232/pyke/intra
copp.pdf.

107 *And never will be*: https://irows.ucr.edu/cd/courses/232/pyke
/intracopp.pdf.

108 *"anti-semitism is a light sleeper"*: https://www.oxfordreference
.com/display/10.1093/acref/9780191826719.001.0001/q-oro
-ed4-00016287.

109 *attacked in broad daylight*: https://www.nytimes.com/2022
/04/26/nyregion/antisemitic-attacks-new-york.html.

109 *marred or toppled*: https://abcnews.go.com/US/dozens-graves
-jewish-cemetery-defaced-swastikas-offensive-graffiti
/story?id=93325341; and https://www.cnn.com/2019/03/21
/us/hebrew-cemetery-vandalism-trnd/index.html.

109 *Jews in American history*: https://www.washingtonpost.com
/nation/2018/10/28/victims-expected-be-named-after-killed
-deadliest-attack-jews-us-history/.

109 *don't need their job*: https://fortune.com/2023/01/11/hiring
-jewish-people-antisemitism-workplace-study/.

109 *spreads like wildfire*: https://www.theguardian.com/media
/2021/aug/01/a-safe-space-for-racists-antisemitism-report
-criticises-social-media-giants.

109 *Jokers to the Right*: "Stuck in the Middle With You" by Stealers
Wheel.

110 *January 6th*: https://www.adl.org/resources/report/antisemitic

-conspiracies-about-911-endure-20-years-later; and https://
www.adl.org/resources/blog/antisemites-implicate-jews
-zionists-dc-violence.

110   *China and Iran*: https://www.jstor.org/stable/pdf/resrep26356
.12.pdf.

14: The Holocaust, Part I: The (Very Real) History

118   *every single day*: https://encyclopedia.ushmm.org/content/en
/article/gassing-operations.

119   *one million people died*: https://www.auschwitz.org/en/history
/auschwitz-and-shoah/the-number-of-victims/.

122   *struggling national identity*: https://www.theholocaustexplained
.org/stab-in-the-back-myth/.

124   *over the course of twelve years*: https://www.statista.com/chart
/24024/number-of-victims-nazi-regime/.

124   *"Holocaust is a myth"*: https://d3nkl3psvxxpe9.cloudfront.net
/documents/econTabReport_tT4jyzG.pdf?utm_source
=Holocaust+Center&utm_campaign=9a3eae595d-EMAIL
_CAMPAIGN_2023_07_17_10_37_COPY_01&utm_medium
=email&utm_term=0_-41d61e4ad8-%5BLIST_EMAIL
_ID%5D.

124   *two million or fewer*: https://www.claimscon.org/millennial
-study/.

124   *ghettos overall*: https://www.claimscon.org/millennial-study/.

124   *who caused the Holocaust*: https://www.claimscon.org/millennial
-study/.

125   *"psychological distress"*: https://www.axios.com/2023/01/07/holo
caust-genocide-education-state-laws; and https://www.sltrib
.com/religion/2021/10/18/commentary-there-are-no/.

125   *House Bill 3979*: https://www.theatlantic.com/magazine/archive
/2023/05/holocaust-student-education-jewish-anti-semitism
/673488/.

127   *existence in Germany*: Deborah Hertz, *How Jews Became Germans: The History of Conversion and Assimilation in Berlin* (New
Haven, London: Yale University Press, 2007), www.jstor.org
/stable/j.ctt5vktjn.

127   *military service*: https://www.ushmm.org/teach/fundamentals
/holocaust-questions.

128   *Jewish-led grab for world domination*: https://www.amazon
      .com/Specter-Haunting-Europe-Myth-Judeo-Bolshevismdp
      /0674047680?asin=0674047680&revisionId=&format=4&
      depth=1.

128   *plotting to take over the world*: https://www.amazon.com
      /Specter-Haunting-Europe-Myth-Judeo-Bolshevismdp
      /0674047680?asin=0674047680&revisionId=&format
      =4&depth=1.

128   *the Nazi Party*: https://encyclopedia.ushmm.org/content/en
      /article/world-war-i-aftermath.

129   *attempting to control Germany*: https://encyclopedia.ushmm
      .org/content/en/timeline-event/holocaust/before-1933/adolf
      -hitler-issues-comment-on-the-jewish-question.

129   *book*, Mein Kampf: https://www.yadvashem.org/docs/extracts
      -from-mein-kampf.html.

129   *world-domination aspirations*: https://www.facinghistory.org
      /resource-library/myth-jewish-conspiracy.

129   *"stab-in-the-back myth"*: https://encyclopedia.ushmm.org/con
      tent/en/timeline-event/holocaust/before-1933/hindenburg
      -spreads-stab-in-the-back-myth.

130   *"member of the nation"*: https://encyclopedia.ushmm.org/content
      /en/article/nazi-party-platform.

130   *regardless of social status*: https://encyclopedia.ushmm.org
      /content/en/article/nazi-party-platform.

130   *humanity itself*: https://www.csustan.edu/sites/default/files
      /honors/documents/journals/thresholds/Farhadian.pdf.

130   *Romany (formerly Gypsies), the Polish, and above all: Jews*:
      https://www.csustan.edu/sites/default/files/honors/documents
      /journals/thresholds/Farhadian.pdf.

131   *suppress publications*: https://encyclopedia.ushmm.org/content
      /en/timeline-event/holocaust/1933-1938/reichstag-fire
      -decree.

131   *became a police state*: https://encyclopedia.ushmm.org/content
      /en/article/the-enabling-act.

131   *wrote … Mein Kampf*: https://encyclopedia.ushmm.org/content
      /en/timeline-event/holocaust/before-1933/beer-hall-putsch.

131   *"devoid of men"*: https://www.yadvashem.org/docs/extracts-from
      -mein-kampf.html.

132   limits to his authority: https://encyclopedia.ushmm.org/content

/en/timeline-event/holocaust/1933-1938/death-of-german -president-von-hindenburg.

132 *outside of Munich*: https://encyclopedia.ushmm.org/content/en /timeline-event/holocaust/1933-1938/establishment -of-dachau-camp.

132 *forced to leave German schools*: https://encyclopedia.ushmm.org /content/en/timeline-event/holocaust/1933-1938/law-limits -jews-in-public-schools.

132 *boycott Jewish-owned businesses*: https://encyclopedia.ushmm .org/content/en/article/boycott-of-jewish-businesses.

132 *"race defilement"*: https://encyclopedia.ushmm.org/content/en /article/the-nuremberg-race-laws.

132 *justified by "aryanization"*: https://www.smithsonianmag.com /history/1938-nazi-law-forced-jews-register-their-wealth making-it-easier-steal-180968894/.

132 *"Decree for the Reporting of Jewish-Owned Property"*: https: //www.smithsonianmag.com/history/1938-nazi-law-forced -jews-register-their-wealthmaking-it-easier-steal-180968894/.

133 *when in public*: https://encyclopedia.ushmm.org/content/en /article/the-nuremberg-race-laws.

134 *plumbing or heating*: https://encyclopedia.ushmm.org/content /en/article/life-in-the-ghettos.

134 *"None is too many"*: https://www.thecanadianencyclopedia.ca /en/article/none-is-too-many; and https://cbra.library.utoronto .ca/items/show/38794.

134 *254 of them died*: https://encyclopedia.ushmm.org/content/en /article/voyage-of-the-st-louis.

135 *lovers' spat*: https://en.wikipedia.org/wiki/Herschel_Grynszpan #:~:text=The%20problem%20was%20their%20belief,been%20 court%2Dmartialed%20for%20homosexuality.

135 *"Night of Broken Glass"*: https://encyclopedia.ushmm.org /content/en/article/kristallnacht.

135 *$400 million*: https://encyclopedia.ushmm.org/content/en/article /kristallnacht.

136 *and Sobibor*: https://www.jewishvirtuallibrary.org/how-many -concentration-camps.

137 *"extermination through labor"*: Marc Buggeln, *Slave Labor in Nazi Concentration Camps* (Oxford: Oxford University Press, 2014), 335; https://www.timesofisrael.com/german-car-maker

-audi-reveals-nazi-past/; and https://encyclopedia.ushmm.org
/content/en/article/bayer#:~:text=Most%20of%20the%20
experiments%20were,%2C%20dipht.heria%2C%20and%20
other%20diseases.

137 *cataclysmic event*: https://www.theatlantic.com/magazine/archive
/2023/05/holocaust-student-education-jewish-anti
-semitism/673488/.

15: The Holocaust, Part II: The (Very Real) Aftermath

140 *Oskar Schindler*: https://encyclopedia.ushmm.org/content/en
/article/oskar-schindler.

140 *Raoul Wallenberg*: https://encyclopedia.ushmm.org/content
/en/article/raoul-wallenberg-and-the-rescue-of-jews-in
-budapest.

140 *"individual choices"*: https://www.ushmm.org/teach/fundamentals
/holocaust-questions.

141 *distortion content*: https://www.un.org/en/delegate/un-report
-social-media-feeds-holocaust-denial-and-distortion.

141 *committed during the Holocaust*: https://www.ushmm.org/anti
semitism/holocaust-denial-and-distortion/holocaust-denial
-antisemitism-iran/2016-holocaust-cartoon-contests-in-iran
/timeline; https://time.com/5128341/poland-holocaust-law/;
and https://www.npr.org/2018/06/27/623865367/poland-back
tracks-on-a-controversial-holocaust-speech-law.

142 tons *of records*: "Combating Holocaust Denial: Evidence of the
Holocaust Presented at Nuremberg," United States Holocaust
Memorial Museum, retrieved June 4, 2020.

142 *Database of Survivor and Victim Names*: https://www.ushmm
.org/online/hsv/source_view.php?SourceId=32662.

143 *anxiety and the posttraumatic stress disorder (PTSD)*: https://www
.sciencedirect.com/science/article/abs/pii/S0165032723003348;
and https://www.ncbi.nlm.nih.gov/pmc/articles/PMC9175561/.

143 *have PTSD*: Emmanuel Acho, *Uncomfortable Conversations
with a Black Man* (New York: Flatiron Books, 2020), 139.

146 *and get stronger*: https://www.apa.org/monitor/2016/11/growth
-trauma.

16: How This Book Almost Didn't Happen

151 *"bean counting"*: https://www.democracynow.org/2023/10/13 /noura_erakat_palestine_gaza_israel.

151 *designated terrorist organization*: https://twitter.com/4noura /status/1710679040389239044; https://twitter.com/4noura /status/1710722756663480821; and https://twitter.com /4noura/status/1580932481892913153?lang=en.

152 *through the streets of Gaza*: https://www.dailymail.co.uk/news /article-12757487/Hamas-terrorist-spat-paraded-Shani -Louks-body-Gaza-killed-rabbi-claims.html.

154 *countries in the 1800s*: https://www.jewishvirtuallibrary.org /the-damascus-blood-libel.

155 *explicitly states their mission*: https://www.palestine-studies.org /sites/default/files/attachments/jps-articles/2538093.pdf.

17: The Z Word

161 *"You are my brother"*: Tishby, *Israel*, 65; and Theodore Herzl, *The Old New Land* (Leipzig: Hermann Seemann Nachfolger, 1902).

161 *form this state*: https://www.jewishvirtuallibrary.org/first-zionist -congress-and-basel-program-1897.

165 *Second Temple of Jerusalem*: https://www.jewishvirtuallibrary .org/the-return-to-zion-538-142-bce.

166 *national sovereignty*: https://www.britannica.com/topic/Macca bees.

166 *a couple hundred years*: https://www.britannica.com/topic /Hasmonean-dynasty.

166 *crush the uprising*: https://www.britannica.com/event/First -Jewish-Revolt.

166 *(which they also did)*: https://www.worldhistory.org/The_Bar -Kochba_Revolt/.

166 *nod to the Philistines*: https://www.britannica.com/place/Palestine.

166 *most likely Greeks*: https://www.newscientist.com/article/220 8581-ancient-dna-reveals-that-jews-biblical-rivals-were -from-greece/.

167 *in the Bible*: https://www.biblicalarchaeology.org/daily/people -cultures-in-the-bible/who-were-philistines-where-did-they -come-from/.

167   *Khalil Beidas in 1898*: https://en.wikipedia.org/wiki/Palestin
       ians.

167   *emerged in the late nineteenth century*: https://yplus.ps/wp
       -content/uploads/2021/01/Khalidi-Rashid-Palestinian-Iden
       tity.pdf.

167   *how that went for the Jews*: Tishby, *Israel*, 32.

168   *the Caliphate*: Ibid., 32.

168   *lower than their neighbors'*: Ibid., 32.

168   *enslavement of the rest*: https://www.jewishvirtuallibrary.org
       /the-crusades.

168   *conversions to Islam, or exile*: Tishby, *Israel*, 33.

169   *Wilderness of Zin*: https://www.amazon.com/Wilderness-Zin
       -T-Lawrence/dp/1575060779.

169   *a Russian Jew*: https://stevenewmanwriter.medium.com/t-e
       -lawrence-chaim-weizmann-7b507f486962.

169   *wanted to help the Arabs*: Tishby, *Israel*, 44.

169   *"spots in a desert"*: Ibid., 44.

170   *Balfour Declaration*: https://www.britannica.com/topic/Balfour
       -Report; https://avalon.law.yale.edu/20th_Century/balfour.asp.

170   *Sykes-Picot Agreement*: https://www.britannica.com/event
       /Sykes-Picot-Agreement.

171   *pissing off both Arabs and Jews*: https://www.britannica.com
       /place/Palestine/World-War-I-and-after.

172   *"wrestles with God and prevails"*: https://www.biblegateway
       .com/passage/?search=Genesis%2032%3A22-32&
       version=CEV.

18: Peace, Love, and Hummus

174   *land titles*: https://slate.com/news-and-politics/2001/10/the
       -roots-of-arab-anti-semitism.html.

174   *"bent on world domination"*: https://slate.com/news-and-politics
       /2001/10/the-roots-of-arab-anti-semitism.html.

175   *1936 to 1939*: https://www.britannica.com/place/Palestine
       /The-Arab-Revolt.

175   *Haj Amin Al-Husseini*: https://encyclopedia.ushmm.org/con
       tent/en/article/hajj-amin-al-husayni-key-dates.

175   *"Five Million Jews"*: https://slate.com/news-and-politics/2001
       /10/the-roots-of-arab-anti-semitism.html.

176   *volunteers from Egypt*: Tishby, *Israel*, 107.

176   *partition of Palestine*: https://encyclopedia.ushmm.org/content /en/article/hajj-amin-al-husayni-key-dates.

177   *ordered them to leave*: and https://content.time.com/time/sub scriber/article/0,33009,798519,00.html; and https://www.jewish virtuallibrary.org/myths-and-facts-the-refugees#24.

177   *impending war*: https://content.time.com/time/subscriber/article /0,33009,798519,00.html.

177   *becoming Israeli citizens*: https://www.cfr.org/backgrounder /what-know-about-arab-citizens-israel#:~:text=After%20 more%20than%20700%2C000%20of,about%20half%20of%20 Israel%27s%20population.

177   *"has died down"*: https://www.jewishvirtuallibrary.org/myths -and-facts-the-refugees#24.

178   *"overthrow the situation"*: https://www.nytimes.com/2023/11 /08/world/middleeast/hamas-israel-gaza-war.html.

179   *$6.5 billion*: https://jij.org/wp-content/uploads/2017/05/JIJ -Fact-Sheet-2-Money-EN-A4-ver-12.pdf.

19: The New Face of Antisemitism

183   *Legitimacy of the State of Israel*: https://en.wikipedia.org/wiki /Legitimacy_of_the_State_of_Israel.

185   *convert to Communism*: https://www.jewishpolicycenter.org /2022/04/08/exposing-the-soviet-lie-of-israeli-apartheid/.

185   *falsely confess*: https://www.britannica.com/event/Doctors-Plot.

186   *calculating, bloodthirsty Jew*: https://www.jewishvirtuallibrary .org/the-doctor-s-plot.

186   *lobbed a bomb*: https://israeled.org/soviet-embassy-bombed-in -tel-aviv/.

186   *interchangeable with antisemitism*: https://www.international affairs.org.au/australianoutlook/red-terror-how-the-soviet -union-shaped-the-modern-anti-zionist-discourse/; https://www .ncbi.nlm.nih.gov/pmc/articles/PMC139050/; and https://en .wikipedia.org/wiki/Doctors%27_plot.

186   *United Nations subcommission*: https://legal.un.org/avl/pdf/ha /cerd/cerd_ph_e.pdf.

186   *"elimination of all forms of racial discrimination"*: https://www .un.org/unispal/document/auto-insert-181963/; https://www

.jstor.org/stable/23605353; and https://legal.un.org/avl/ha/cerd
/cerd.html.

186 *So, the Soviets*: https://www.academia.edu/35771145/The
_USSR_and_the_analogy_between_Zionism_and_racism
_Precedents_of_UNGA_Resolution_3379.

186 *promoted racial superiority*: https://www.ajc.org/news/10-tough
-questions-on-antisemitism-explained.

187 *"racism and racial discrimination"*: https://www.academia.edu
/35771145/The_USSR_and_the_analogy_between_Zionism_
and_racism_Precedents_of_UNGA_Resolution_3379.

187 *"selective prosecution"*: https://unwatch.org/database/.

187 *To Israel?*: https://unwatch.org/database/; and https://docs
.house.gov/meetings/FA/FA06/20230622/116138/HHRG
-118-FA06-Wstate-NeuerH-20230622.pdf.

187 *members of Hamas*: https://forward.com/fast-forward/569283
/rape-kits-forensic-evidence-oct-7-times-of-israel/.

187 *condemnation of antisemitism*: https://legal.un.org/avl/ha/cerd
/cerd.html.

187 *"international sanction"*: https://www.americanrhetoric.com
/speeches/danielpatrickmoynihanun3379.html.

188 *tool of war in Sudan*: https://www.ohchr.org/en/press-releases
/2023/11/sudan-un-experts-appalled-use-sexual-violence
-tool-war.

188 *rest of humanity*: https://bdsmovement.net/.

188 *allegations were credible enough*: https://www.nytimes.com
/2024/01/28/world/middleeast/gaza-unrwa-hamas-israel
.html; and https://www.forbes.com/sites/zacharyfolk/2024/
01/29/what-we-know-about-the-dossier-accusing-190-un
-employees-of-ties-to-hamas/?sh=70f06ee8725d.

189 *"Jewish state in Palestine"*: https://www.jewishvirtuallibrary.org
/bds-in-their-own-words.

189 *"you say you are"*: https://www.jewishvirtuallibrary.org/bds-in
-their-own-words.

190 *eradicate Israel*: https://www.nytimes.com/2019/07/27/world
/middleeast/bds-israel-boycott-antisemitic.html.

190 *do business with Israel*: https://ustr.gov/sites/default/files/2013
%20NTE%20Arab%20League%20Final.pdf.

193 *martyrdom and jihad do*: https://www.samharris.org/blog/the
-bright-line-between-good-and-evil.

20: How to Not Lose Friends and Alienate People

199 *Islam is the official state religion*: https://www.pewresearch
.org/religion/2017/10/03/many-countries-favor-specific
-religions-officially-or-unofficially/#:~:text=Nine%20of%20
these%20countries%20are,as%20their%20official%20state%20
religion.

199 *Christianity is the official state religion*: https://www.uscirf
.gov/publications/did-you-knowmuslim-constitutions#:~:text
=The%2023%20countries%20where%20Islam,United%20
Arab%20Emirates%2C%20and%20Yemen.

199 *hundreds if not thousands of rockets*: https://www.jewishvirtual
library.org/palestinian-rocket-and-mortar-attacks-against
-israel.

201 *US Presidential Medal of Freedom*: https://www.jpost.com
/international/sharansky-gets-presidential-medal-of
-freedom.

201 *Department of State in 2010*: Tishby, *Israel*, 205.

201 *sites of other religions*: Ibid., 280.

202 *larger British colonies*: https://www.history.ox.ac.uk/why-was
-british-india-partitioned-in-1947-considering-the
-role-of-muhammad-ali-0#:~:text='The%20Long%20Part
ition',%2C%20present%2Dday%20Bangladesh).

21: Soul Food Shabbat

207 *National Association for the Advancement of Colored People*:
https://www.loc.gov/exhibits/naacp/founding-and-early-years
.html#:~:text=Moskowitz's%20involvement%20in%20the%20
NAACP,and%20Herbert%20Lehman%20contributed%20
funds.

207 *and Langston Hughes*: https://www.britannica.com/biography
/Julius-Rosenwald.

207 *including the Freedom Riders*: https://cupola.gettysburg.edu/cgi
/viewcontent.cgi?article=1271&context=ghj.

208 *"you're talking antisemitism"*: https://scholar.harvard.edu/files
/martinkramer/files/words_of_martin_luther_king.pdf.

208 *the first Black–Israel summit*: Dumisani Washington, Founder
and CEO of the Institute for Black Solidarity with Israel.

208 *"death con 3" on Jewish people*: https://www.cbsnews.com /sanfrancisco/news/the-rapper-ye-who-has-a-long-history -of-making-antisemitic-comments-issues-an-apology-in -hebrew/.

208 *"financial engineering"*: https://www.ajc.org/news/5-of-kanye -wests-antisemitic-remarks-explained.

208 *denies the Holocaust happened*: https://www.cnn.com/2022 /10/31/sport/kyrie-irving-brooklyn-nets-antisemitic-movie -spt-intl/index.html.

208 *Jews controlling Hollywood*: https://www.cnn.com/2022/11/14 /entertainment/dave-chappelle-adl-antisemitic/index.html.

209 *Africa's mineral wealth*: https://www.nytimes.com/2024/01/18 /magazine/black-jewish-activists-palestine.html; and https: //reviews.history.ac.uk/review/1582.

209 *Zionism and the Black Church*: Dumisani Washington, *Zionism and the Black Church* (Charlotte, NC: Umndeni Press, 2021).

22: Be a Mensch: Show Up as an Ally

218 *"ends with the Jews"*: https://archive.nytimes.com/www.nytimes .com/books/98/03/29/specials/baldwin-antisem.html? fbclid=IwAR09N1nHAdgTseVmfOY_ypLQCbqp2R VauSJ4W_emCc80tR5j9sz8BcJS3KM; and https://www.new statesman.com/encounter/2018/08/rabbi-jonathan-sacks-hate -begins-jews-never-ends-jews.

Appendix A: An Antisemitic Appendix

255 *to defeat him*: https://www.washingtonpost.com/wp-srv/politics /special/clinton/frenzy/jackson.htm.

Appendix B: Ask Me Anything: Jewish Edition

263 *average of $1,749*: https://theconversation.com/american-jews -and-charitable-giving-an-enduring-tradition-87993#:~:text =Most%20Jews%2C%20regardless%20of%20their,house holds%20in%20that%20income%20bracket; and https://giving usa.org/.

263 *same income bracket*: https://theconversation.com/american-jews

-and-charitable-giving-an-enduring-tradition-87993#:~:text
=Most%20Jews%2C%20regardless%20of%20their,house
holds%20in%20that%20income%20bracket.

264 *many and tangled*: https://mankindquarterly.org/files/sample
/vanStratenJewishMigrations.pdf.

264 *were Yiddish speakers*: https://www.jhi.pl/en/articles/call-for
-papers-yiddish-and-the-holocaust-new-approaches,7309#:~:-
text=Of%20the%20approximately%206%20million,85%20
percent%20were%20Yiddish%20speakers.

264 *an endangered language*: https://www.europarl.europa.eu/Reg
Data/etudes/BRIE/2022/698881/EPRS_BRI(2022)698881
_EN.pdf.

About the Authors

EMMANUEL ACHO is the #1 *New York Times* bestselling author of *Uncomfortable Conversations with a Black Boy* and the *New York Times* bestseller *Uncomfortable Conversations with a Black Man*. He is the host/producer of the Emmy Award–winning YouTube series of the same name, whose mission is to promote dialogue around racial insensitivity and ignorance. A former NFL linebacker, Acho is a Fox Sports analyst and television personality. Raised in Dallas, he holds a master's degree in sports psychology from the University of Texas at Austin. He lives in Los Angeles.

NOA TISHBY is the *New York Times* bestselling author of *Israel: A Simple Guide to the Most Misunderstood Country on Earth* and Israel's former Special Envoy for Combatting Antisemitism and Delegitimization. A native of Tel Aviv, she served in the Israeli army before moving to Los Angeles and launching a career in the entertainment industry. An award-winning producer, Tishby made history with the sale of *In Treatment* to HBO, the first Israeli television show to become an American series. One of the most visible activists on social media, Tishby is the founder of several nonprofit organizations, including Act for Israel and Eighteen, which combats antisemitism and inspires Jewish pride. She lives in Los Angeles and is a proud Jewish mother to her son, Ari.